The Wetland Revolution in Prehistory

*Proceedings of a conference
held by The Prehistoric Society and WARP
at the University of Exeter
April 1991*

edited by Bryony Coles

WARP

The Prehistoric Society

First published in 1992 by
The Prehistoric Society &
 WARP (Wetland Archaeology Research Project)

© The editor and individual authors 1992

ISBN 0 9519117 0 8

WARP Occasional Paper 6

Department of History and Archaeology
University of Exeter
Exeter EX4 4QH
UK

Typeset by Department of History and Archaeology
University of Exeter
Printed in UK by Short Run Press Ltd, Exeter

Contents

Contributors' names and addresses ... iv

1 Introduction: the Wetland Revolution in Prehistory? ... 1
Bryony Coles

2 Wetland sites in Japan ... 5
Akira Matsui

3 Wetland agriculture in New Guinea Highlands prehistory ... 15
Tim Bayliss-Smith and Jack Golson

4 Recent developments in Irish wetland research ... 29
Barry Raftery

5 Flag Fen, Fengate, Peterborough II: further definition, techniques and assessment ... 37
Francis Pryor and Maisie Taylor

6 River valley bottoms and archaeology in the Holocene ... 47
John Evans

7 Noyen-sur-Seine: a mesolithic waterside settlement ... 55
Claude Mordant and Daniel Mordant

8 Friesack mesolithic wetlands ... 65
Bernhard Gramsch

9 Recent developments in wetland archaeology in Poland ... 73
Wojciech Brzeziński

10 Biskupin fortified settlement and its environment in the light of new environmental and archaeological studies ... 81
Władysław Niewiarowski, Bożena Noryśkiewicz, Wojciech Piotrowski and Wiesław Zajączkowski

11 Evolution of lakes and prehistoric settlement in Northwestern Russia ... 93
Pavel Dolukhanov

12 An evolving revolution in wet site research on the Northwest Coast of North America ... 99
Dale Croes

13 Florida's archaeological wet sites ... 113
Barbara Purdy

14 Problems and potential of wet sites in North America: the example of Windover ... 125
Glen Doran

15 The *Pfahlbauland* exhibition, Zürich 1990 ... 135
Ulrich Ruoff

16 The Wetland revolution: a natural event ... 147
John Coles and Bryony Coles

Contributors

Tim Bayliss-Smith — Department of Geography, University of Cambridge
Downing Place, Cambridge CB2 3EN, UK

Wojciech Brzeziński — Państwowe Muzeum Archeologiczne
ul. Długa, 52, 00-950 Warszawa, Poland

Bryony Coles — Department of History and Archaeology
The University, Exeter EX4 4QH, UK

John Coles — Fitzwilliam College, Cambridge, UK

Dale R. Croes — Washington State University, 13719 54th Drive SE
Everett, Washington 98208, USA

Pavel Dolukhanov — Department of Archaeology, The University
Newcastle upon Tyne NE1 7RU, UK

Glen H. Doran — Department of Anthropology, Florida State University
Tallahassee, Florida 32306, USA

John Evans — School of History and Archaeology, University College of Wales
PO Box 909, Cardiff CF1 3XU, UK

Jack Golson — Research School of Pacific Studies, Australian National University
Box 4, Canberra ACT2601, Australia

Bernhard Gramsch — Museum für Ur-und-Frügeschichte, Schloss Babelsberg,
Potsdam, D (O)-1570, Germany

Akira Matsui — Centre for Archaeological Operations
Nara National Cultural Properties Research Institute
2-9-1, Nijo-cho NARA 630, Japan

Claude Mordant — Service régional de l'Archéologie
30 rue Vannerie, 21000 Dijon, France

Daniel Mordant — DM Archéologue départemental, Service du Patrimoine
248 avenue Charles Prieur, 77190 Dannemarie-les-Lys, France

Władysław Niewiarowski — Institute of Geography, Nicholas Copernicus University in Torun
Fredry 6/8, 87-100 Torun, Poland

Bożena Noryśkiewicz — Institute of Geography, Nicholas Copernicus University in Torun
Fredry 6/8, 87-100 Torun, Poland

Wojciech Piotrowski — Biskupin Department, Państwowe Muzeum Archeologiczne
ul. Długa 52, 00-950 Warszawa, Poland

Francis Pryor — Fenland Archaeological Trust, Flag Fen Excavations
Fourth Drove, Peterborough PE1 5UR, UK

Barbara Purdy — Department of Anthropology, University of Florida,
Gainesville, Florida 32611, USA

Barry Raftery — Department of Archaeology, University College
Belfield, Dublin 4, Ireland

Ulrich Ruoff — Büro für Archäologie, Neumarkt 4,
CH-8001 Zürich, Switzerland

Maisie Taylor — Fenland Archaeolgical Trust, Flag Fen Excavations
Fourth Drove, Peterborough PE1 5UR, UK

Wiesław Zajączkowski — Biskupin Department, Państwowe Muzeum Archaeologiczne
ul. Długa 52, 00-950 Warszawa, Poland

1

INTRODUCTION: THE WETLAND REVOLUTION IN PREHISTORY ?

Bryony Coles

In April 1991 the Prehistoric Society and WARP (Wetland Archaeology Research Project) held a joint conference: two hundred people filled a lecture theatre at the University of Exeter in the southwest of England, and for three days they listened to and debated papers on wetland archaeology from around the world. Was this a revolution? Hardly so, given the similar conference held by the Prehistoric Society in 1983 on *European Wetlands in Prehistory* (Coles and Lawson 1987), followed in 1986 by the Association of Environmental Archaeologists with *The Exploitation of Wetlands* (Murphy and French 1988) and by *Wet Site Archaeology*, held across the Atlantic in Florida (Purdy 1988). Back in the Old World, there was then a virtual spate of wet meetings, headed by the sequence of one-day events organised by WARP jointly with various bodies (Coles and Coles 1989, Coles, Coles and Dobson 1990, Coles and Goodburn 1991).

But all good revolutions can be likened to the floodwaters that pour forth at the bursting of a dam, their previous slow build-up recognized only with hindsight. Was the meeting held on the northwest coast of North America the first trickle from the New World (Croes 1976), and in Europe should we go back as far as the meeting which celebrated the centenary of Keller's first publication of the Swiss Lake Villages (Guyan *et al* 1955; Keller 1854)? Clearly, wetland archaeology as the theme of an international conference had precedents on either side of the Atlantic.

The meaning intended by the title of the conference, and of this volume, was therefore something different, something for readers to ponder in going through the diverse papers that follow, something that is explored in the concluding paper. It should be said at the outset, though, that the title was intended to be provocative and to encourage debate about whether or not wetland archaeology was of particular significance in the study of prehistory.

The papers given at the conference ranged geographically from Japan to the Americas via Europe, and in time from the Lower Palaeolithic to recent centuries. There were, nevertheless, many aspects of wetland archaeology omitted. In particular, we would have liked to increase the

ethnographic content of the conference, and to have had more reference to the wetlands of continental Asia, Africa and Australasia. But, for a mixture of political, financial and personal reasons, several potential speakers were unable to attend. Optimistically, we could hope that the *Wetland Revolution* turns out to have been one of the last archaeology conferences which East Europeans had difficulty in attending. And we were fortunate that Gela Gamkrelidze from Tbilisi in Georgia was able to be present. He spoke (at a preliminary seminar) about under-water archaeology in his country and described some of the exciting finds that were being made despite severe technical difficulties and shortage of equipment. It is to be hoped that expansion of archaeological work keeps pace with any developing threat to the Georgian wet sites.

Several papers were given at the conference which are not published here. Naama Goren-Inbar of the Hebrew University, Jerusalem, reported on her work at Gesher Benet Ya'aqov in the present valley of the river Jordan in northern Israel. Here, excavation of stone tools and animal bones also revealed waterlogged plant materials including wood, fruits and seeds. The distribution of worked stone, butchered bone and wood suggested a deliberate accumulation by people rather than a natural accumulation by water, and the location was a marshy lake margin at the time. The wood was sufficiently well-preserved to allow discussion of whether or not it had been worked. There was, for example, a lump of willow wood, of polished appearance and perhaps deliberately shaved down. An oak log or branch lay over a stone artefact and adjacent to an elephant skull and a heavy basalt core; something had been used to break open the skull, perhaps the log.

The significance of Gesher Benet Ya'aqov lay not simply in the survival of waterlogged wood in a part of the world most of us consider arid, but above all in its date: the lithic industry was Acheulean, the people who were very likely using and maybe also working the wood were *Homo erectus*, and the wood had survived in a waterlogged state for an estimated 500,000 years. Further details of this very early wetland site are now published (Belitsky *et al* 1991).

1

At a previous wetland conference, Søren Andersen introduced the underwater site of Tybrind Vig (Andersen 1987). On the present occasion, he persuaded us that that remarkable site was but the tip of the iceberg as far as the Danish Mesolithic was concerned. Although it was likely that all inland wetland sites had been drained to destruction, long-term changes in the relative levels of land and sea had ensured the preservation of settlements around the coasts of southern Scandinavia, now submerged beneath the sea. Systematic survey had suggested that Denmark might have 5000-10,000 submerged Stone Age settlements (Fischer 1988). They were legally protected in the same way as dryland sites, the National Forest and Nature Agency was responsible for their registration, new techniques of underwater exploration were being adapted to archaeological ends, and a lectureship in marine archaeology now existed. Andersen demonstrated convincingly that waterlogged Stone Age sites survive in great number, and that steps are being taken to investigate and to safeguard them. We can, therefore, look forward to a great expansion in evidence from the Stone Age of southern Scandinavia, new categories of information to study and new means of studying them, typified perhaps by the recent discovery underwater of a late Mesolithic burial of a man, laid in a tree-trunk coffin and covered over with bark (Skaarup and Grøn 1991).

Wetland agriculture in Latin America was the subject of a paper given by David Harris, prepared with Warwick Bray. In that extensive region, the investigation of wetlands has concentrated on field systems and agricultural localities, rather than on domestic sites. Drained fields have been studied in tropical zones from Mexico to Bolivia, and at all altitudes from sea level to over 3000 m. In size these field systems range from a few hectares to the major schemes of landscape reorganization discovered by air photography and ground survey in the Maya lowlands and the San Jorge basin of Colombia. Drained fields were constructed from the first millennium BC to the Spanish Conquest, thus not all are of the same age, nor does the archaeological evidence suggest a unitary phenomenon or a single centre of origin. More probably, there were similar responses to a common environmental opportunity.

Drained fields, or 'raised fields', are found mainly in seasonally flooded savanna zones or at the swampy margins of lakes and lagoons. The ditches deal with surface run-off, and control the level of the subterranean water table. Earth excavated from the ditches is piled between them to raise the planting surfaces and to prevent waterlogging of roots. In lowland regions drainage is the critical factor, but in the high Andes where night frosts are a problem the construction of ditched fields creates a distinct microclimate with higher temperatures and fewer hours of frost than in surrounding areas. In the Titicaca Basin, abandoned field systems were reactivated in the 1980s by archaeologists and agronomists working together. The experiment has produced spectacular increases in crop yields, perhaps twice the dryland average. The yields appear to be sustainable, and Government agencies in several countries are now showing an interest in wetland agriculture. Harris and Bray's survey revealed extensive current work on identifying, recording and sometimes excavating a vast body of evidence for wetland agriculture which in due course will be available for comparison with data from Japan and New Guinea (see Matsui, and Bayliss-Smith and Golson, this volume).

The papers published here start with Matsui's eye-opening survey of rescue work on wetland sites in Japan, the huge scale of which is documented in diagrams and tables, and was brought home to us at the conference with slides of vast excavations carried out in advance of motorway building and other such projects. Matsui selects a few wetland sites from successive periods of Japan's prehistory to illustrate the nature of the evidence becoming available, in particular the site of Awazu which he has investigated himself. As he points out, wetland environments accounted for a relatively high proportion of settled areas in prehistoric Japan, and now provide the main context for the survival of bone as well as wood and other plant materials. Therefore, the study of Japanese prehistory depends heavily on the evidence from wetland sites, much as Dutch prehistory does, for example, and more so than in Britain.

In New Guinea, as in Japan and in Latin America, wetland crops were cultivated, but in New Guinea they appear to have had a much greater antiquity, as the work of Bayliss-Smith and Golson has demonstrated. Their combined ethnographic and archaeological fieldwork in the Kuk region of the New Guinea Highlands documents the existence of systems of ditched cultivation plots as early as 9000 BP, remarkably early in the history of controlled crop-raising whether wetland or dryland. But the main focus of their paper in this volume is a later phase, some 2000 years ago, when an intensification of production from wetlands became apparent. They examine the changing inter-relationships of crop species, labour input, pest control and yields, and suggest that the challenges and rewards of exploiting a wetland environment may promote communal, co-operative schemes of water control. These in turn may encourage particular types of social development seen not only in the New Guinea Highlands but in other regions too where wetland cultivation was practised on a local scale.

Raftery's survey of results from his work in central Ireland introduces a new theme, trackways to cross the wetlands. It also introduces new work, for up until the mid-1980s, virtually no archaeological investigations were taking place in the central Irish bogs despite the horrific pace of peat extraction (Coles 1988). Since then, in the space of a few seasons of wetland fieldwork, Raftery has made numerous significant discoveries, confirming the archaeological richness of the Irish bogs and persuading various authorities of the need for a properly funded wetland archaeology unit, which is now at work. The trackways reported here are just the beginning, the tip of another iceberg, which promises when further investigated enough evidence to rewrite substantial areas of Irish prehistory.

Pryor and Taylor discuss recent results from their continuing rescue project at Flag Fen near Peterborough in eastern England. Their fieldwork in this region began on the dryland fen edge, with Neolithic and Bronze Age settlements and field systems at Fengate. Subsequently, via other sites in the region, they moved out to waterlogged Flag Fen. Thus they have practised both dryland and wetland field-work in one relatively small area, and gathered together evidence which will form a sound basis for examining the prehistoric inter-relationships between the two environments. They have also discovered a tangible link between the wet and the dry, in the form of a massive post alignment running from the dryland field system out across the wet, through the Flag Fen Platform and probably beyond. The nature and first implications of this evidence are explored in their contribution.

Evans provides a theoretical paper which considers river valley archaeology and palaeoenvironments, and draws attention to the fallibility of some common assumptions about valleys and the ways in which past peoples may have used them. Essentially, he argues that there has probably been more change during the Holocene than we generally allow for, and therefore the past characteristics of valleys and the attractiveness of what they had to offer to people need careful consideration for each case.

If the reader so wished, the Mordants' account of the Mesolithic riverside site of Noyen-sur-Seine could provide a specific archaeological context for testing Evans' theoretical considerations. The Noyen material is early, and unusual for Europe west of the Rhine, with fish traps and basketry and a boat. As for a great number of wetland sites, what has been preserved and discovered is largely the debris which fell into water from a settlement placed on the adjacent dry land. At Noyen, this material has provided good environmental and economic data, which the Mordants use to build up a picture of the mosaic of local environments and the ways in which early Mesolithic people may have exploited them.

Friesack has yielded material of similar antiquity to Noyen, but from a different type of wetland environment, a region of shallow lakes and sandy islands. Gramsch introduces the great wealth of organic material culture recovered from this site, where material accumulated for several millennia. As at Noyen, much of it is material discarded from a settlement, but there are also a few preserved *in situ* features. Gramsch raises several points for discussion, including the question of the contribution of organic artefacts to the study of human cultures and population movements, a study which is commonly based on lithics and pottery and other dryland durables.

Moving eastwards from Friesack, Brzezinski provides a survey of recent work on wetland sites in Poland. To do this was not an easy task, as publication has been difficult, and not always in a readily accessible form. Brzezinski's survey is all the more welcome. It reveals that several major wetland sites have been investigated in the last two decades, of surprisingly diverse character, ranging from multi-period settlement on the peatbog island of Dudka to a probably ritual riverside site at Otalazka to a later trading and craft centre at Janów Pomorski.

The classic site of Polish wetland archaeology is of course Biskupin, known since the 1930s. The paper given by Niewiarowski and Piotrowski, prepared with their colleagues Noryskiewicz and Zagaczkowski, presents the results of recent investigations focussed on the environment and economy of the Biskupin region, which provide for the first time detailed evidence of the setting of the famous fortified settlement. Local vegetation and lake levels are discussed, along with the question of whether the site was an island or a peninsula at the time of occupation. Helped by several seasons of experimental archaeology, the authors examine the economy of the settlement and its likely demands on local resources, from where they speculate about population levels. Their results demonstrate that, although a site may have been extensively investigated in the past, there can still be much to learn from applying new techniques and new approaches to interpretation.

Dolukhanov's paper moves east again, to the wet landscapes of northwestern Russia. After a brief discussion of the geology and hydrology of lakes in the region, Dolukhanov examines the archaeological evidence for Mesolithic and Neolithic settlement, paying particular attention to the site of Rudnya Serteya. He demonstrates that although pottery appeared at a relatively early stage, domestic animals were introduced only gradually and on a small scale into the economy of the prehistoric lakeshore inhabitants.

The three North American papers describe sites that have the same abundance of organic material as those from Old World wetlands, and yet all three authors deplore the relative neglect of wetland archaeology in the New World. Croes traces its very recent growth on the Northwest Coast, where environmental conditions conspire to provide excellent contexts for the preservation of settlements and allied features as well as their debris. Focussing primarily on material from his own excavations at Hoko River, with reference to other sites from the region, Croes argues the case that the study of organic material culture reveals a different prehistory to that indicated by lithics and other dryland evidence. His theme finds an echo in Gramsch's paper, and elsewhere, and the implications for the wider study of prehistory are considerable.

Purdy's wetland fieldwork has taken place on the opposite side of North America, in Florida. Her survey of the prehistoric finds from the abundant wetlands of that state reveals an extraordinary amount of sometimes quite astonishing material, and yet most of it is ignored or neglected by North American prehistorians. The wooden figures and masks from Key Marco are perhaps reasonably well known, but even they have deteriorated sadly since their discovery at the end of the nineteenth century. The curation of other, lesser known items is frequently worse or non-existent (a situation which is not restricted to Florida by any means). Purdy's tale is not entirely one of woe, but it is certainly dispiriting to learn in one paragraph of some great archaeological bounty from Florida's wetlands, and in the next to read of its loss.

Doran takes one Florida site, Windover, and examines it against the same background of the general disinterest in wetland sites in North America. He makes some suggestions as to why wetland archaeology has not prospered, places a part of the blame on the archaeologists concerned, and uses the Windover example to show how the situation might be improved. At the same time he provides an overview of the evidence from the site, which is early in the North American record and best-known for the preservation of many human skeletons in a mortuary pond, some of the skulls still containing brain tissue. Windover also yielded textiles and other artefacts, and it provides yet another example of a wetland site significantly enhancing the overall archaeological record.

One of Doran's themes, and one taken up by Pryor and Taylor also, is the need to involve the general public in wetland sites. Ruoff's paper describes how this was done on a grand scale in the summer of 1990 when the *Pfahlbauland* exhibition took place on the shores of Lake Zürich. Ruoff discusses the initial aims of the exhibition, its planning, and some of the difficulties of its realisation. He notes how prehistorians need to be clear in their own minds about what the evidence is, before they can present it to the questioning public, and he gives some examples of the considerable feedback gained during a summer of interaction with the public. The exhibition was enormously successful, bringing in several hundred thousand visitors, many of whom tried out dugout canoes, bows-and-arrows, querns and bake ovens, weaving and basketry, and a host of other crafts and activities based directly on excavated prehistoric evidence.

Some of the themes common to these papers are taken up again in the final chapter, but nothing on paper can do justice to the discussions that took place during the conference, whether in the lecture hall or less formally outside it, and during the excursions that followed. But perhaps readers will find material in these papers to stimulate their own debates, and enough different views on what is significant in wetland archaeology for them to draw their own conclusions about the Wetland Revolution.

A note about dates

We have tried to make clear the nature of all dates used in this volume. This has made the text clumsy in places, but we hope that a more accurate representation of time has been achieved, and that comparisons between sites and regions are facilitated. Radiocarbon dates are identified as 'uncal BP', 'cal BP', 'cal BC' etc., and where the calculation of time elapsed is based on radiocarbon dating this is noted, e.g. 'The second occupation lasted approximately 700 radiocarbon years'. It is not yet possible to give all radiocarbon dates in calibrated form, as calibration curves have yet to be established in many parts of the world. Dendrochronological dates are identified as such in the text.

Acknowledgements

Financial support for the Wetland Revolution conference was received from the British Academy, the British Council, the University of Exeter Research Fund, and a number of individual sponsors: their contributions are gratefully acknowledged. The preparation of this volume could not have been achieved without the work of Tina Tuohy, who did much of the initial word-processing assisted by Jennifer Warren, and the Drawing Office staff, Department of History and Archaeology, University of Exeter: Nigel Code, Seán Goddard, Mike Rouillard and Sue Rouillard, who prepared the text and illustrations for printing; their time and skills have been much appreciated. Many people have helped with specialist knowledge, notably Andrew Jones with his rapid checking of foreign fish identifications. Finally, my thanks to Dr J.M.Coles for advising with equal authority on editorial and on wetland matters.

BIBLIOGRAPHY

Andersen, S. 1987. Tybrind Vig: A submerged Ertebølle Settlement in Denmark. In J.M. Coles and A.J. Lawson (eds), *European Wetlands in Prehistory*, 253-280. Oxford: Clarendon Press.

Belitsky, S., Goren-Inbar, N. and Werker, E. 1991. A Middle Pleistocene wooden plank with man-made polish. *Journal of Human Evolution* 20, 349-353.

Coles, J.M. 1988. The Peat Hag. In B.A. Purdy (ed.), *Wet Site Archaeology*, 43-53. Caldwell, New Jersey: Telford Press.

Coles, J.M. and Coles, B.J. (eds) 1989. *The Archaeology of Rural Wetlands in England*. Exeter and London: WARP and English Heritage.

Coles, J.M., Coles, B.J. and Dobson, M.J. (eds) 1990. *Waterlogged Wood: the recording, sampling, conservation and curation of structural wood*. Exeter and London: WARP and English Heritage.

Coles, J.M. and Goodburn, D.M. (eds) 1991. *Wet Site Excavation and Survey*. Exeter and London: WARP, Museum of London and Nautical Archaeology Society.

Coles, J.M. and Lawson, A.J. (eds) 1987. *European Wetlands in Prehistory*. Oxford: Clarendon Press.

Croes, D. (ed.) 1976. *The Excavation of water-saturated archaeological sites (wet sites) on the Northwest Coast of North America*. Ottawa: National Museum of Man Mercury Series No.50.

Fischer, A. 1988. Submerged Mesolithic in Denmark. *Mesolithic Miscellany* 9(1), 9-10.

Guyan, W.U., Levi, H., Lüdi, W., Speck, J., Tauber, H., Troels-Smith, J., Vogt, E., and Welten, M. (eds) 1955. *Das Pfahlbauproblem*. Basel: Birkhäuser Verlag.

Keller, F. 1854. Die Keltische Pfahlbauten in den Schweizerseen. *Mitteilungen der Antiquarischen Gesellschaft im Zürich* 9.

Murphy, P and French, C. (eds) 1988. *The Exploitation of Wetlands*. Symposia of the Association for Environmental Archaeology No.7. Oxford: British Archaeological Reports, British Series 186.

Purdy, B.A. (ed.) 1988. *Wet Site Archaeology*. Caldwell, New Jersey: Telford Press.

Skaarup, J. and Grøn, O. 1991. Den vade grav. *Skalk* 1991 (1), 3-7.

2

WETLAND SITES IN JAPAN

Akira Matsui

Wetland sites occupy an important part in Japanese archaeology (Figs. 2.1, 2.2). For long, the majority of people in Japan have chosen alluvial plains for their residences and a number of sites are located on alluvial plains. These sites are characterized by excellent preservation of organic materials owing to their waterlogged condition.

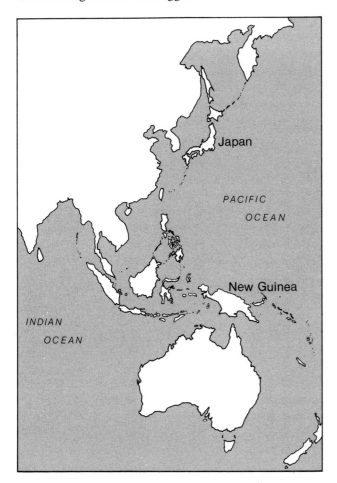

Fig. 2.1 Location Map

Drastic increases in construction and development works since the 1970s have resulted in the excavation of numerous sites on the alluvial plains. Owing to the advances in excavation techniques necessary for wetland site excavations, such as the steel sheet pile method and 24-hour motor pump drainage, and improved preservation techniques of organic materials, wetland site excavation has greatly contributed to understanding the prehistory of Japan. Ironically, the construction companies and other developers who destroy important wetland sites have helped to make wet site excavation technically possible by financing the excavation of even deeply stratified sites (see Appendix).

Before discussion of wetland sites in Japan, it is necessary to introduce a chronology of Japanese prehistory to be covered in this paper.

General Chronology of Japanese Archaeology (Table 1)

The oldest Palaeolithic site in Japan is still uncertain, but there are several sites that have been excavated below deep stratified volcanic soils in Miyagi prefecture and Tokyo. These sites are dated to more than one hundred thousand years BP by a variety of physical dating methods, especially tephra chronology. The origin of the people who came to live in Japan is still under discussion (Serizawa 1979).

Although more than 20,000 Late Palaeolithic sites have been found throughout Japan, few sites preserve organic materials such as faunal or floral remains because most of these sites are covered with volcanic or other acid soil. The changes in fauna and flora during the late and post Pleistocene are therefore unclear. It is worthy of note here that the earliest pottery appeared during the end of the Pleistocene. Fukui cave in Nagasaki prefecture yielded such pottery radiometrically dated back to 12,000 uncal BP. This chronological phase is called the Incipient Jomon period.

TABLE 1.
OUTLINE CHRONOLOGY OF JAPANESE
PREHISTORY

Period		Comments
Palaeolithic		
Lower	?150,000-30,000 BP	Hunting and gathering
Late	30,000-12000 BP	Lower Palaeolithic sites rare but number rising.
Jomon		
Incipient	12,000-10,000 BP	Stable hunting and gathering
Initial	10,000-7000 BP	culture with pottery and
Early	7000-4500 BP	without any significant
Middle	4500-3500 BP	agriculture. Beginning marked
Late	3500-3000 BP	by appearance of pottery in Late
Final	3000-2400 BP	Pleistocene; ceases in north
	(1000-400 BC)	slightly later than in south.
Yoyoi		
I	400-250 BC	Agricultural society
II	250-100 BC	Wet rice cultivation established
III	100-1 BC	A few written records from China
IV	AD1-100	concerning Japan.
V	AD100-300	Yoyoi V usually considered as final phase of Japanese prehistory.
Kofun		
Early	AD300-400	Period of Great Burial Mound; so-
Middle	AD400-500	call Key-hole shaped tombs are
Late	AD500-600	representative. Some written records
Final	AD600-700	of oracles have survived from Japan and China,thus the Kofun period is considered historic.

Fig. 2.2 Principal wetland sites in Japan

The next phase is the Initial Jomon, once thought the oldest phase of the Jomon culture. It is characterized by the emergence of shell middens in the Kanto district which is clear evidence of adaptation to maritime environments. During the later part of this period, the climate became warmer thereby causing a marine transgression. As a result, shallow rich marine environments occurred especially along the Tokyo bay and other Kanto districts. A large number of shell middens were formed during Early, Middle and Late Jomon periods in this area (Pearson and Pearson 1978). Throughout the Jomon period, the number of wetland sites increased in general. This might indicate that people had succeeded in adapting to various kinds of environments including wetlands, but most of the settlements themselves were restricted to dry environments.

The succeeding Yayoi Culture is characterized by rice agriculture in the wetlands. Because of their main subsistence the Yayoi people were more orientated toward wetland environments than Jomon people. The population increased. Many large sites have been discovered in the deep soil of the alluvial plains and the major portions of these sites still remain unexcavated (Sahara 1987).

EXAMPLES OF WETLAND SITES FROM THE PALAEOLITHIC AND JOMON PERIODS

A. Tomizawa

Recently a Late Palaeolithic waterlogged site, Tomizawa, was excavated in Sendai city of Miyagi prefecture. It preserved an area of late Pleistocene forest, radiocarbon dated 23,000 uncal BP; there were not only well-preserved trees but also many ecological remains, such as deer prints and droppings in association with a scatter of stone tools and open fires. The trees have been identified as *Picea glehnii, Pinus koraiensis, Abies* sp. *et al*, which suggests a cold climate of the ice age. This Palaeolithic level was superimposed by a Yayoi Period rice paddy field. This horizon was also waterlogged and preserved a large number of wooden implements for rice cultivation as well as piles and planks used for water management. The municipal authorities relocated the intended school building and designated this site for a field museum of archaeology and natural history (Hayasaka 1989).

B. Awazu (Figs. 2.3-2.5)

The Awazu site is located on the bottom of Lake Biwa at its southern tip. Since the lake level has been fluctuating, several archaeological sites have been discovered on the bottom, one to three metres deep. After underwater archaeological surveys had been conducted for several years by the Board of Education, a new excavation at the Awazu site was planned as part of a new development and construction programme for Lake Biwa.

The precise area and artefact distribution of Awazu site were confirmed by boring, scuba diving, and use of an underwater pump, and two separate shell middens were detected (Maruyama 1984). These shell middens and settlements are mainly distributed on the west side of the lake

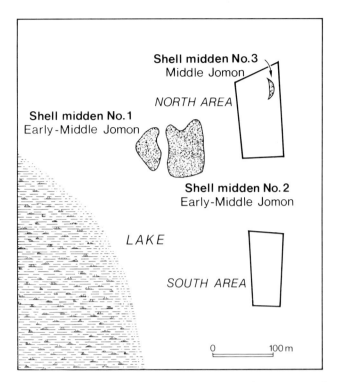

Fig. 2.3 The Awazu site. (After The Board of Education of Shiga Prefecture et al 1991 p.3)

bottom, and are located on the current ship route (Fig. 2.3). In view of the significance of this site, not only as shell middens but also as rich sources of well preserved organic remains, such as wooden articles, *urushi* Japanese laquer ware, plant and animal remains, the Shiga Prefectural government decided to relocate the ship route in order to preserve the two large middens and main part of the site.

Within a proposed new ship route, underwater archaeological survey detected still further occupation layers in two areas(north and south areas). These areas were surrounded by iron sheet piles and then drained in the summer of 1990. Although there were no significant features in the south area, well preserved occupation layers were found in the north area (Fig. 2.4).

After removing the surface deposits of the lake bottom layers of the north area, two sets of occupational layers were found: (1) occupation debris of organic materials and a series of clay and sand layers, dating to the Initial Jomon Period 9500 uncal BP; and (2) a shell midden primarily consisting of fresh water clams and layers of floral remains, both dating to the Middle Jomon Period 4500 uncal BP. Because these layers were thereafter covered by lake water an enormous quantity of organic remains was preserved in an extremely good condition as in the case of the shell middens no.1 and 2.

In the Initial Jomon debris we have discovered plant remains including Japanese chestnuts (*Castanea crenata*), acorns (*Quercus* sp. and others), water caltrop (also known as water chestnut) which were probably people's food items. The size of chestnuts is more than 2 cm and some-

times 3 cm, which is larger than that of wild species (1.5 cm). This has led botanists to suggest that the Jomon people intentionally looked after a chestnut forest by pulling weeds, eliminating unnecessary branches, etc. Similarly, the frequent discovery of seeds and skins of bottle gourds (*Lagenaria siceraria*)leads us to debate whether the bottle gourd was domesticated or not. Bottle gourds may have drifted to the coast of the Sea of Japan facing the Asian Continent, and it is quite likely that Jomon people transported them to such an inland area as Lake Biwa for utilization.

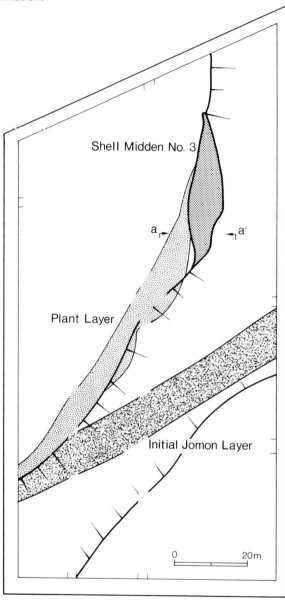

Fig. 2.4 The distribution of occupation debris in the northern excavation area of Awazu. (After The Board of Education of Shiga Prefecture et al 1991 p.5)

The Middle Jomon level yielded a crescent-shaped shell midden, which measures 40 x 15 m and 1 m thick at the deepest section. In one of the cross-sections of this shell midden, we observed a series of layers of shellfish, plant remains, and sand. The proportion of edible nuts against the total amount of plant remains is more than 90%. It is likely

a  a'

☐ Shell ■ Nuts ▨ Sand

0   3 m

Fig. 2.5. Cross section of Awazu shell midden No.3. (After The Board of Education of Shiga Prefecture et al 1991 p.5)

that the Awazu inhabitants of 4500 uncal BP already possessed the skills to remove the harsh taste of horse chestnuts and the acorns of some species of *Quercus* to make them edible. Generally, sophisticated techniques such as boiling nuts with ash and exposing them in running water, are necessary to remove the harsh taste, especially in the case of horse chestnuts. Consequently, it used to be believed that Jomon people acquired these techniques in Western Japan during the Late Jomon period, and the Awazu discovery has disproved this hypothesis.

The distribution of the layers of floral remains extended about 50 m to the south from the shell midden. They are probably secondary deposits from the flow of water during the Middle Jomon. The shell midden also contains floral remains, and the quantities of plant remains are relatively poor in the northern part of the shell midden. Probably the water came up to the shell midden and washed out some of the plants at times in the rainy season during the Middle Jomon, and formed the plant layer to the south.

At first the Middle Jomon inhabitants of this shell midden apparently did not utilize shellfish but specialized in processing plant food suitable for preservation and storage (Fig. 2.5). This is evident from four or five cycles of intermittent layers of nuts and of sand. After the cycle of nuts and sand layers, shellfish come into use and we see the next cycle of sand, shell and nut shells intermittently. The hypothesis of food processing is supported by the following evidence:

1. Freshwater clams (*Corbicula sandai*) comprise more than 90% of the shells in this midden, and there are very few other artefacts and ecofacts. This indicates that a large number of shellfish were discarded at once.

2. Similarly in the plant layers we discover a large number of the shells of horse chestnuts, acorn etc. This again suggests that a considerable amount of nuts was processed here in a short period of time.

3. In the cross section, we see thirteen or fourteen cycles of plant, sand and shellfish layers. These cycles probably resulted from intensive shellfish processing alternating with intensive nut processing over thirteen or fourteen years.

4. In the shell and plant layers, we rarely discover occupation debris, such as pot sherds, fragmentary lithics, broken bone tools etc. nor daily food items such as fish, bird, and mammal bones. This is unlike the ordinary situation in other shell middens in the eastern parts of Japan. There, occupation debris and daily food remains tend to be recovered from the same layers.

5. Based on these facts and interpretations, it is not an unlikely hypothesis that the Awazu residents collected and preserved shellfish in spring and early summer and nuts in autumn. This hypothesis explains why a sand layer formed between a shellfish layer and a plant layer.

6. It is probable that the area named shell midden no.3 was used for seasonal work carried out by the people who settled near the shell middens no. 1 and 2 of the Awazu site. Since there were few hunting and fishing tools, and the area was primarily devoted to food processing, this area must have been a special work space and may have been for women .

Results of excavations at the Awazu site show evidence of climatic changes. While chestnut was abundant in the Initial Jomon Period, it was rare in the Middle Jomon layers. This probably indicates that evergreen forest of chestnut and Japanese beech (*Abies crenata*) flourished in Lake Biwa area around 9500 uncal BP in the early post-Pleistocene phase. By 4500 uncal BP (Middle Jomon) vegetation in this area became similar to that of the present, characterized by deciduous forest.

Unfortunately we could not obtain faunal remains dating to the Initial Jomon Period at Awazu, but we suspect that it was more or less unchanged until the Middle Jomon Period. The nearby Ishiyama Shell Midden which was formed in the later half of the Initial Jomon period has yielded wild boar, Japanese deer, wolves, dogs, monkey, racoon dogs etc. which are common to most of the Jomon shell middens, and this should be the case at Awazu. In the Middle Jomon shell midden, I have identified the faunal remains, which are most common in Jomon shell middens (Table 2).

TABLE 2.
FAUNAL REMAINS RECOVERED FROM THE
AWAZU SHELL MIDDEN NO. 3

Fish

Carp	*Cyprinus carpio*
Catfish	*Parasilurus asotus*
Bagrid catfish	*Pelteobagrus nudiceps*

Reptiles

Snapping turtle	*Trionyx sinensis japonicus*

Birds

Mallard	*Anatidae gen. et sp.indet*

Mammals

Wild Boar	*Sus scrofa leucomystax*
Sika-deer	*Cervus nippon*
Domestic Dog	*Canis familiaris*
Racoon dog	*Nyctereutes procyonoides*
Japanese monkey	*Macaca fuscata*

Probably because this area was not used for residence but as a special labour area, the number of faunal remains is not large in this shell midden even though fine sieving was utilized for recovery.

C.Ondashi

The Ondashi site is located at the north entrance of the Yonezawa basin in Yamagata Prefecture. This site is dated to the Early Jomon period *c* 5000 uncal BP. In this location, a cold climate encouraged peat bog development. A large lake, or rather marsh, existed in the middle of the Yonezawa basin during the Early Jomon period. There was a settlement on the north shore of this marsh. The Ondashi site was first found when a small drainage ditch was dug, and then recently excavated prior to the construction of the bypass for the National road which was planned by the National Corporation for the Road Construction. The excavation was carried out in 1986, 1987 and 1988. High underground water levels and the cold climate preserved incredible organic remains in the uniform peat-like soil. Among the materials recovered were mushrooms for food, ropes, baskets and *urushi* implements such as wooden bowls, combs and woven textiles. Many posts, planks and timber structures with some indications of woodworking shed new light on the oldest architecture in Japan (Fig.2.6).

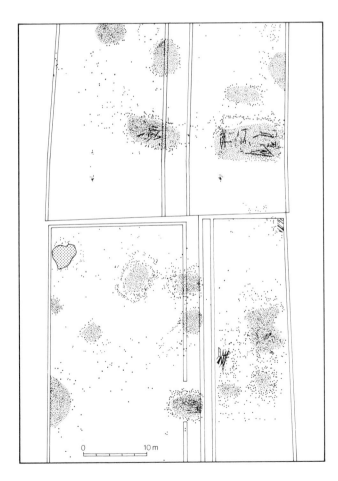

Fig. 2.6 Plan of the houses on the Ondashi site. (After Yamagata Pref. Gov. ed. 1987 Fig. 3)

Although dwellings during the Jomon period are mostly thought to be only semi-subterranean houses, the discoveries at this site show that plain ground-level pile and plank houses were also popular, although they were rarely preserved. The horizontal plans of these houses are divided into two types, rectangular and circular. Some of them were rebuilt and enlarged at the same place, which can be observed from the distribution of the posts. These houses were accompanied by small mounds with piles and planks, and sometimes woven mats could be observed on these mounds.

D. Juno

The Juno site is located in a small river valley, cutting through solid dry land. The Board of Education of Saitama Prefecture planned to construct a prefectural museum in this area. Because some Jomon pottery had been found, the museum staff first carried out a test excavation. Doing so they found many organic remains including several pieces of *urushi* lacquer ware, combs and other objects, as well as many pot sherds and lithics. They decided to excavate all the area for construction, which is about 11,000 sq. m. This excavation continued for four years from 1978 till 1981.

Sediment analyses indicate that the valley was below sea level during the early half of the Early Jomon, that is the time of transgression of the sea. A few pottery fragments of this period were recovered from the bottom of the site.

Most of the archaeological remains from Juno, particularly the wetland features, are dated between the later half of Middle Jomon (4000 uncal BP) and the early half of Late Jomon. During the Middle Jomon, the valley turned to a marshy area, and the river formed thick alluvial deposits.

The excavation has revealed many important features including two wooden tracks and lines of wooden piles. The lines of piles cross the lowland from one side of the stable land to the other. Using ethnographic analogy with premodern Ainu, it is assumed that these features were used as special hunting traps, where the chasers run the animals against such fences to catch them. This was the first discovery of such features from the Jomon period. The structure of the two trackways is similar, and simple (Fig. 2.7). Two or three horizontal timbers were laid on the wet ground and stabilized by many obliquely driven wooden pegs. A broken dugout canoe was also reused as a platform. The trees used were mostly chestnut, oak and some others. These features are dated to about 4100 - 4000 uncal BP.

Since this excavation, other similar wooden tracks have been found in the Kanto region. Such sites include Ushiroya and Akayama (Kanehako 1990) of Saitama prefecture and Umenoyato in Kanagawa prefecture, all of which are dated to the Late Jomon or later. Juno's trackways remain the oldest examples in Japan.

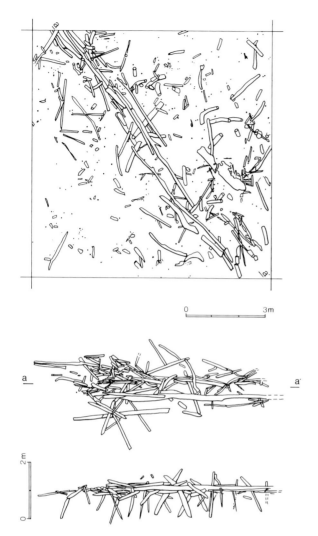

Fig. 2.7 Structure of the trackways at Juno. (After Saitama Pref. Museum 1984; Fig. 82, 92)

E. Other important wetland Jomon sites

There are many other important wetland Jomon sites in Japan which have been excavated. Among them the following sites are worthy of mention in this paper.

The Shidanai site in Tsunagi town of Iwate prefecture was excavated as a rescue project before the construction of a dam in 1977. This was one of many sites about to be flooded by the reservoir. It was located on a river terrace and its slope. The excavators found a fish trap in the stream of the Jomon period. This feature dated to the Late Jomon period. Such fish traps of various periods after the Jomon period have been excavated in Hokkaido.

The Mawaki site is dated to the Early Middle Jomon period and is located north of the Noto peninsula in Ishikawa Prefecture. The excavations of this site were carried out in 1982 and 1983. Most of the faunal remains were sea mammals, such as porpoise and small kinds of whales. This site is located at the deep end of a small bay, which suggests that probably these sea mammals were captured by communal hunting which involved both chasers by canoes and watchers on the top of the hill at the entrance of the bay.

The same technique was used up until World War II in the vicinity of the Mawaki site.

The discovery of at least three superimposed wood circles indicates that this site was also used as some kind of ceremonial centre for the area for a long time. Large half-cut timbers of Japanese chestnut were used for the posts. Circles of the same type have been excavated in the Hokuriku region, but their purpose and function are still unknown, as in the case of stone circles in northern Japan dating to the same periods. One of these wood circles is reconstructed and open for the public at Chikamori site near Kanazawa city in Ishikawa Prefecture, about 70 km south of the Mawaki site.

EXAMPLES OF WETLAND SITES FROM THE YAYOI PERIOD

A. Yayoi culture in Osaka Plain

During the Jomon period, the middle part of the Osaka plain was a shallow bay, named Kawachi bay after the old name for the eastern part of Osaka prefecture (Fig. 2.8). Only three small shell middens and a small number of other types of sites have been located along the coast of this ancient bay, which indicates that the Jomon people in this area did not actively exploit this environment. However during the beginning of the Yayoi period, or in the very final phase of the Jomon period[1], people began to exploit this marshy environment, where they constructed rice paddy fields. At the same time, Kawachi bay turned into Kawa-chi-gata, which was a lagoon or marsh. Many early agricultural settlements were located on this coastal alluvial plain. However, the rapid accumulation of alluvial deposits of the

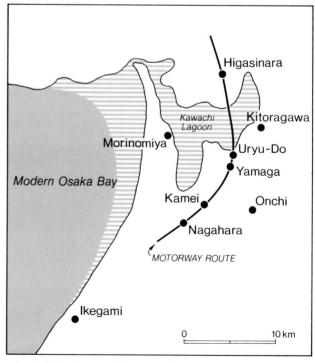

Fig. 2.8 The Kawachi-gata or lagoon and distribution of sites

rivers concealed these first agricultural settlements under deep deposits. The fact that some large settlements were covered with mud indicates that these sites were abandoned because of disastrous floods. For instance, Uryudo Site, which is one of the biggest settlements of this area, was destroyed by a flood and never inhabited again until historic times. Deep alluvial soil and a high level of underground water have preserved these sites in a good condition. The accumulation of these deposits averages about 6 m: the deepest features, such as the bottom of a ditch, are as deep as 8 m or more from the present surface. Because of the deep wet clay soil, the environment of these sites is suitable for the preservation of wooden artefacts and other floral, faunal and organic remains.

At the end of the 1960s a major motorway was planned to pass through the middle of the former Kawachi lagoon and its surroundings from north to south. The Board of Education of Osaka Prefectural Government negotiated with the motorway construction corporation to carry out a survey along the planned route. Osaka Archaeological Centre[2] was engaged in this rescue project. According to the survey and test excavations, although a few sites were found within the former Kawachi-gata, it also became clear that from the southern coast of the lagoon to the edge of the Quaternary terrain, many large settlements were superimposed on each other all through the planned area. In all researchers totally excavated 16 km of the route which measured 16.5 km in length! Their "test trench" was about 8 m wide and they had to carry their excavation sometimes 7 to 8 m below the ground surface. Moreover, at many sites multiple cultural layers were found mostly dated from the end of the Jomon period up to the recent pre-modern period. The archaeologists utilized the steel sheet pile method and 24-hour motor pump during the excavations for the sake of safety. Although it occupied the large part of the excavation budget for this project, this method has become popular for deep stratified excavations all over Japan

This project was carried out for more than 10 years and involved a huge budget, but as a result 13 major sites were excavated and a great deal of information was gathered. The Yamaga and Kamei sites are only two of these sites which were investigated prior to the motorway construction.

B. Yamaga

Yamaga site was formed mostly during the first three phases of Yayoi Period, that is roughly from about 300 BC for three centuries. It was then abandoned and turned into rice paddy fields for other settlements. There were many wooden agricultural implements and other equipment like basketry fish traps, and plank and timber lines for irrigation ditches. These features threw a new light on our knowledge of how people lived in this alluvial plain during the Yayoi period. Many semi-subterranean houses, wells, burial mounds and irrigation ditches were found. The basketry fish traps (Fig. 2.9) were also found on the bottom of a stream in this site. Several such fish traps have been found at Yayoi sites in Western Japan.

C. Kamei Site

Kamei site was inhabited from the first phase of Yayoi period through to the Kofun period. The excavations revealed the plan of this site during these phases. Because some parts of the ditches enclosing the settlement were also used as garbage pits, many faunal and plant remains were recovered from the waterlogged fills of these ditches. The present author's analysis of the faunal remains shows that $2/3$ of their remains consisted of wild boar (*Sus scrofa leucomystax*), almost all the remaining $1/3$ were sika deer (*Cervus nippon*), and other mammals such as wolves, racoon dogs and marten were rare in fragment number. The variety of the faunal remains at the Kawachi settlement sites decreased from the Jomon period to the Yayoi period in general (Table 3; Matsui 1991).

Recently Nishimoto mentions that a large number of the boar had already been domesticated, and seemed to have been imported from China or Korea at the beginning of the Yayoi Period, because a high percentage of periodontal

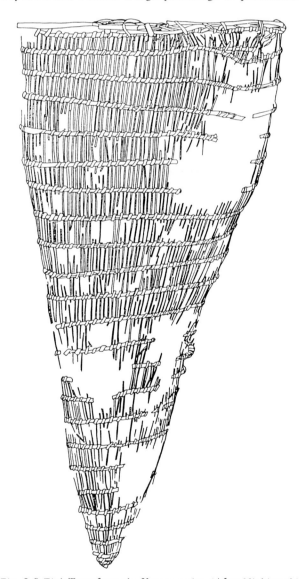

Fig. 2.9 Fish Trap from the Yamaga site. (After Nishiguchi et al 1984 Fig. 17)

11

TABLE 3

FAUNAL REMAINS RECOVERED FROM THE KAWACHI PLAIN

| Site / Period | **Mammal** | | | | | | | | | | | | | | | **Bird** | **Fish** | | | | | | | | | | | | | | | **Reptile** | | | **Amphibian** |
	Whale	Rat *Rattus sp.*	Marten *Martes melampus*	Badger *Meles meles*	Japanese monkey *Macaca fuscata*	Hare *Lepus brachyurus*	River otter *Lutra lutra*	Giant flying squirrel *Petaurista leucogenys*	Fox *Vulpes vulpes*	Racoon dog *Nyctereutes procyonoides*	Wolf *Canis lupus*	Black bear *Selenarctos thibetanus*	Sika-deer *Cervus nippon*	Wild Boar *Sus scrofa leucomstax*	Dog *Canis familiaris*	bird	Spanish mackerel *Scomberomorus niphonius*	Putterfish *Tetraodontidae sp.*	Arabian pike-eel *Muraenesox cinereus*	Japanese flounder *Paralichthys olivaceus*	Sea bass *Lateolabrax japonicus*	Mullet *Mugil cephalus*	Grunt *Plectorhynchus cinctus*	Red sea bream *Pagrus major*	Black sea bream *Acanthopagrus schlegeli*	Bagrid catfish *Bagridae sp.*	Catfish *Parasilurus asotus*	Crucian carp *Carassius auratus*	Carp *Cyprinus carpio*	Ray	Shark	Snapping Turtle *Trionyx sinensis*	Turtle	Snake	Frog
Morinomiya Jomon	●	●	●	●	●		●		●						?	●	●	●	●	●	●	●	●	●	●		●	●	●	●	●	●	●	●	●
Kitoragawa Yayoi		●								●	●					●	●	●	●		●			●	●				●			●	●	●	●
Ikegami Yayoi	●											●				●	●	●																	
Uryu-do Yayoi																●	●	●	●										●	●		●	●		
Higashi-nara Yayoi																●	●	●																	
Kamei Yayoi	●	●	●		●	●			●	●	●	●	●	●	●	●	●	●							●		●		●	●		●	●	●	●
Onchi Yayoi																●	●	●	●													●	●		
Nagahara Yayoi																●																			

disease could be observed in their teeth rows. He argues that a large number of the boar which have been reported as "wild" should have been "domesticated" boar in western parts of Japan during Yayoi 1 phase (Nishimoto 1991). Further analyses of the morphological features of the zoological remains are necessary.

CONCLUDING REMARKS

As discussed above, wetland archaeology in Japan has greatly contributed to our understanding of prehistoric lifestyles. Owing to excellent preservation of organic remains at wetland sites, we have discovered fish traps, ground-level dwellings, trackways, etc. of the Jomon Periods. For the Yayoi Period, the discovery of paddy fields associated with highly advanced irrigation systems, a variety of wooden agricultural tools, such as ploughs, and the clear transition from the hunting-gathering economy to subsistence primarily based on rice cultivation are worthy of note. I believe that future discoveries at wetland sites will greatly add to the picture of prehistoric lifestyles in Japan.

APPENDIX : Rescue Archaeology in Japan

(based largely on Tanaka 1984, with new information also from him.)

The law for the protection of cultural properties (1952), which covers archaeological remains in the same way as fine arts and historical architecture, is the backbone for Japanese rescue archaeology. Although it does not say that the developers should be responsible for all expenses for rescue excavations, public consensus or agreement that it be so seems to have been established for many years, excepting nonprofitable developments such as personal housing or land improvements for agriculture, when a government subsidy covers expenses. Since the early 1970s, the number of rescue excavations has increased rapidly. The number of research excavations undertaken by universities or museums has not increased significantly, and the number of rescue excavations has been many times larger than those of academics for some years (Fig. 2.10).

In 1989, there were 8446 rescue excavations and 5723 watching brief cases, making a total of 14,169 archaeological sites investigated under the direction of the Agency for Cultural Affairs. Archaeologists specializing in rescue excavations and site protection administration numbered 4366 hired by local governments or public corporations in 1991. The budget for rescue excavations in 1989 is given in Table 4. As a result of this huge number of investigations the amount of site reports has also increased in recent years. In 1987, more than 3000 publications covering 5500 individual sites were published (Centre for Archaeological Operations 1989).

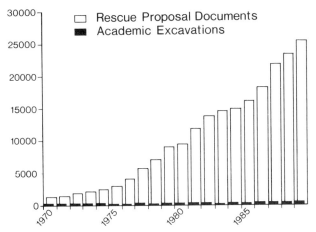

Fig. 2.10 The number of rescue and academic excavations 1970-89

TABLE 4
1989 RESCUE EXCAVATION BUDGETS

DEVELOPER	JAPANESE YEN	£ STERLING
Local Government	26,493,000,000	105,972,000
Public corporations, local	1,773,000,000	7,092,000
National government	12,672,000,000	50,688,000
Public corporations, national	17,182,000,000	68,728,000
Private enterprises	14,089,000,000	56,356,000
Total	**72,209,000,000**	**288,836,000**

As the role of the national government, *i.e.* the Agency for Cultural Affairs, is limited to providing advice and guidance to local rescue bodies, the Centre for Archaeological Operations was established at the Nara National Cultural Properties Research Institute (NABUNKEN), where the author is one of the members. The principal roles of this centre are as follows:

1. Training of rescue excavators from local governments or public corporations.
2. Supervision of rescue excavations, if it is necessary.
3. Developing new techniques relating to the excavation and preservation of archaeological remains.
4. Collection and publication of information concerning archaeological excavations .

Notes.

1. Definition of the Yayoi period is one of the controversial topics in Japanese archaeology. Some archaeologists suggest that the existence of Yayoi style pottery is an indispensable part of definition of the period. Others, including myself, emphasize the significance of economic changes, that is, a shift from Jomon style hunting and gathering subsistence to an agricultural economy of the Yayoi type, wet rice agriculture, is the crucial mark of the Yayoi period. Recently, in northern Kyushu and some areas in Honshu and Shikoku, many excavations have revealed rice paddy fields associated with final Jomon pottery. From the author's point of view, these sites should be classified as Yayoi sites.

2. Some of the local archaeological centres are run by their governments directly. Others are not completely run by their local governments but are public corporations. The Osaka archaeological centre is one of the latter cases.

Acknowledgements.

I wish to acknowledge, with thanks, many colleagues and friends. Especially the following persons have helped with my research and translation into English. M.Tanaka and M. Sahara have been advising me since I started my research in this institute in 1982. Dr G. Barnes informed me of the Wetland Revolution conference and recommended me to take part in it. Dr P. Bleed, who was my adviser at University of Nebraska Lincoln, helped me to translate this paper into English. K. Sasaki and J. Habu also discussed the contents of this paper and helped to write it in English.

BIBLIOGRAPHY

The Board of Education of Shiga Prefecture *et al* 1991. *Awazu Kotei Iseki (Awazu, the lake bottom site).* Text for the public lecture held at Otsu City Museum on March 17 1991.

Centre for Archaeological Operations 1990. *C.A.O. News No 67.* Nara National Cultural Properties Research Institute. (In Japanese)

Hayasaka, S. 1989. Outline of Tomizawa Site, Sendai, Northeast Honshu, Japan. *The Quaternary Research* 28 (3), 292-301. Japan Association for Quaternary Research. (With English summary)

Kanehako, F. (ed.) 1990. *Akayama* Vol 1. Kawaguchi-shi Iseki chousa-kai (Kawaguchi City Archaeological Unit). (In Japanese)

Kato, S. 1987. Jomon Culture. In Tsuboi (ed.), *Recent archaeological discoveries in Japan*, 24-36. The Centre for East Asian Cultural Studies and UNESCO.

Matsui, A. 1987. Kamei Iseki Shutudono Doubutuizontai (Faunal analysis of Kamei site). *Kamei Site Report (Part 2)*,423-484. Osaka Archaeological Centre. (In Japanese)Matsui, A.1991.Yayoi Jidai No Dobutu-shoku (Faunal remains in the Yayoi period. *Yayoi Bunka*, 89-91. Osaka Prefectural Yayoi Museum. (In Japanese)

Maruyama, R. (ed.) 1984. Awazu Kaiduka Kotei Iseki (Awazu shell middens in the bottom of Lake Biwa). The Board of Education, Shiga Prefecture Government. (In Japanese)

Nishiguchi, Y., Mijono, J. and Venishi, M. 1984. *Yamaga site (part 3)*. Osaka Archaeological Centre. (In Japanese)

Nishimoto, T. 1991. Buta No Shiso-noro (Pyorrheal pigs of Yayoi period) *Yayoi Culture*, 140-141. Osaka Yayoi Museum. (In Japanese)

Pearson, R. and Pearson, K. 1978. Some problems in the study of Jomon subsistence. *Antiquity 52*, 21-27.

Sahara, M. 1987. The Yayoi Culture. In Tsuboi (ed.),*Recent Archaeological discoveries in Japan*, 37-54. The Centre for East Asian Cultural Studies and UNESCO.

Saitama Prefecture Museum (ed.) *Juno Site - Features and Artifacts*. The Board of Education, Saitama prefecture. (In Japanese)

Serizawa, C. 1979. Cave Sites in Japan. *World Archaeology* 10 (3), 340-349.

Tanaka, M. 1984. Japan. In H. Cleere (ed.), *Approaches to the Archaeological Heritage*, 82-88. Cambridge University Press.

Tohoku Rekishi Shiryo-kan 1990. *Jomon-jin no kurashi* (The subsistence of the Jomon People). (In Japanese)

Yamada (ed.) 1986. *Mawaki Site*. The Board of Education, Noto Town (In Japanese)

Yamagata Prefectural Government (ed.) 1985, 1986, 1987. *Ondashi Site*, On-site public lecture,Text Nos 1-3. Yamagata Prefectural Government Board of Education. (In Japanese)

3

WETLAND AGRICULTURE IN NEW GUINEA HIGHLANDS PREHISTORY

Tim Bayliss-Smith and Jack Golson

INTRODUCTION: WETLAND LAND USE FROM A TEMPERATE PERSPECTIVE

Temperate wetlands are today the great granaries of the industrialised nations. Our growing capacity to regulate rivers, to dig and pump deep drains, and to plough with heavy machinery has transformed the economics of wetland farming, and has provided the means for a widespread conversion of heavy clay soils into fertile arable land. But in the past the role of wetlands has been very different. Most of the major plains and valleys of Europe were areas of either persistent or seasonal waterlogging, and in prehistory they were reserved as the prime sites for animal grazing rather than being seen as an arable resource.

Around the Mediterranean the wetlands were the areas that solved for transhumant stock-keepers the problem of seasonal variation in grazing, in particular the summer droughts of the lowlands and the winter snows of the mountains (Barker 1985, 57). Similarly in Northern and Eastern Europe, when wetlands were reclaimed from waste they usually became hayfields or summer pastures. Particularly where communities had access to floodplains and fens rather than acid raised bogs, the wetland resources enabled farmers to maintain much larger herds and flocks, and this in turn provided the extra manure to keep the better-drained wetland margins under perennial cultivation. Fish, wild fowl, peat and sedge were other valued fen products, and apart from some marginal reclamation in the late medieval period, arable land use was seldom attempted (Pryor 1976; Dolukhanov 1979; Louwe Kooijmans 1980; Brandt *et al* 1984).

In the Somerset Levels, for example, Coles and Coles (1986) have pointed to the lack of evidence for any arable use of wetlands in the pre-Roman period. Clarke (1972) imagined for Late Iron Age Glastonbury 'ditched field agriculture' based on infields of winter barley and outfields of spring wheat and beans planted as the flood waters receded, but the model is implausible. If the Glastonbury people were farmers, their fields were on the islands not in the marsh: "they had better sense than to attempt to drain the latter" (Coles and Coles 1986, 183).

Even where the capability existed for effective drainage, as in Fenland in Romano-British times, the wetland economy was still largely based on improved grazing. Until the 17th century Fenland was largely cattle country with sheep on the seaward margins. Arable farming only became predominant when the technology and economics of the Industrial Revolution transformed the costs and risks of crop production (Ravensdale 1974; Godwin 1978; Darby 1983).

TROPICAL WETLANDS: AN ALTERNATIVE PERSPECTIVE

In the lowlands of the humid tropics the situation is quite different. Large domesticated animals capable of utilising wetlands as pasture were altogether absent until introduced by contact with other regions. There was an indigenous process of animal domestication within communities that were more-or-less sedentary and mainly horticultural with some hunting, fishing and collecting, but the species domesticated were not primarily grazing animals of the wetland (Donkin 1985). The indigenous domesticated animals were pig, common fowl and duck in south and southeast Asia and Melanesia, bush pig (reared) and guinea fowl in west and central Africa and peccary (reared) and muscovy duck in the American lowland tropics.

Both the bush pig and the peccary were probably on the way to full domestication at the time of European expansion

(Donkin 1985, 100). Like the Asian pig, their rearing involved hand feeding with a range of foods, but primarily surplus crops or crop residues. For these animals grass is not important in the diet, although rooting in wetlands for earthworms can provide an important dietary supplement.

For crop production, on the other hand, tropical wetlands possess many advantages over dryland sites. Whereas dryland soils are subject to a collapse in productivity unless their nutrients are replenished by forest recycling processes, wetlands are sites of sediment accumulation, a much slower breakdown of organic matter, nitrogen fixation on moist surfaces, and an enhanced availability of phosphorus under waterlogged conditions (Vasey *et al* 1984). With even a modest lowering of the water table these soils dry out and a wide range of dryland crops can be grown. If swampy conditions are re-established by seasonal or periodic flooding then the growth of weeds will be checked. In this way flooding not only replenishes nutrients but also removes an important reason for the shifting cultivator deciding to shift (Vasey 1979). It is clear that where wetland resources were available, we no longer need to assume that people in tropical lowlands were forced to depend upon shifting cultivation with a forest fallow, or that such areas could only support sparse and semi-sedentary populations (Denevan 1982; Brookfield 1986).

In Central America, for example, archaeological work in Belize and Guatemala indicates that Maya wetland agriculture dates back at least 3000 years, with ditching systems becoming widespread as a phase of intensification in the Late Preclassic period (Denevan 1982). It is argued that wetlands were initially attractive to the Maya because they offered the possibility of long-term cultivation, so reducing the work of felling forest trees. Seasonal flooding controlled weeds, and the floodplain soils were considerably richer in nutrients than most others that were available. The role of flooding in pest control, or what Mathewson (1990, 33) calls "the entomological dimension of wetland agriculture", has also been emphasised. In summary, and in the light of the known hazards of swidden cultivation in Central American tropical forests, it is now thought that "wetland cultivation provided a significant strategy for reducing risk to farmers and increasing surplus" (Pohl *et al* 1990, 235).

However, neither of the New World staples of maize and manioc are properly adapted to water-saturated soils. If they are to be cultivated in wetlands, they can only be grown successfully when the water table has been lowered. Swamps need to be drained with ditches, and the fields elevated (as well as fertilised) with the muck and sediment dug out of the ditches. The same intolerance of waterlogging is characteristic of the yam (*Dioscorea* spp.), which in coastal swamps in New Guinea can only be grown through the elaborate construction of 'island beds' accessible only by canoe (Serpenti 1965).

The yam (*D. rotundata*) is the presumed indigenous staple of agrarian populations in the West African rain forests, for example around Benin. There is no evidence

for the use of wetlands in this forest zone in prehistory. On the other hand, archaeological survey efforts have so far been concentrated on the urban centres, with questions of their subsistence base receiving little attention (Connah 1987, 129-141). Basing his argument on surface finds, Darling (1984, 71) suggests that around Benin the interfluves were densely settled and the forests were cleared, whereas the river valleys were avoided because of their reputation for disease and sorcery. It was further north, in the savanna zone, that the wetlands became a key agricultural resource in the Iron Age period. Both African rice (*Oryza glaberrima*) and sorghum were grown as flood-recession crops in the Inland Delta of the Niger, in the Benue floodplains, and along the margins of Lake Chad (Connah 1985, 1987; Adams 1989; Harlan 1989).

In Southeast Asia and the Pacific, in contrast, two of the primary indigenous staples are perfectly adapted to wetland conditions. Neither rice nor taro are obligate wetland species, but both tolerate water-saturated soils and yield most heavily as pondfield crops. In southeast Asia, rice (*Oryza sativa*) is well known as the predominant crop of the historical period. Taro (*Colocasia esculenta*) is one of the root crops that are presumed to predate rice, as part of the ancient horticultural base of the region (Spriggs 1982). However, we can only conjecture at the relative importance of taro and the role of the wetlands in its cultivation. As Golson (1989, 680) has pointed out, what is striking so far is "the failure of archaeological research on the Southeast Asian mainland to throw light on the antiquity, indeed the presence, of root-crop, tree-crop agriculture".

Rice and taro both thrive with shallow inundation but cannot tolerate stagnant water. In Island Melanesia the water control techniques for growing taro have much in common with rice terracing and pondfield irrigation in places like Luzon in the Philippines. Spriggs (1982, 1990) has suggested that the similarity in technology implies that the two crops share a common origin in prehistory, linked through the expansion of Austronesian-speaking cultures out of Southeast Asia 5-6000 years ago. The alternative view of endogenous development of water control technology in Melanesia derives from evidence for the antiquity of wetland cultivation in New Guinea, which was also an independent centre for plant domestication (Yen 1990).

It is not yet known whether *Colocasia* is among the species that were domesticated in New Guinea, or whether it first arrived through diffusion, perhaps with the main yam species (*Dioscorea alata* and *D. esculenta*), which according to Yen (1990, 260) "are almost certainly of Southeast Asian origin". If *Colocasia* is indigenous, then the ultimate origins of the Oceanic wetland systems that are based on taro may lie in dryland systems for the manipulation of wild plant populations in the lowland rain forests. Groube (1989) has proposed that in Pleistocene New Guinea there was a long pre-horticultural phase of manipulation of forest canopy, using a distinctive type of heavy stone blade waisted for hafting. According to this model trees were killed to stimulate the growth of edible wild plants such as taro. Only much later did mixed swidden agriculture develop out of these extensive systems of rain forest management, with wetlands providing an opportunity for the intensification of taro production in certain circumstances.

WETLAND AGRICULTURE IN NEW GUINEA

The object of this paper is to consider for the New Guinea Highlands what were the circumstances in which wetlands became agricultural resources for those communities having access to them. The paper provides a selective review and interpretation of data in previous publications, integrating Golson's information on the archaeology of wetlands agriculture with Bayliss-Smith's material on the technology and economics of taro production. The paper also provides a new synthesis of one particular drainage phase which, we argue, constituted a revolution in highlands production systems.

How can we reconstruct the potential advantages and disadvantages of wetlands for New Guinea farmers in prehistory? The sparse and partial nature of the evidence available from archaeology, palaeobotany and geomorphology makes any such reconstruction highly dependent upon ethnographic inference. However, New Guinea ethnography requires careful interpretation if it is not to be misleading, since there is reason to suppose that much of what we now see in the Highlands is an artefact of comparatively recent changes in environment, economy and society.

The Highlands occupy a zone that extends 1100 km from west to east and about 160 km from north to south (Fig. 3.1). Agrarian populations live at all altitudes between 1000 m and about 2700 m, but most of the 1.5 million highlanders live in the major valleys between 1500 m and 1900 m, for example the Baliem, Lai, Wahgi and Chimbu valleys. Since the introduction of the sweet potato (*Ipomoea batatas*) possibly 1200 years ago but more probably 400 years ago, an enlargement of the subsistence base has led to a great increase in population, both of people and pigs. The agricultural frontier has expanded into drier and less fertile areas and to higher altitudes, and the area converted from forest to grassland has also increased (Sorenson 1972; Golson 1977, 1982; Bayliss-Smith 1985a, 1991).

As well as taking account of this 'Ipomoean Revolution', we must also bear in mind the impact of new technology. Almost all observations of highlands agriculture since European contact in the 1930s have some bias because of the impact of steel tools. Steel axes and knives very soon replaced stone tools for cutting wood and grass. The adoption of steel spades for digging ditches and tilling the soil soon followed, although even today the wooden digging stick is still used for certain tasks (Sorenson 1972; Steensberg 1980). Nevertheless the impact of new tools on labour inputs and the feasibility of cultivating marginal land was far-reaching, and surplus production for the wealth economy also became easier to achieve. The wealth economy itself was affected by an over-supply of traditional valuables such as shells, and by new sources of wealth from the monetary economy.

Ethnographic studies in New Guinea are therefore not altogether dependable as analogues of prehistoric land use. However, if used with care they can greatly enrich our understanding of wetland management in prehistory. We consider first of all insights from data on the subsistence economics of taro production in dryland and wetland sites. Following this we review the archaeological evidence for wetland drainage at the Kuk site in the upper Wahgi

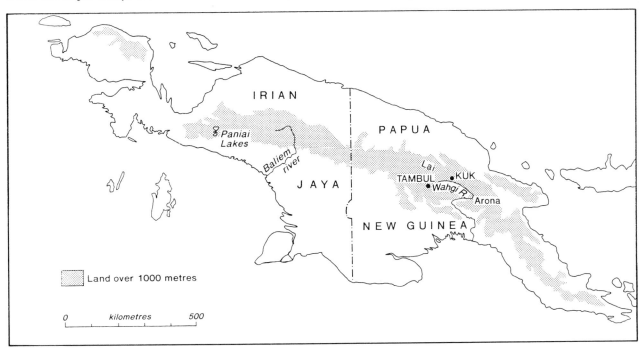

Fig. 3.1 New Guinea

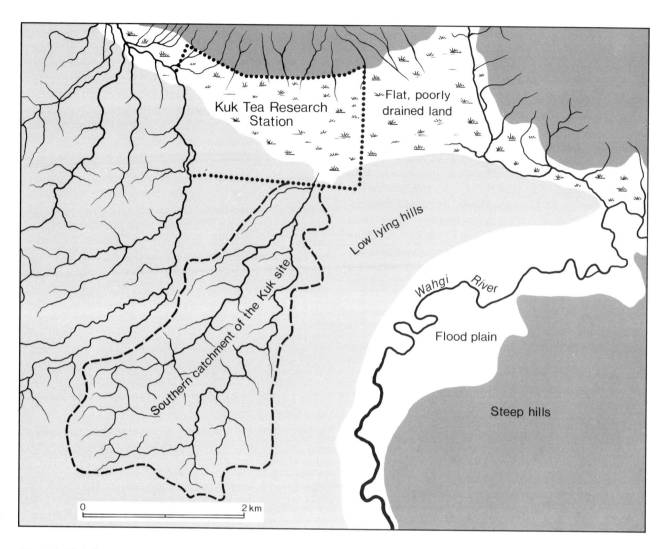

Fig. 3.2 Kuk Swamp

valley (Fig. 3.2), and discuss ways in which the evidence can be interpreted.

The subsistence economics of taro cultivation

Taro is sometimes grown in New Guinea as a wetland crop, but usually in the Highlands today it is found as a rainfed crop on dryland sites. Rainfed taro is not feasible in the seasonally dry Eastern Highlands, and it is here that we find archaeological evidence in the Arona valley for moisture retention devices in benched landscapes (Golson and Gardner 1990, 410), and in a few places the modern practice of irrigation using bamboo pipes to transfer water from springs (Loving 1976). In the Central and Western Highlands the rainfall is sufficient for taro to sustain itself as a dryland crop, but for other reasons it tends to be restricted in its occurrence. In these regions taro is found today only in swidden plots cleared from a bush or forest fallow, or alternatively as a minor crop planted in wet gullies or around house sites.

One reason that taro cultivators favour forested or wetland sites is the low fertility of degraded grassland soils

(Clarke 1977). Another reason is the likelihood of pest damage. Taro corms are eaten by several species of the *Papuana* beetles which thrive in deforested areas, and especially in areas of *Miscanthus floridulus*, the dominant tall cane grass of the Central and Western Highlands of Papua New Guinea. Powell *et al* (1975, 21) recorded that in the Mount Hagen area "while the taro crops are still growing flat stones are laid near the stalk on the surface of the ground to prevent beetles from boring holes in the tubers". To grow taro on a large scale and to avoid the pest damage that can otherwise overwhelm their crops, farmers usually locate their gardens either in wetlands or in forest swiddens (Bayliss-Smith 1985a, 1985b; Bayliss-Smith and Golson 1992).

Data on labour inputs for taro cultivation are rather sparse. Most observations refer to labour inputs and yields from the sweet potato, which today is the predominant staple in most of the Highlands. In the the Paniai lake basins of Irian Jaya, for example, the Kapauku studied by Pospisil (1963, 182, 444) have 90 per cent of all cultivated land under the sweet potato, and 82 per cent of the sweet potato yield comes from dryland gardens . Wetland cultivation of sweet potato requires twice the labour input of the hillside swiddens, but gives twice and sometimes three times the yield for the same area of land (1963, 126-7). Despite this advantage, the Kapauku people cannot rely on valley cultivation for all their sweet potato, since despite drainage the wetlands are susceptible to flooding in very wet years. When flooded the sweet potato crop is completely destroyed (1963, 86). As a well-adapted wetland crop, taro would of course be less vulnerable to the flood hazard.

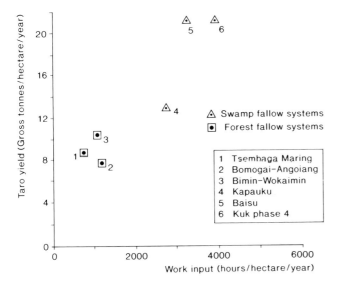

Fig. 3.3   Yields and labour inputs in taro cultivation: a comparison of dryland and wetland sites in the New Guinea Highlands

Wetlands have the further advantage for the Kapauku of allowing them a diversity of crops that cannot easily be grown on the degraded and infested soils of dryland slopes. For this reason taro, banana and sugar cane are all concentrated on the wetland sites (Pospisil 1963, 87). It seems likely that in pre-sweet potato times the advantage enjoyed by communities like this with access to wetlands would have been even greater. Pospisil's surveys of taro yields were not as thorough as those for sweet potato, but the data suggest an average yield of about 13 tonnes of taro per hectare per year of cropping (Fig. 3.3). This output was gained in return for less than 1200 hours of labour in draining and cultivating the swampy sites (1963, 423, 436-444).

For the Paniai lakes region a comparison cannot be made with taro grown in swiddens, but three separate studies from the Fringe Highlands indicate that in swiddens both labour and yields are less substantial (for sources, see Bayliss-Smith 1985a). Under modern conditions labour input into swiddens averages around 1000 hours per hectare-year, while yields are in the range 8-10 tonnes. In prehistory the use of stone axes would have necessitated more labour for certain tasks, and the total input might have been around 1500 hours.

Like most studies, the Kapauku survey concentrated on sweet potato, and for wetland taro the data are unsatisfactory. More complete surveys were carried out by Bayliss-Smith at Baisu Corrective Institution which is only 4 km from the archaeological site at Kuk. In its environmental characteristics Baisu is a close analogue of Kuk swamp, but being a prison farm obviously it is organised somewhat differently from any village production system. Detailed surveys at Baisu indicated a somewhat higher level of labour intensity than was estimated for the Kapauku, and this was confirmed by surveys at Tambul where men were draining swamps on river terraces and floodplains in the upper Kaugel valley (Bayliss-Smith 1985a). Labour inputs at Baisu averaged 3295 hours per hectare per year, but this was rewarded by excellent yields averaging per hectare just under 21 tonnes (Bayliss-Smith and Golson 1992, Table 4).

The Baisu management uses insecticide to counter *Papuana* damage, and this permits repeated crops of taro. Experience without insecticide at Baisu and also at Kuk and Wau in experimental plots, as well as the testimony of local farmers, indicate that in the Highlands today taro grown in drained soils in deforested areas usually suffers severe losses from beetle attack (Powell *et al* 1975, 21; Clarke 1977; Swift 1985; Bayliss-Smith and Golson 1992). Similarly in wetlands after drainage only a single taro crop can be taken unless insecticides are used. After one crop the plot reverted to fallow or, in the present day context, it was planted with sweet potato.

In Fig. 3.3 is also shown an estimate for the economics of the Phase 4 system at Kuk, about 2000 -1200 uncal BP. The estimate is based on the Baisu data modified to take into account the differences in technology in prehistory. The use of steel spades at Baisu rather than heavy digging sticks and paddle-shaped wooden spades is one obvious difference. Single-ended and, occasionally, double-ended paddles have been found in prehistoric contexts at a number of sites in the upper Wahgi valley (Golson and Steensberg 1985, 376). The oldest one that has been dated was found at Tambul and had a radiocarbon age of 3930 uncal BP. Similar tools were observed in use by Heider (1970) in the Baliem valley of Irian Jaya:

> *The paddle digging stick, cut down from a plank, is the same length [1.5-2.0 m] as the heavy stick, but one end splays out to a thin paddle 10 to 15 cm wide, which is fire hardened. It is used exclusively for slicing the ditch mud into chunks that can be easily lifted on to the fields by hand.* (Heider 1970, 379)

The similarity of these spades to tools found in peat bogs in Denmark has been noted by Steensberg (1980, 84), while Mowat (1991) has described a similar artefact from Lochlea crannog, Strathclyde, Scotland. These tools are illustrated in Fig. 3.4.

Experiments at Kuk by Steensberg (1980, 90, revised in Golson and Steensberg 1985, 362-3) demonstrated the superior performance of the steel spades compared to wooden ones. When excavating ditches, on average the modern spades increased a man's productivity from 0.6 to 2.2 cubic metres per hour. Gorecki's data (1985, 341) for steel spades show an even higher rate. He records that in the Mid-Wahgi wetlands today gangs of plantation labourers are required to dig ditches at a rate of 15 cu. m per man per day, a task which they can usually accomplish within 5 hours. On the other hand surveys covering longer periods of work at Baisu and Tambul show much less impressive rates (0.5-0.8 cu. m/hour), while Pospisil's (1963, 106) observations from Kapauku indicate a somewhat higher productivity for wooden tools than in Steensberg's experiments. Clearly there are many variables to be considered as well as type of tool, such as dimensions of ditch, cohesiveness and wetness of soil, and skill and motivation of the workforce. The data all seem to refer to men, who today provide the main workforce for ditch digging.

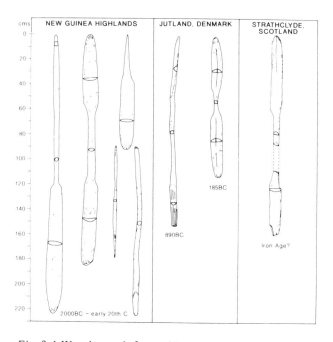

Fig. 3.4 Wooden tools for prehistoric wetland management

Digging ditches in Phase 4 is estimated to have required 472 hours/ha/yr compared to 159 hours in the modern Baisu system, while the total input is estimated at 3978 hours/ha/yr, a 20 per cent bigger input than in the modern system (Bayliss-Smith and Golson 1992, Table 5). Overall these data imply that wetland cultivation is about three times more labour intensive than forest swidden cultivation, and produces in return twice or two and a half times the yield of taro.

However, the wetland / forest swidden comparison is probably not relevant to Kuk over the last 2000 years at least, since the pollen evidence suggests a landscape that in the upper Wahgi valley was largely deforested well before this time (Powell *et al* 1975; Powell 1982). If areas under forest fallow in which swiddening could be carried out did not exist, then swidden cultivation does not represent a realistic alternative to the drainage of wetlands. To assess the relative advantages of the wetland side of production, we would need comparative data on labour inputs to dryland gardens under grassland fallow, and the associated yields. For pre-sweet potato times yams and bananas are the most likely dryland staples, but at present there is almost no information about the performance of these crops in the Highlands.

Archaeological evidence for drainage

The Kuk site was first revealed in 1969 during the initial drainage of Kuk Agricultural Research Station. Kuk is located in a swampy area amid the grasslands of the upper Wahgi valley at an altitude of 1580 m. It proved to have a long and complex history of agricultural use, characterised by episodes of large-scale drainage for cultivation separated by often substantial periods of abandonment. The most recent termination of drainage occurred about 100 years ago, perhaps because the full development of dryland systems for sweet potato cultivation had by then made the continued drainage of wetlands unnecessary. However, warfare and epidemic malaria are other possible reasons for this latest abandonment, which led to swampy conditions becoming re-established until the beginnings of research station activities in the late 1960s.

The evidence for agriculture consists of a stratified sequence of features cut into the swamp deposits. These are interpreted as representing two kinds of features: planting areas, either mounds separated by basins or beds separated by small ditches; and major disposal channels by which water was removed from the site. These features form virtually the totality of the archaeological evidence. There is no evidence for habitation in the wetland until the very end of the sequence; there is no recognisable evidence for cultivated plants until the same period (Phase 6), and then always in association with houses; and there is no evidence for agricultural tools (almost exclusively of wood) until about 500 years ago, older ones presumably having rotted because of fluctuating water levels in the swamp caused by its periodic drainage.

The archaeological evidence, although abundant, is therefore very restricted in its range. It can be supplemented by inference from geomorphology (Hughes *et al* 1991), palynology (Powell 1982), phytoliths (Wilson 1985), and (as outlined above) the ethnography of current agricultural practices in the Highlands. There has also been some archaeological work at nearby sites, which shows that the sequence at Kuk represents regional events and is not merely a local story (Golson 1982, 120-121; cf. Gillieson *et al* 1985). Golson and Gardner (1990) go further than this, and suggest that the sequence of vegetation changes in the Baliem valley and the management of benched landscapes in the Arona valley indicate that the Kuk model is representative of the Highlands as a whole.

The agricultural systems at Kuk, of which only one has so far been fully described (Bayliss-Smith and Golson 1992), fall into two groups. Drainage phases 1-3 date from 9000 uncal BP to about 2500 uncal BP. Unlike the more recent phases, they are not easily interpreted by reference to ethnographic analogues:

They are simpler in drainage organisation and they appear to be separated by long periods of inactivity in the swamp. Most importantly, their structural features are not linear and uniform but consist in part of small basins and interconnecting runnels which can admit and circulate water, as well as dispose of its excess. In contrast to the monoculture of taro and subsequently sweet potato proposed for Phases 4-6, these earlier systems are thought to represent mixed gardening with the intercropping of different plant species and allowance for their varying soil and moisture requirements. (Golson 1990, 145)

The communities operating these systems probably lived at low population densities, and they were managing a less degraded environment than in the more recent period. With hunting and gathering resources available in nearby forests, pig husbandry (if pigs were present) would not need to have been so systematic.

Phases 4-6 (after 2000 uncal BP to about 100 uncal BP), on the other hand, are interpreted as "representing the development of the pig-centred societies of modern times" (Golson 1990, 145). Phase 4 (after 2000-1200 uncal BP) is thought to represent intensive taro production, and Phase 6 (250 uncal BP to about 100 uncal BP) wetland cultivation of sweet potato in an economy based largely on dryland sweet potato production and pig husbandry, as at Paniai lakes today. The status of Phase 5 (about 400-250 uncal BP) is uncertain, but has been interpreted (Golson 1982, 132) as pre-sweet potato and hence the last of the taro-based systems.

Kuk Phase 4: intensification of wetland production

The evidence for Phase 4, which we discuss elsewhere in more detail (Bayliss-Smith and Golson 1992), consists of widespread networks of field ditches which articulate with the newly-dug major disposal channels. The ditches have a distinctive cross-sectional shape and network characteristics. They are typically gutter-like slots 35-40 cm deep and 25-30 cm wide, narrowing to 10-15 cm wide at their base. From the modest lowering of the water table that these ditches seem designed to achieve, we can infer that a water-tolerant crop was being grown, probably taro. Fragments of this Phase 4 system are encountered in about 75 ha of the 125 ha of alluvial fan that makes up the greater part of the wetland area of the Kuk site, the fan being the product of deposition by Kuk creek, a small stream which drains the southern catchment. Phase 4 ditches have also been found below Ep Ridge on the site's northern border, and they are known from elsewhere in the upper Wahgi valley (Golson 1976; Harris and Hughes 1978; Golson and Steensberg 1985).

Phase 4 ditches join each other at right angles, so the networks define grid patterns of small fields. Five such grid patterns were reconstructed using archaeological evidence from Block A9 at Kuk. The average field dimensions

(measured from the midpoints of surrounding ditches) were 8.8 x 12.2 m, with individual fields varying in shape from square to rectangular. Examples are shown in Fig. 3.5, which also shows the supposed direction of flow of drainage water deduced from the elevations of the bases of ditches.

As in the upper Kaugel valley today, these ditches may have been abandoned and re-used repeatedly, the soft peaty infill being easier to dig out than the clay substrate. Thus whole networks can be re-established after a period of swamp fallow. There is evidence that this practice was attempted in Phase 4, but not always successfully. Golson (1976, 215) has illustrated the case of two almost parallel Phase 4 ditches which diverge at an acute angle, suggesting that sometimes the infilling of a former ditch was so complete that no trace of it remained when the time came to recut the ditch along the same line. We do not know how quickly this infilling took place, as a result of the blockage of the main disposal channels, the growth of fallow vegetation, and fan alluviation processes. However, if we assume that *Papuana* beetles were as common and as destructive in the deforested landscape around 2000 uncal BP as they are today, then the removal of taro beetle infestation, and also weeds, would be most easily achieved by deliberate swamp fallowing.

We also know that within Block A9 of the Kuk site not all Phase 4 field systems were in simultaneous use. This can be inferred from the thin and discontinous horizon of air-fall volcanic ash, known as Olgaboli tephra, which is dated to 1190 uncal BP (Golson 1976, 212) and marks the end of Phase 4 activities at the site. In some ditch networks Olgaboli tephra is found almost at the bottom of ditches, while in other cases the ditches were nearly infilled at the time of this volcanic ash shower. Again this would be consistent with a shifting cultivation system where the swamp was a mosaic of plots, some in use but most under fallow.

Rather similar systems of ditches can be observed today in the upper Kaugel valley near Tambul, 40-50 km southwest of Kuk, where they are used to reclaim swampy areas for either taro or sweet potatoes (Bayliss-Smith 1985a, 1988). An example from Kiripia is shown in Fig. 3.5. Compared to the Phase 4 system at Kuk the Kiripia ditches are more closely spaced, and this probably reflects the greater soil drainage problems at the Kiripia site because of its cooler and wetter climate and the proximity of the Kaugel river.

The potential level of labour intensity in Phase 4 and the system's population capacity can be calculated if we make certain assumptions based on the ethnographic and archaeological evidence. We assume firstly that what we see in Phase 4 is a form of taro shifting cultivation using swamp fallow. We have used for calculation purposes a 20-year cycle, the same taro yields as at Baisu, and Baisu labour inputs increased to take account of wooden tools. Our calculated labour requirement and population capacity is much affected by other assumptions that must be made,

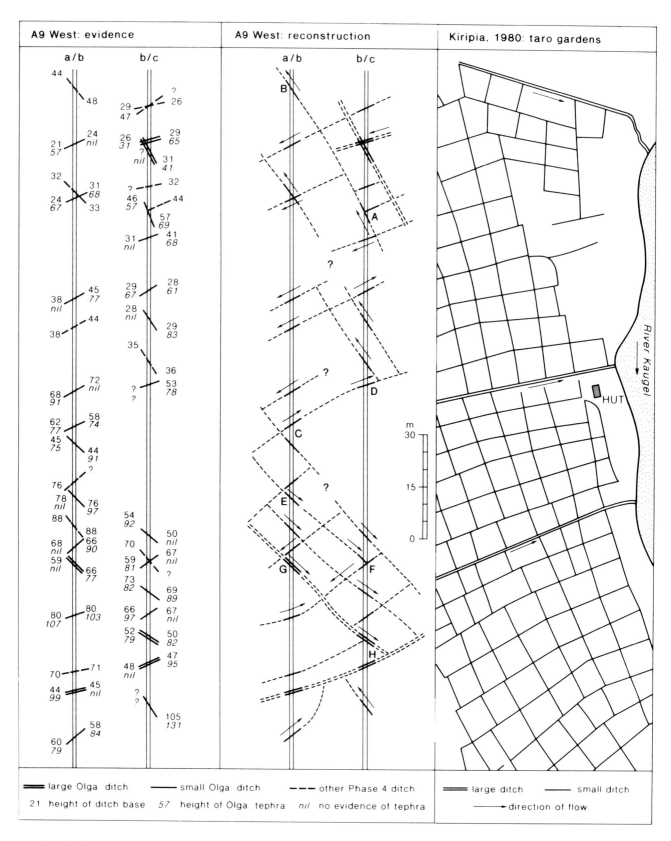

Fig. 3.5 Kuk Phase 4 ditches and field systems compared to modern taro gardens at Kiripia, upper Kaugel valley

firstly about the importance of wetland production in the total economy of the area, and secondly about the amount of surplus production required, for example for pig fodder. Making reasonable assumptions about both variables provides for us a range of 'standard populations' ranging from 78 to 480 people for Kuk swamp as a whole. The upper level would imply population densities as great as those achieved today under the sweet potato economy. As regards labour intensity, our calculations suggest that taro production, itself only one part of the economy of Phase 4, would have required 1.8-10.8 hours per adult person per week, depending again on the level of taro demand that we assume (Bayliss-Smith and Golson 1992, Table 6).

Despite sources of uncertainty, what is clear from these calculations is that the Phase 4 system of production did have a considerable potential for intensification. If more labour had been applied then greater surplus production could certainly have been achieved. These findings support Golson's earlier conclusion, that probably the onset of Phase 4 saw the the genesis of Wahgi society as known ethnographically:

> *The character of [Wahgi] society, defined by the role of the pig as a symbol of wealth and the key to exchanges of every kind, would have been determined by the particular ecological developments that I have suggested began 2500 years ago, the permanent replacement of woody regrowth by grassland. Differential access to land of high quality and the opportunities for some individuals to advance themselves through pig breeding could in the fullness of time lead to those inequalities between individuals and between clans that are described in the documents of the contact period* (Golson 1990, 144)

Elsewhere we have suggested that these fundamental changes in Phase 4 constituted a 'Colocasian Revolution' for those communities with the wetland resources to allow the intensification of land and labour use that is envisaged (Bayliss-Smith and Golson 1992). In this way certain Highlands communities could sidestep the growing ecological problems of dryland agriculture, they could forge new social relations of production that allowed a greater exploitation of women's labour, and they could also develop more complex exchange networks based on a surplus of taro produced from wetlands.

The various pre-conditions for this revolution are summarised in Fig. 3.6. Unfortunately the onset of this phase is poorly dated, and its predicted effects upon Wahgi society are so far poorly documented archaeologically. The reasons for the abandonment of the wetland manifestation of this new production system about 1200 radiocarbon years ago may be linked to the success of deliberate tree fallowing as a means of rehabilitating dryland soils. These are all ideas that will need to be tested in future research, both within and outside the wetlands.

CONCLUSION: WETLANDS AS SOCIETAL SEEDBEDS

In proposing that there occurred a Colocasian Revolution in the New Guinea Highlands in the second millennium uncal BP, we erect a local hypothesis which will need to be rigorously tested using local data. But in another sense what we propose is simply a local version of a much broader hypothesis, namely that wetlands were an environment which challenged prehistoric societies in a distinctive way that tended to produce a distinctive outcome.

In this connection much attention has been given to the centralised, despotic 'hydraulic civilisations' of Steward (1949) and Wittfogel (1957), since most authors have assumed that drainage and irrigation are equivalent (Mitchell 1973). Hydraulic societies are perhaps best exemplified in the Pacific by the socially-stratified chiefdoms of Polynesian high islands, where taro irrigation was the most developed in places and periods where power was the most centralised (Earle 1978; Spriggs 1990). But irrigation offers to authority the ability to withhold water as well as to allocate it, whereas drainage and terracing do not offer this power (Brookfield 1986).

The social and political structures encouraged by the needs of wetland drainage may therefore be rather different in character from those found in the 'hydraulic societies'. Wetland drainage can be simple in its technology and incremental in its evolution, and it need not require large-scale territorial control, centralised management or forced labour. In such circumstances drainage activity will tend to encourage the development within communities of reciprocal and co-operative relationships. As Blaikie and Brookfield (1987, 75) have pointed out, the role of co-operation in rural communities is a complex one, involving production and consumption, social control, religion and ceremony. Land management is only one of the functions of co-operation but it is certainly an important one, and one that they argue has been neglected. The technical demands of an activity like wetland drainage provide a good example of a land management practice which, at least in its initial stages, does seem to encourage the collective management of a common property resource.

The same may be said of temperate wetlands. Beresford and St Joseph hint at this tendency in their account of medieval Lincolnshire:

> *Country such as heaths and woodland ... led to the growth of scattered communities. Fenland and marsh, on the other hand, limited the degree to which individuals could maintain a separate economic existence. The effort at reclamation and the continuing need to maintain defences against flood waters have always called for a communal effort, and the characteristic village of the medieval fenland is a nucleated settlement...* (Beresford and St Joseph 1979, 100)

The Fenland village of Cottenham provides extraordinarily detailed evidence of communal wetland management from medieval times onwards. Ravensdale (1974, 68) refers to "the power and range of the commoners' organisation", and "the skill and flexibility with which the Cottenham ordermakers responded to the vagaries of water-level and climate". At Ramsey access to the various fen products was controlled by detailed regulations, leading to "many ... disputes caused by the array of complicated rights and interlocking interests" (Darby 1983, 24).

In more recent times this peasant power over the fens was considered by entrepreneurs to be a conservative force that

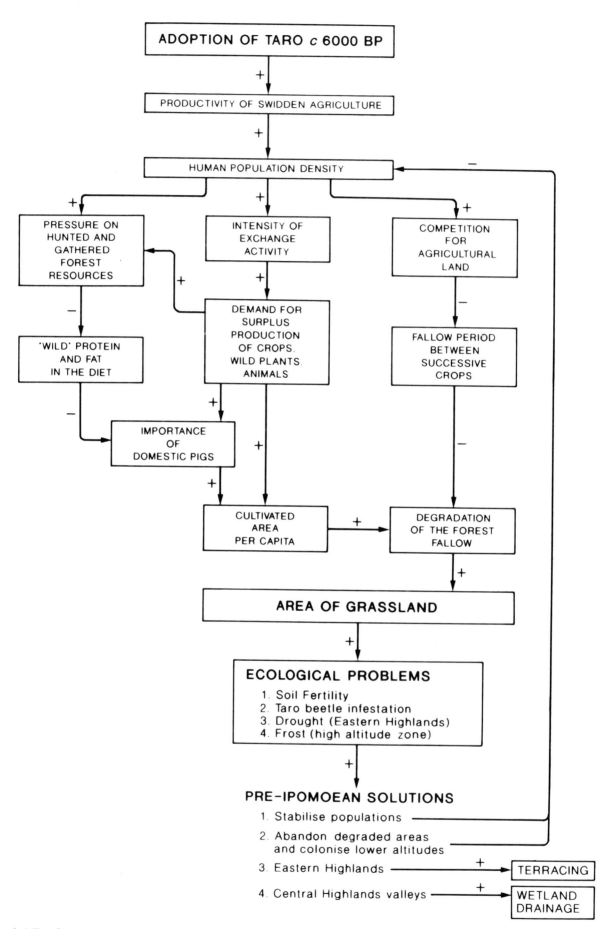

Fig. 3.6 The Colocasian Revolution in the New Guinea Highlands: social processes, ecological problems and regional solutions

obstructed 'improvement', and this points to a paradox of wetland management. Successful drainage by co-operative management, if sustained, can also provide an opportunity for the expropriation of wealth and the emergence of inequality, and this tendency may be resisted. In the English Fenland as in the New Guinea Highlands, what set limits on egalitarian relationships of co-operation within communities was the additional wealth that could be gained from wetlands once they had been successfully reclaimed.

As Spriggs (1990, 179) pointed out with reference to irrigation on the Melanesian island of Aneityum, "the potential for intensification is the potential to increase surplus production to meet the demands of the socio-political system". In Fenland the profit-seeking 'adventurers' saw their drainage efforts resented and resisted by the ordinary fenmen whose common rights to grazing and fen produce

were about to be expropriated. Is it fanciful, in the very different societies of New Guinea, to see a structural parallel in the tensions that also emerge in areas of agricultural intensification such as wetlands? These tensions arise between the 'big men' who benefit from the surplus extracted after wetland drainage, and either their followers whose labour is being exploited or their rivals whose power is being eclipsed.

In these ways we believe that the Colocasian Revolution in New Guinea could prove to have some structural features in common with similar 'revolutions' in wetland management in other parts of the world. At the beginning of this paper we emphasised some contrasts between the prehistory of temperate and tropical wetlands, but it may well be that wetland researchers ultimately find that they are converging on the same piece of theoretical high ground.

BIBLIOGRAPHY

Adams, W.M. 1989. Definition and development in African indigenous irrigation. *Azania 24*, 21-27.

Barker, G. 1985. *Prehistoric Farming in Europe.* Cambridge: Cambridge University Press.

Bayliss-Smith, T.P. 1985a. Pre-Ipomoean agriculture in the New Guinea highlands above 2000 metres: some experimental data on taro cultivation. In I.S. Farrington (ed.), *Prehistoric Intensive Agriculture in the Tropics 1,*285-320.Oxford: BAR International Series 232.

Bayliss-Smith, T.P. 1985b. Subsistence agriculture and nutrition in the Bimin valley, Oksapmin sub-district, Papua New Guinea. *Singapore Journal of Tropical Geography 6*, 101-115.

Bayliss-Smith, T.P. 1988. Prehistoric agriculture in the New Guinea Highlands: problems in defining the altitudinal limits to growth. In J. Bintliff and D. Davidson (eds), *Conceptual Issues in Environmental Archaeology*, 153-160. Edinburgh: Edinburgh University Press.

Bayliss-Smith, T.P. 1991. Food security and agricultural sustainability in the New Guinea Highlands: vulnerable people, vulnerable places. *IDS Bulletin* 22(3), 5-11.

Bayliss-Smith, T.P. and Golson, J. 1992. A Colocasian Revolution in the New Guinea Highlands? Insights from Phase 4 at Kuk. *Archaeology in Oceania.*

Beresford, M.W. and St Joseph, J.K.S. 1979. *Medieval England: An Aerial Survey*, 2nd edn.Cambridge: Cambridge University Press.

Blaikie, P. and Brookfield, H.C. 1987. *Land Degradation and Society.* London: Methuen.

Brandt, R.W., Van der Leeuw, S.E. and Van Wijngaarden-Bakker, L.H. 1984. Transformations in a Dutch estuary: research in a wet landscape. *World Archaeology 16*(1), 1-17.

Brookfield, H.C. 1986. Intensification intensified. *Archaeology in Oceania 21*, 177-180.

Clarke, D.L. 1972. A provisional model of an Iron Age society and its settlement system. In D.L. Clarke (ed.), *Models in Archaeology*, 801-870, London: Methuen.

Clarke, W.C. 1977. A change in subsistence staple in prehistoric New Guinea. *Proceedings of the Symposium of the International Society of Root Crops, 3rd, Ibadan 1973*, 159-163. Ibadan.

Coles, B. and Coles, J. 1986. *Sweet Track to Glastonbury The Somerset Levels in Prehistory.*London: Thames and Hudson.

Connah, G. 1985. Agricultural intensification and sedentism in the firki of N.E. Nigeria. In I.S. Farrington (ed.), *Prehistoric Intensive Agriculture in the Tropics 2*, 765-785. Oxford: BAR International Series 232.

Connah, G. 1987. *African Civilisations. Precolonial Cities and States in Tropical African Archaeological Perspective.* Cambridge: Cambridge University Press.

Darby, H.C. 1983. *The Changing Fenland.* Cambridge: Cambridge University Press.

Darling, P.J. 1984. *Archaeology and History in Southern Nigeria*, 2 vols. Oxford: BAR International Series 215.

Denevan, W.M. 1982. Hydraulic agriculture in the American tropics: forms, measures and recent research. In K. V. Flannery (ed.), *Maya Subsistence*, 181-204, London: Academic Press.

Dolukhanov, P.M. 1979. *Ecology and Economy in Neolithic Eastern Europe.* London: Duckworth.

Donkin, R.A. 1985. The Peccary -- with observations on the introduction of pigs to the New World. *Transactions of the American Philosophical Society 75*(5), 1-152.

Earle, T. 1978. *Economic and Social Organisation of a Complex Chiefdom the Halelea District, Kaua'i, Hawaii.* Anthropological Papers 63, Museum of Anthropology, University of Michigan, Ann Arbor.

Gillieson, D., Gorecki, P.,P. and Hope, G.S. 1985. Prehistoric agricultural systems in a lowland swamp, Papua New Guinea. *Archaeology in Oceania 20,* 32-37.

Godwin H. 1978. *Fenland: Its Ancient Past and Uncertain Future.* Cambridge: Cambridge University Press.

Golson, J. 1976. Archaeology and agricultural history in the New Guinea Highlands. In G. de G. Sieveking, I.H. Longworth and K.E. Wilson (eds), *Problems in Economic and Social Archaeology,* 201-220. London: Duckworth.

Golson, J. 1977. No room at the top: agricultural intensification in the New Guinea Highlands. In J. Golson, J. Allen and R. Jones (eds), *Sunda and Sahul: Prehistoric Studies in Southeast Asia, Melanesia and Australia,* 601-638. London: Academic Press.

Golson, J. 1982. The Ipomoean Revolution revisited: society and the sweet potato in the upper Wahgi valley. In A. Strathern (ed.), *Inequality in New Guinea Highlands Societies,* 109-136. Cambridge: Cambridge University Press.

Golson, J. 1989. The origins and development of New Guinea agriculture. In D.R. Harris and G.C. Hillman (eds), *Foraging and Farming: the Evolution of Plant Exploitation,* 678-687. London: Unwin Hyman.

Golson, J. 1990. Kuk and the development of agriculture in New Guinea: retrospection and introspection. In D.E. Yen and J.M.J. Mummery (eds), *Pacific Production Systems. Approaches to Economic Prehistory,* 139-147. Occasional Papers in Prehistory 18, Department of Prehistory, Research School of Pacific Studies, Australian National University, Canberra.

Golson, J. and Gardner, D.S. 1990. Agriculture and sociopolitical organisation in New Guinea Highlands prehistory. *Annual Review of Anthropology 19,* 395-417.

Golson, J. and Steensberg, A. 1985. The tools of agricultural intensification in the New Guinea Highlands. In I.S.Farrington (ed.), *Prehistoric Intensive Agriculture in the Tropics 1,* 347-384. Oxford: BAR International Series 232.

Gorecki, P.P. 1985. The conquest of a new 'wet and dry' territory: its mechanism and its archaeological consequence. In I.S. Farrington (ed.), *Prehistoric Intensive Agriculture in the Tropics,* 321-345. Oxford: BAR International Series 232.

Groube, L. 1989. The taming of the rain forests: a model for Late Pleistocene forest exploitation in New Guinea. In D.R. Harris and G.C. Hillman (eds), *Foraging and Farming: the Evolution of Plant Exploitation,* 292-304. London: Unwin Hyman.

Harlan, J.R. 1989. The tropical African cereals. In D.R. Harris and G.C. Hillman (eds), *Foraging and Farming: the Evolution of Plant Exploitation,* 335-343. London: Unwin Hyman.

Harris, E.C. and Hughes, P. J. 1978. An early agricultural system at Mugumamp Ridge, Western Highlands Province, Papua New Guinea. *Mankind 11,* 437-444.

Heider, K.G. 1970. *The Dugum Dani: a Papuan Culture in the Highlands of West New Guinea.* Viking Fund Publications in Anthropology 49, Wenner-Gren Foundation, New York.

Hughes, P.J., Sullivan, M.E. and Yok, D. 1991. Human induced erosion in a highlands catchment in Papua New Guinea: the prehistoric and contemporary records. *Zeitschrift fur Geomorphologie,* N.F. Suppl. -Bd. 83, 227-239.

Louwe Kooijmans, L.P. 1987. Neolithic settlement and subsistence in the wetlands of the Rhine/Meuse Delta of the Netherlands. In J.M. Coles and A.J. Lawson (eds), *European Wetlands in Prehistory,* 227-252. Oxford: Clarendon Press .

Loving, R. 1976. Use of bamboo by the Awa. *Journal of the Polynesian Society 85,* 521-542.

Mathewson, K. 1990. Rio Hondo refelections: notes on Puleston's place and the archaeology of Maya landscape. In M.D. Pohl (ed.), *Ancient Maya Wetland Agriculture: Excavations on Albion Island, Northern Belize,* 21-52. Boulder: Westview Press.

Mitchell, W.P. 1973. The hydraulic hypothesis: a reappraisal. *Current Anthropology 14,* 532-534.

Pohl, M.D., Bloom, P.R. and Pope, K.O. 1990. Interpretations of wetland farming in northern Belize: excavations at San Antonio Rio Hondo. In M.D. Pohl (ed.), *Ancient Maya Wetland Agriculture: Excavations on Albion Island, Northern Belize,* 187-278. Boulder: Westview Press.

Pospisil, L. 1963. *Kapauku Papuan Economy.* Publications in Anthropology 67, Yale University Press, New Haven.

Powell, J.M., Kalunga, A.,Moge, R., Pono, C., Zimike F. and Golson, J. 1975. *Ancient Traditions of the Mount Hagen Area.* Occasional Paper 12, Department of Geography, University of Papua New Guinea, Port Moresby.

Powell, J.M. 1982. History of plant use and man's impact on the vegetation. In J.L. Gressitt (ed.),*Biogeography and Ecology of New Guinea,* 207-227. The Hague: Junk.

Pryor, F. 1976. Fen-edge land management in the Bronze Age: an interim report on excavations at Fengate, Peterborough, 1971-5. In C. Burgess and R. Miket (eds), *Settlement and Economy in the Third and Second Millennia b.c.,* 29-49. Oxford: BAR British Series 33.

Ravensdale, J.R. 1974. *Liable to Flood. Village Landscape on the edge of the Fens, A.D. 450-1850.* Cambridge: Cambridge University Press.

Serpenti, L. 1965. *Cultivators in the Swamps. Social Structure and Horticulture in a New Guinean Society.* Assen: Van Gorcum.

Sorenson, E.R. 1972. Socio-ecological change among the Fore of New Guinea. *Current Anthropology 13,* 349-383.

Spriggs, M.J.T. 1982. Taro cropping systems in the Southeast Asian-Pacific region: archaeological evidence. *Archaeology in Oceania 17*, 7-15.

Spriggs, M.J.T. 1990. Why irrigation matters in Pacific prehistory. In D.E. Yen and J.M.J. Mummery (eds), *Pacific Production Systems. Approaches to Economic Prehistory*. Occasional Papers in Prehistory 18, Research School of Pacific Studies, Australian National University, Canberra.

Steensberg, A. 1980. *New Guinea Gardens: a Study of Husbandry with Parallels in Prehistoric Europe*. London: Academic Press.

Steward, J.H. 1949. Cultural causality and law: a trial formulation of the development of early civilisation. *American Anthropologist 51*, 1-27.

Vasey, D. 1979. Population and agricultural intensity in the humid tropics. *Human Ecology 7*, 269-284.

Vasey, D., Harris, D.R., Olson, G.W., Spriggs, M.J.T. and Turner B.L. 1984. The role of standing water and water-logged soils in raised-field, drained-field and island-bed agriculture. *Singapore Journal of Tropical Agriculture 5*, 63-72.

Wilson, S.M. 1985. Phytolith evidence from Kuk, an early agricultural site in Papua New Guinea. *Archaeology in Oceania 20*, 90-97.

Wittfogel, K.A. 1957. *Oriental Despotism*. New Haven: Yale University Press.

Yen, D.E. 1990. Environment, agriculture and the colonisation of the Pacific. In D.E. Yen and J.M.J. Mummery (eds), *Pacific Production Systems. Approaches to Economic Prehistory*, 258-277. Occasional Papers in Prehistory 18, Department of Prehistory, Research School of Pacific Studies, Australian National University, Canberra.

4

RECENT DEVELOPMENTS IN IRISH WETLAND RESEARCH

Barry Raftery

SYNOPSIS

The paper deals with the results of 6 seasons' excavations between 1985 and 1990 on wooden trackways in Irish midland bogs. During this period more than 60 tracks were investigated. Dating, both by dendrochronological and radiocarbon means, indicated a chronological range for the tracks between the mid-fourth millennium cal BC and the 6th century AD. A wide range of structural types was encountered,including tracks of brushwood hurdles and of massive, transversely-laid oak planks.The most impressive construction was a 2 km long road of transverse oaks,which was dated to 148 BC.Under the timbers of this track an interesting series of wooden artefacts was found. Following on the success of the campaign of excavation and the associated survey, an Irish Archaelogical Wetland Unit has been established. This is a 4-person team,based on the UCD Campus, which has a five-year brief to carry out a comprehensive survey of archaeological features in Irish bogs.

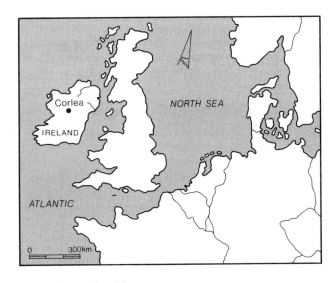

Fig. 4.1 Location Map

In 1984 the existence of a very large trackway of split oak planks in Corlea bog, Co. Longford (Fig. 4.1) was brought to scientific attention. In the same year wood samples were taken from it to Queen's University, Belfast and these were dated by dendrochronological analysis to 148 BC. The demonstrated Iron Age dating of the structure allied to its exceptional dimensions clearly emphasised its importance and the writer was invited by the National Monuments Branch of the Office of Public Works to carry out rescue excavation on the track in the summer of 1985. Initial results were promising and the campaign continued with State funding over the following two seasons. During this period,while work was concentrated on the big Iron Age track, superficial examination of the surrounding bogland revealed the presence of an alarming number of hitherto unrecorded trackways. Almost all of these were under threat of imminent destruction.In 1988 a joint wetland

project was initiated, financed by the European Social Fund and involving students and staff from Exeter University and University College Dublin.This continued during 1989 and 1990 and has been approved until 1993. The basic purpose of the funding was the training of students in all aspects of wetland archaeology. In the course of this training programme it was possible to carry out extensive survey and excavation on a large number of the threatened trackways.

At the time of writing almost 70 tracks have been examined archaeologically, the most important on an extensive scale. Radiocarbon dates are now available for almost all the excavated tracks, thanks to the generous cooperation of the Biologisch-Archaeologisch Instituut,Rijksuniversiteit, Groningen in the Netherlands.Dates have also been made available recently for wood samples from older trackway

Fig. 4.2 Mid-fourth millennium BC trackway, Corlea 9, Co. Longford

excavations preserved in the National Museum. In addition in five instances,where suitable oak timbers were present,dendrochronological dates from Belfast have been forthcoming.

The obvious value of the work since 1985 has given rise to the creation of the Irish Archaeological Wetland Unit in the autumn of 1990. This is staffed by four specialists in wetland research under the general direction of the writer with Aonghus Moloney as Field Director. It is under the joint auspices of the Office of Public Works and the Department of Archaeology, University College, Dublin. Newly refurbished and fully-equipped premises have been provided on the campus of University College, Dublin to serve as the unit headquarters.Its mandate is to carry out a systematic survey of the bogs of Ireland over a period of five years, recording, planning and, in selected instances, excavating archaeological features which are discovered. Though still only in its initial stages the unit has already discovered some four hundred new trackways and has carried out a largescale excavation on a recently discovered palisaded settlement of the later Bronze Age at Clonfinlough, Co. Offaly.

A further development arising from the Corlea excavations has been the decision to build a permanent wetland interpretative centre at the site. This followed the direct intervention of the Taoiseach Charles J. Haughey,T.D., who visited the site in the summer of 1990. Monies from the European Structural Fund will finance the project. The ly concentrated on trackways in Co. Longford (Fig 4.1). Most of the work has been in the townlands of Corlea, Derryoghil, Annaghbeg and Cloonbony. Other recent trackway excavations have been carried out at Bloomhill, Co. Offaly (Breen 1988) and by the National Museum in Derrynaflan and Littleton bogs, Co. Tipperary. A bronze sword of Late Bronze Age date was found associated with the Littleton trackway site (Michael Ryan, pers. comm.).

THE CORLEA PROJECT

In the course of the six-year campaign (Raftery 1990) it has been possible to recognise a wide range of differing forms of trackway construction varying in date from around the middle of the fourth millennium cal BC to the 6th century AD (based on dendrochronology). The earliest are of simple construction. They are made of longitudinally-placed branches and brushwood with occasional transverse supports providing a walking surface 1.20 m to 1.50 m in width (Fig. 4.2). Pegs were only occasionally used to help stabilise the mass of the material. Axe-marks, when present, are clearly recognisable as having been made by stone implements. They take a consistent form. The facets are short, narrow and markedly concave and have been produced by chopping downwards at a sharp angle.

There is a greater variety among the tracks dated by dendrochronology and by calibrated radiocarbon dates to the third millennium BC. The simplest is exemplified by Derryoghil 7 which was a pedestrian walkway consisting of straight stems of ashwood, placed logitudinally in groups of three, and supported at intervals by short transverse timbers. A more substantial track of the third millennium cal BC is that uncovered at Cloonbony. This was a corduroy road of tightly-packed roundwood stems, mainly of alder, laid on a substructure of longitudinal timbers and brushwood. Parallel rows of pegs helped to keep the timbers in place. Preservation of axe facets was poor on this track but a number, clearly the marks of stone tools, were recognisable.

Another third millennium BC track of transverse timbers was that designated as Corlea 6 (Fig. 4.3). This differed in a number of significant aspects from Cloonbony for it was entirely without pegs and both roundwood and split stems were used in its construction. These were predominantly of oak and ash. Tree-ring analysis of one of the oaks gave a felling date of 2259 BC. Axe facets present on timbers from this track were especially interesting. They differed in every way from those of demonstrably Neolithic character. They were broader and flatter than the facets of stone axes and had crisp and regularly convex jamb-curves (Raftery 1990, fig. 80). In addition, some of the oaks present had been chopped cleanly and deeply across the grain. It is thus difficult not to conclude from these axe-marks that metal tools had been used. If true this is a matter of considerable significance for the origins of metallurgy in the west.

Tracks made of longitudinally-laid bundles of brushwood, as already known in the fourth millennium cal BC,

Fig. 4.3 Corlea 6, Co. Longford, dated to 2259 BC

centre, an impressive modern construction designed to harmonise with its bogland surroundings, will house a full archaeological display illustrating the results of six years' excavation in the region, and will contain as a centre-piece a gallery in which a conserved 20 m stretch of the great Iron Age roadway found at Corlea will be exhibited. It is proposed that the timbers, lifted specially for the display, will be pre-treated in a low molecular solution of PEG 400 after which they will be freeze-dried. The initial process will be carried out in custom-made tanks locally housed in premises supplied by Bord na Móna (the Irish Turf Board). The final conservation takes place in Portsmouth where suitably large freeze-drying facilities are available.

The six year campaign conducted by the writer has, with the exception of a single site in Co. Galway, been exclusive-

Fig. 4.4 Late third/early second millennium BC hurdle trackway, Annaghbeg 2, Co. Longford

continued to be used in the third and second millennia. This is scarcely surprising for such a basic method of simply and effectively providing a safe, dry passage across a bog is essentially timeless. In fact, accounts of the construction of such trackways are known from the recent past. One track, however, of which only a single example was uncovered in the course of the campaign, was of short, straight rods regularly laid in transverse arrangement on a bed of brushwood. There were also several, dating around the middle of the second millennium cal BC, which consisted of no more than a few long stems laid down directly on the bog surface. These represent the minimum effort to provide footing for agile travellers across stretches of soggy bogland.

Tracks incorporating panels of woven hurdles are common in the second millennium cal BC especially during its later phases. No fewer than nine examples have been investigated to date. These were generally of hazel rods and there is considerable evidence that coppicing was practised. In most instances the panels were quite narrow, being no more than 50-60 cm wide on average and they were in general 1.50 m to 3 m in length. One track in Corlea contained in its construction a woven panel which was 2.50 m long and 1.50 m in width.

The finest hurdle track was that designated Annaghbeg 2 which dated to the late third/early second millennium cal BC. Three overlapping panels were uncovered in the course of excavation. Two were damaged by a drainage channel, the third, however, was intact (Fig. 4.4). This was 5.20 m long and 1.10-1.20 m wide. It had been superbly constructed of long straight hazel rods skilfully and tightly

Fig. 4.5 Corlea 1, Co. Longford, dated to 148 BC

woven around 12 (or possibly 13) sails. This panel showed the hurdle maker's craft at its best.

A date early in the last millennium BC has been established by dendrochronology for two tracks. One, Derryoghil 1, is made of sizable oak planks laid transversely on a brushwood substructure. It was dated to 938 ± 9 BC. The second track, in Garryduff bog, Co. Galway, was composed of exceedingly thin oak planks, many of which were mortised at their ends but which were only occasionally pegged in position. Indeed, the presence in some instances of three mortices along the length of a plank suggested that these might have been reused timbers brought from a dismantled structure of some sort. The technique of construction at Garryduff was unique. Three main layers were present, a basal layer of rough brushwood and random planks, upon which lay a level of transverse planks which in turn was overlain by a narrow walking surface of longitudinally placed planks. This interesting example was dated to 892 ± 9 BC.

The great Iron Age road (Corlea 1) which first drew scientific attention to the area dominates all the other tracks investigated by its sheer size and by the magnitude of the work which was clearly involved in its construction. It has now been established that there were once two stretches which are likely to be contemporaneous, one in Corlea bog the other in Derraghan More, separated from one another by a small island of dry land. Each length of trackway was about 1 km in length. Most of this track was in the state-owned section of the bog and has been almost entirely obliterated there largely as a result of intensive peat-milling activities. In the east, however, in a small area of privately owned bog, about 80 m of the track survives intact under a cover of about 1.20 m of peat.

In the course of the six-year campaign most of the surviving stretches in the Bord na Móna bog were investigated and a section some 35 m in length was excavated at the eastern edge of the privately-owned bog. In all some 150 m of Corlea 1 have been examined.

Constructional details were largely consistent along the length of the track. Long straight roundwood stems were laid in parallel pairs, 1.20 m apart on average, to serve as supports for the upper timbers. Occasionally the number of these runners was increased, doubtless because the track builders encountered local problems of excessive wetness. In places too, to counteract the difficulties caused by the hummocks and hollows of the bog, concentrations of branches, brushwood, scrap timbers, miscellaneous off-cuts and even discarded wooden artefacts were thrown down to give additional support to the structural elements of the road and to try to level the surface upon which the timbers were laid.

The superstructure of the road was made of transverse oak planks varying between 3 m and 4 m in length (Fig. 4.5). The largest were as much as 60 cm wide and 10-15 cm thick. Rectangular mortices had usually, though not always, been chopped into the ends of the planks and through these pegs

Fig. 4.6 Carved end of runner from substructure of Corlea 1

of birch or oak had been hammered deep into the bog. Some of the larger planks had a double mortice at one end. In one section of the track two sleepers were encountered each with a pair of deep rectangular notches cut into their undersides. These notches fitted perfectly over the two underlying runners and their purpose seems to have been to counteract the excessive projection of the two sleepers above the level of the walking surface.

One short stretch of the roadway, towards the centre of the Corlea bog, differed from that encountered elsewhere. Here the timbers were in a confused jumble with sleepers lying on top of one another at varied angles and longitudinals placed randomly on top of these. Some of the timbers in this area had been heavily burnt. It is possible that the track was never finished here or that it had been deliberately and systematically dismantled. The latter explanation certainly applies to a stretch excavated in 1990. Here there was clear evidence of intensive burning which had caused major damage to several of the massive oak sleepers. At a later stage, where gaps had appeared, some of the surviving sleepers had been replaced lengthwise along the centre of the track to facilitate its continued use by pedestrians.

As noted above a number of wooden artefacts, the majority broken and useless, were brought to light in the fill directly under the timbers of the track (Raftery 1990, 51-59). Commonest are the hand-carved staves of flat-bottomed, bucket-like containers. Most identified pieces are of willow. There is also a large fragmentary object of oak which might be part of the frame of a cart. This is a straight rectangular-sectioned bar of wood, 1.45 m in length, pierced by thin slots into which flat planks have been inserted. Several other carved pieces of oak recovered in the same area might also be parts of a vehicle. A particularly fine object is a polished board of ash which has a series of delicate tenons and other elements fitted into it with the aid of tiny transverse dowels. It is an exceptional example of Iron Age joinery but its purpose is entirely unknown. Other finds included a troughlike object of oak, two notched pegs, one barbed at the end like a modern tent peg, a knife(?) handle, an ard-head of oak, a heavy mallet-like object of the same material and a thin rod of yew wood, 95 cm in length, with carefully rounded and polished ends. It is possibly a herdsman's switch.

Of especial interest was a 5 m long ash stem which served as one of the runners of the substructure. One end of this has been worked smooth and 16 cm from this a deep notch has been cut around its circumference (Fig. 4.6). Projecting a short distance from the knob thus formed was a short length of branch the end of which had also been cut smooth. A second similar stump of a branch projected from the log, in the same direction as the first stump, a short distance just below the notch. Though the workmanship is crude the clear impression is that the shape produced was deliberately intended. The purpose of this strange artefact is, of course, speculative but it might conceivably once have served as some sort of cult emblem akin perhaps to the crude wooden renderings known from parts of northern Europe and from Thuringia in Germany (Schutz 1983,332-6; Krüger 1988, Tafeln 52,53; Coles 1990,328-9).

The only trackway encountered which postdated the birth of Christ was a simple plank path dated by dendrochronology to 587 ± 9 AD. In the Bord na Móna bog this had been completely obliterated, surviving only in a small area where it had been covered by one of the ridges of milled peat. In the privately owned bog to the east, however, it was well preserved under about 60 cm of peat. It consisted of a series of individual planks laid end-to-end or with overlapping ends, supported at intervals by short transverse lengths of oak roundwood. Regularly drilled circular holes occurred in the ends of some of the planks and short square-sectioned pegs of oak had been pushed into these to secure the planks in place.

DISCUSSION

The excavations to date have revealed a wealth of information, both archaeological and environmental, and the work of processing and interpreting the data is now in progress. It will take some time before all the available strands of evidence have been fully assessed. It is clear, however, that many questions have been raised for which answers are not readily forthcoming.

Obviously the problem of crossing the waterlogged bogs was a recurrent one which presented itself at intervals from the Neolithic to the Early Historic period. Those dwelling in the bog environs, using the available resources of their immediate neighbourhood, sought to overcome that problem in a variety of different ways and with varying degrees of ingenuity. It is evident that climatic fluctuations influenced the intensity of trackway construction and the available series of dates suggests that there were prolonged periods of excessive wetness, especially during the second millennium cal BC.

Most of the tracks were built essentially for pedestrian traffic but it is possible that animals too could have been brought along them. Our absence of information, however, concerning the nature of contemporary settlement on the drylands surrounding the bogs makes it difficult to be specific about the ways in which the tracks were used. Nor can we estimate in detail the numbers involved in the construction, and subsequent use, of any of the tracks. In most cases, however, especially where tracks of simple brushwood or hurdle construction are concerned, no great numbers of people need have been necessary for their manufacture. A rather greater concentration of manpower would have been required in the construction of tracks such as Corlea 6 for here larger trees had to be felled and the timbers trimmed and split before transporting them to the site. It is thus not immediately clear why tracks of the proportions of Corlea 6 or Cloonbony were built in the third millennium BC. They seem unnecessarily large for solely pedestrian use and even if intended for cattle droving as well the work involved seems still to be excessive. There is no evidence that wheeled vehicles existed in Ireland at this time so we must wonder whether there was an element of communal prestige inherent in the planning and construction of these large, early tracks.

As regards Corlea 1, the Iron Age road, this seems certainly to have been the case. The huge oaks employed imply a largescale and highly coordinated use of manpower. It is difficult not to regard this as a tribal undertaking the significance of which superseded purely local considerations. The possibility that the building of Corlea 1 is in some way linked to some of the Iron Age sites of major ceremonial significance such as Cruachain, the ancient focus of Connacht, across the Shannon to the west, cannot be discounted though this can scarcely be demonstrated (Raftery 1990, 50-1). It seems, at any rate, that the intention was to build something big and impressive, something which might almost be described as monumental. Nowhere else in Ireland is there a contemporary wooden roadway of equal dimensions. This was a roadway meant for display and ostentation. Its construction in 148 BC could well be an element in the important cultural developments which seem to be taking place in the country during this period. The evidence is incomplete but still tantalising for this was probably the time when La Tène influences were becoming established in the land. It was certainly the time when some at least of the great linear earthworks were being built (Lynn 1982, 121-8: Baillie and Brown 1989, 11) and when the imposing 40 m diameter structure was erected at Navan Fort, the Iron Age capital of Ulster (Lynn 1986, 11-19; Baillie 1986, 20-22; 1988, 37-40).

It is difficult not to assume that the Corlea road was intended for the passage of wheeled vehicles. Indeed, as noted above, some of the fragmentary timber artefacts recovered in the fill under the road could have come from a cart. Nothing which may definitively be regarded as from a vehicle was found, however, and there were no wheel ruts or wear on the surface of the road which could indicate that vehicles were used.

It may be that the great roadway was in use for only a very limited period. The two disturbed sections referred to above suggest that deliberate destruction took place. The possibility that this happened soon after the building of the track is implied by detailed palaeobotanical examination of the peat immediately underneath the timber of the road. This revealed no trace of the crushing and compression which would inevitably result from the movement of vehicles across the road for any extended period. Indeed, the examinations gave rise to the view that the very weight of the timbers was such that in little more than ten years they had sunk into the bog. Thus the seeming emphasis on size rather than practicality rapidly made the road unusable.

Nowhere in Britain are comparable trackways known. On the European mainland, however, remarkably similar constructions occur in Lower Saxony (Hayen 1979; Coles and Coles 1989,168). Their dating overlaps with that of Corlea 1. Despite the restricted distribution of tracks of this type it seems nonetheless unwise to regard such structural similarities as evidence of cultural ties between the two regions. The similarities can readily be interpreted as no more than convergence, the product of unrelated groups finding common solutions to common problems posed by the necessity of crossing wet bogs. It is however interesting to note that the tracks of Lower Saxony occur in an area which, by the 1st century AD at least, and probably before this, was occupied by the Germanic Cauci (Krüger 1988, 50, Abb. 62) and that the same tribe, later to become the historic Ui Cuaich, are marked on Ptolemy's second century map (Byrne 1984) as occurring in the general area of east central Ireland.

BIBLIOGRAPHY

Baillie, M.G.L. 1986. The Central Post from Navan Fort. *Emania* 1, 20-21.

Baillie, M.G.L. 1988. The Dating of the Timbers from Navan Fort and the Dorsey, Co. Armagh. *Emania* 4, 37-40.

Baillie, M.G. and Brown, D.M. 1989. Further dates from the Dorsey. *Emania* 6, 11.

Breen,T.C. 1988. Excavation of a roadway at Bloomhill Bog, County Offaly. *Proceedings of the Royal Irish Academy* 88 C 10, 321-339.

Byrne, F.J. 1984. Map 14 (Ptolemy's Map). In T.W. Moody, F.X. Martin and F.J. Byrne (eds), *A New History of Ireland*. Vol.9 Part 2, 98. Oxford: Clarendon Press.

Coles, B. 1990. Anthropomorphic wooden figurines from Britain and Ireland. *Proceedings of the Prehistoric Society* 56, 315-333.

Coles, B. and Coles, J. 1989. *People of the Wetlands*. London: Thames and Hudson.

Hayen, H. 1979. *Der Bohlenweg VI(PR) im grossen Moor am Dümmer* Materialhefte zur Ur-und Frühgeschichte Niedersachsens, Heft 15 .

Krüger, B. (ed.) 1988. *Die Germanen*. Berlin: Akademie-Verlag.

Lynn, C. 1982. The Dorsey and other linear earthworks. In B.G. Scott (ed.), *Studies on Early Ireland: Essays in honour of M.V. Duignan*, 121-128. Belfast.

Lynn, C. 1986. Navan Fort; A Draft Summary of D.M. Waterman's Excavations. *Emania* 1, 11-19.

Raftery, B. 1990. *Trackways Through Time*. Dublin: Headline Publishing.

Schutz, H. 1983. *The Prehistory of Germanic Europe*. New Haven and London: Yale University Press.

5

FLAG FEN, FENGATE, PETERBOROUGH II: FURTHER DEFINITION, TECHNIQUES AND ASSESSMENT (1986-90)

Francis Pryor and Maisie Taylor

SYNOPSIS

This paper is a general review of work at the Bronze Age site at Flag Fen, Peterborough, England. It updates the last report (Pryor et al 1986), and contains interim statements on continuing research into timber and wood and dendrochronology (by Janet Neve). The two developments of particular importance are the discovery of a kilometre-long alignment of posts, which may have served as a boundary, and the recognition that ritual played a major role in the site's establishment and use.

Flag Fen is a waterlogged site of mainly Bronze Age date situated near the edge of the East Anglian Fens, at Peterborough, Cambridgeshire (Fig. 5.1). The site is close to the Fengate fen-edge where a succession of ancient sites and landscapes was investigated between 1971 and 1978 (Pryor 1974; 1978; 1980; 1984). It was discovered during archaeological survey in 1982 and has been the subject of excavation ever since; apart from a first preliminary season (1983), the excavations have taken place each year, throughout the frost-free months (April-October). Finds have included large quantities of timber, pottery, animal bone and, latterly, metalwork. Environmental evidence is particularly well preserved.

The excavations have been funded by English Heritage as part of the Fenland Project (Hall 1987; Hall and Chippindale 1988; Hall et al 1987). The principal other local waterlogged site of prehistoric age to have been excavated recently is the Neolithic causewayed enclosure at Etton, near Maxey, Cambridgeshire, some ten miles north of Peterborough (Pryor and Kinnes 1982; Pryor et al 1985).

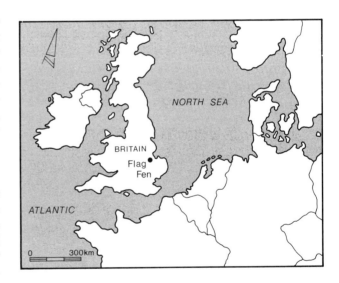

Fig. 5.1 Location map

This report is an overview of progress made at Flag Fen since the first general report (Pryor et al 1986); it is based on the paper delivered at the Exeter Conference and touches on all the main themes considered there; many of the delegates expressed an interest in the excavation, sampling and recording techniques employed on the Flag Fen timbers. This was an aspect of the research that was not considered in detail in the conference paper ; the discussion below of wood storage and other techniques is a response to those enquiries.

Publication

It is hoped that Flag Fen will be a long-term research project, and publication will follow, in essentials, the scheme laid out in the first overview report (Pryor *et al* 1986). The third overview (Pryor in press) will be longer and more comprehensive: it will include detailed results of the dendrochronological and timber and carpentry research projects; it will also consider the Fengate Power Station site, and its relationship to Flag Fen. The overviews will attempt both to assess general trends in the research since the last report, and to present new information of topical interest. Full academic publication of results will be in a series of thematic monographs to be published by Fenland Archaeological Trust. The first will consider the relationship of Flag Fen to the Fengate fen-edge, and its environment, with special reference to the Power Station excavations of 1989 (see below).

Popular publication of research at Flag Fen is given high priority and a general discussion of the site and its place within the Fengate landscape has recently been published (Pryor 1991). The distinction, however, between 'academic' and 'popular' is not necessarily straightforward: two thousand copies of the first overview report, off-printed from the *Proceedings of the Prehistoric Society*, were sold in two summer seasons at Flag Fen, adding considerably to the original journal's circulation.

EXCAVATION, SURVEY & DEVELOPMENT, 1986-1990

Flag Fen Platform Site

The first overview report (Pryor *et al* 1986) considered the discovery of Flag Fen and the first two major seasons of excavation (1984 and 1985). To summarise briefly, work prior to 1986 had shown that a large timber platform had been constructed in the Late Bronze Age in the shallow waters of Flag Fen (Fig. 5.2). Estimates of the platform's size (all phases) now vary between 2.5 and 4 acres. The platform was situated some 400 m east of the alluviated gravel soils of the Fengate fen-edge, close to the natural gravel 'island' of Northey (itself a part of the far larger 'island' of Whittlesey). The platform lay over half a metre below an early Roman road and was cut by a Medieval drainage dyke, the Mustdyke. The plank-built edge revetment of the platform was exposed in excavations along the dykeside and a zone of large posts was interpreted as a domestic building; this interpretation was supported by the discovery of sanded woodchip floors, broken pottery, animal bones and other items of Bronze Age date. Elsewhere the make-up of the platform consisted of an informal crisscross lattice of timbers, many of which had been pegged into position. Finally, it remains to note that the single radiocarbon determination published in the first overview (BM-2123) as 2610 ± 60 uncal BP has subsequently been recalculated: 2830 ± 120 uncal BP. Although a single determination is never significant, this recalculation accords better both with the archaeological evidence and the six provisional Cambridge determinations reported below.

Fig. 5.2 Map showing the Flag Fen platform and post alignment in relation to the Fengate field/drove system. Shaded areas show excavated trenches

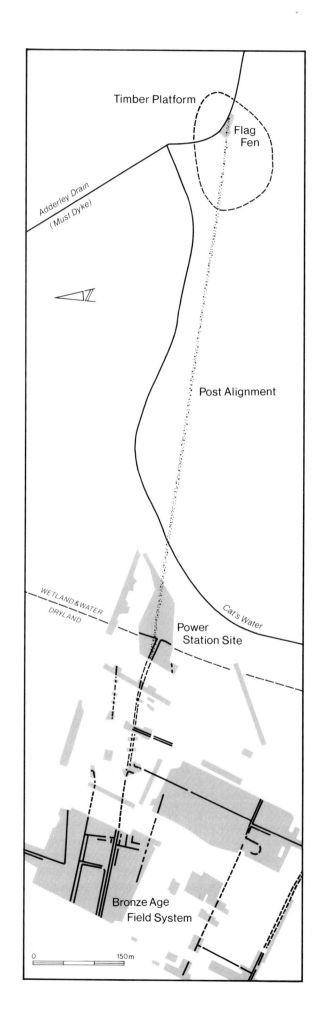

Our approach in 1982-85 was cautious (in retrospect sometimes too cautious): we undertook hand auger survey and very limited trial trenching, the only prospection techniques that could then penetrate to the depths we required (1.5 m) in wet conditions. Hand excavation was slow and painstaking and the recording of thousands of wooden pieces was slow (see below for how this difficult process was expedited). We worked on the principle that acceleration could best be achieved once the size of the problem was understood. We were also concerned with problems of preservation and continuity of research: it was apparent, for example, that the site was important (just how important we did not fully appreciate), but it was drying-out rapidly and we lacked the organisation necessary to raise funds and carry out long-term research. It was clear that piecemeal rescue excavation, however vigorously undertaken, would not be appropriate.

In 1986 the Fenland Archaeological Trust was established, as a company limited by guarantee, with charitable status. Thus established, it was possible to negotiate with the (then) Anglian Water Authority who owned approximately 80% of the timber platform. In 1987 the Trust and the Authority signed a 25-year lease, at a peppercorn rent, of land containing the platform west of the Mustdyke, together with access from Fengate, along the Fen Causeway Roman road.

Monitoring of ground water levels at Flag Fen and elsewhere (French and Taylor 1985) revealed a serious problem of drying-out. So the Trust determined to attempt preservation of those parts of the platform that were still sufficiently wet to be worth the expense involved. The technique employed was simple to describe, but difficult to execute: approximately half the platform was in effect curtained by a damp-proof polythene membrane (1000 gauge) that was inserted through the Holocene peaty alluvial deposits into the underlying Pleistocene clay-capped gravels (Pryor 1991, figs. 9-11). Advice from consulting hydrological engineers in advance of the undertaking suggested that once pumped into the reservoir thus created, and left undisturbed, the water would soon become de-oxygenated; they did not anticipate that it would cause significant damage to underlying anaerobic deposits. A small trial excavation some four years later has confirmed that wood preservation beneath the lakebed is still excellent and that macroscopically visible biological activity (small red worms, burrowing insects etc.), always so apparent outside the flooded area, is seemingly absent.

The insertion of the polythene membrane involved the excavation of a very roughly circular 'trial trench' of some 400 m circumference, around the lake. Large quantities of wood were observed around the entire circuit. Concentrations of posts were observed in five clearly separate locations distributed around the ciruit, and possibly in one other place; two of these locations we now know were part of the post-alignment (see below); the remaining three may be buildings, revetment, raised causeways or other alignments.

Flag Fen was opened to the general public in August 1987. There were two aims behind this important development: first, it is necessary to involve the public in the conduct of archaeology for general theoretical reasons (Binks *et al* 1988; Pryor 1990a; Tilley 1989); second, it was the only means available to us for raising secure, long-term research funds (Pryor 1989).

There were a number of unexpected research benefits which resulted from the display of Flag Fen to the public. First and foremost students and others working on the archaeology were also expected to undertake tours, and to do this they had to have a thorough knowledge of the site and its changing interpretation. This undoubtedly led directly to a far higher general standard of excavation. Second, the public expected to view the excavations in some comfort and the large shelters accordingly erected protected the wood from the elements. Without the stout framework which this provided to hold the camera, for example, the photographic system of planning, described below, could not have been made to work successfully. The third benefit is harder to quantify, but it is important nevertheless: if a complex site is to be understood by a lay person it must, at the very least, be clearly visible. So all unnecessary scaffolding, planks, shoring etc. must be removed. Wood storage or display tanks must be kept free from algae. These measures ensured that the archaeologists, too, could obtain an uncluttered, clear view of their data.

One benefit was most unexpected. Visitors require services such as water and electricity, and the provision of these has necessitated numerous small works, such as the digging of water mains, the sinking of posts, and so on. These works are always carried out under close archaeological supervision. A trial trench to determine a possible location for a new visitor centre north of the Fen Causeway, for example, revealed numerous oak planks, clearly *in situ* and quite well preserved. The construction of a paved walkway to give visitors access to a boardwalk along the west side of the Mustdyke revealed that the platform had a log revetment on its northern side. The southern revetment was mainly of planks (Pryor *et al* 1986, pl.I). It should be recalled that the entire dykeside between the two revetments had shown a continuous spread of wood and timber when it was exposed in 1982 (Pryor *et al* 1986, pl. 4). It seems probable that the northern revetment was not identified in 1982 because humification of the peaty dykesides was especially advanced at that particular point.

The Power Station excavations

Undoubtedly the most significant discovery made during small works took place in 1987, when about 20 mainly oak posts were found driven into the old land surface immediately next to the Cat's Water drain, on the boundary of Flag Fen and Fengate (Pryor 1991, fig. 82). Around the posts were a number of oak planks, probably *in situ* on the old land surface. Six samples were sent to Cambridge University for radiocarbon assay in 1988 and all have given provisional calibrated results within the Late Bronze Age

(R.Switzur, pers. comm.). Confirmation of these results is keenly awaited.

In 1989 it was announced that a consortium was to construct a gas-powered electricity generating station on the fen-edge, immediately east of the Fengate Fourth Drove sub-site. The developers made funds available for an initial exploratory excavation and it was decided to concentrate resources upon the removal of the thick overlying alluvium across as large an area as possible. A 10 m wide alignment of oak posts was revealed, running across what was now termed the Power Station sub-site towards the posts in the water main, which had been revealed two years earlier, and thence eastwards across Flag Fen. At this stage it was assumed that the posts probably formed part of a causeway linking the timber platform to the dryland of Fengate. However, the scale and width of the post alignment did not find ready parallels in other parts of Europe where prehistoric tracks and roads occur frequently. The horizontal timber lay directly on the old land surface and more than one piece had clearly been pegged in position; therefore a raised causeway could almost certainly be discounted.

Fig. 5.3 Metalwork finds from Flag Fen, 1990 season. All were damaged in antiquity. (Photo: Derek Rootes)

A carefully supervised metal-detector survey revealed a number of bronze weapons and ornaments, most of which showed signs of deliberate damage (Fig. 5.3). In many cases broken portions of the same item lay close by one another, as if dropped into the water. The vast majority of identifiable items belonged to the Wilburton industry of the Late Bronze Age. After some 50 items had been revealed in this way English Heritage agreed to fund a major effort to reveal the extent and distribution of the metalwork and other artefacts. Some 15,000 tons of alluvium were then removed over about two months and eventually over 300 metal items were revealed. These were distributed amongst the posts and to the southerly side of them only (Pryor 1991, fig. 89). This distribution pattern is not consistent with the post alignment being a simple road or causeway; the available evidence clearly indicates that ritual played an important part in the site's growth, if not in its inception.

THE WATERLOGGED WOOD

Techniques of Excavation, Sampling and Recording

When work began at Flag Fen the system of excavation and recording was largely the same as that which was then currently employed at the causewayed enclosure site at Etton (Pryor *et al* 1986). The system worked well at Etton, but Flag Fen was a very different site that produced enormous quantities of wood. So in the early years at Flag Fen the wood was exposed in the ground, and every piece was assigned a unique number *in situ*, using a computer-generated list. The *in situ* wood was then photographed from as near to the vertical as possible and plans were drawn independently, using a planning frame in the conventional manner; this procedure, though slow, did lead to a careful examination of the wood in the ground. Each individual piece of wood was then systematically lifted, levels and context were recorded and dimensions were noted; each piece was also given a short descriptive note. The wood was then stored until the wood specialist was available to enter a detailed record onto pre-printed sheets. Later, in the laboratory, data on the pre-printed sheets were transferred to the Project's Cromemco CS1H computer.

The system just described had a number of disadvantages, some of which were unavoidable. In the early seasons (1982-85) the wood specialist was working full-time at Etton, and the Flag Fen wood had to be processed whenever time permitted, as the Neolithic wood had priority, being very much more fragile and unstable. There was no power source on site, and no battery-operated computer was then readily available, so that data could not be entered direct into a computer in the field. This process generated huge quantities of paper. Finally, the actual process of excavation could not be expedited by employing sampling procedures, since a reasonably representative section through the deposits from top to bottom had yet to be completed. It is unwise to define a sampling strategy when the nature of the deposit to be sampled is not at all clear.

By the end of the 1986 season the excavation of the first reasonably-sized trench was nearing completion. Nearly 10,000 timbers had been numbered and lifted, and the site wood record was contained in over fifty A4 ring-binders. A considerable amount of wood was still in store awaiting detailed examination, the computer record had been completed for only a few thousand timbers and virtually no species identification had been attempted. The system and the wood specialist were creaking under the strain. At this time excavation of the waterlogged deposits at Etton was ending and work on a new area at Flag Fen was beginning. It was a good moment to assess the work so far, and to streamline operations.

The system could obviously be speeded up by entering the data direct into computer, and a battery operated Zenith laptop was obtained. The new machine required that the whole database be converted from the Cromemco operating system (a CP/M variant) to the newly standardised IBM-compatible MS-DOS. During this process the database was revised and so improved that it became possible to abandon detailed written records. For security, very brief written notes (provisional measurements and descriptions) are still made on the computer-generated numbers lists. The abandonment of detailed written records was probably the biggest factor in speeding-up the processing of wood on site.

Some areas of the excavation consisted of large quantities of roundwood or woodchips which were simply dumped on the underlying timbers to make up the surface. The numbering and detailed recording of this material on site used to be very time-consuming, and each field record generated inevitably involved time in the laboratory afterwards. It was decided therefore that unworked roundwood or deposits of woodchips should be sampled by metre square and depth, without detailed records and individual numbers. This sampling plan would enable the deposits to be characterised without the expenditure of too much time and effort.

At Etton the practice was to number wood on the plan and in-the ground, at one and the same time. Lifting of the numbered wood took place later. At Flag Fen the far greater quantities of wood often meant that the period between the two processes was extended. Invariably labels became detached and confusion resulted. Today most wood at Flag Fen is only assigned a number when it is lifted. Most other recording is also done at this time: a number is issued from the computer-generated list and a label (Dymo impressed plastic label with backing strip intact and stainless steel pins) is fixed to the timber, and marked on the plan. The timber is measured, briefly described and possibly sketched on the number sheet. It is then lifted from the ground and placed in a light portable water tank before removal to the field centre where it is washed and examined in more detail. The data generated by the more detailed examination is entered direct into a waterproofed laptop computer, together with context details and other information recorded on the field numbers sheets.

The production of site plans was speeded up and improved once the site had been opened to the public in 1987. The excavations were now permanently covered by a large, steel-framed shelter. It was a relatively simple matter to provide a monorail in the roof of the building to carry an automatic camera. Vertical photographs of the wood below could be taken from fixed or moveable points along the rail. Experience has shown that overlapping photographs tend to remove most lens distortion when the final photo-montage is prepared. These compound photographs are used as an underlay in the preparation of drawn plans; detail is still, however, added in the field by hand. This two-part procedure ensures that precise relationships between pieces of wood can be recorded on the plans where these are not clear in the photographs. The plans are modified and added to in the field as lifting proceeds and more detail is revealed. The original photo-montage remains, however, as an important unmodified record of a particular stage in the excavation.

Temporary storage of wood whilst is is undergoing study on archaeological sites is always a problem and it is not one usually addressed by conservators and others interested in permanent conservation or long-term storage (ICOM 1984; Vries-Zuiderbaan 1979). The conditions at every site are different and the financial and technical resources available differ too. Despite these reservations, the following notes on what has proved effective and low-cost at Flag Fen might prove useful.

It was apparent from the outset that it was not sufficient to store Flag Fen wood in damp conditions alone; it had to be kept wet, and preferably under water. Some excavators are still under the misapprehension that if wood is not totally waterlogged when excavated, then it can be stored in damp rather than wet conditions. In our experience storage in anything other than the wet state usually allows significant biological activity. Sealing wood in plastic sleeves can also be very dangerous: the wood may be damaged during insertion into the sleeve, and once sealed, it is often difficult to monitor the extent to which it is air-tight. Many of the large timbers at Flag Fen are very fragile and cannot support their own weight. It was decided, therefore, that the safest policy was to build large plank-and-polythene temporary tanks for short-term storage of timbers on site, and as close to the excavation as possible. This would mean that even large timbers could go straight out of the excavation into water. The sapwood of oak (*Quercus* Sp.) and the heartwood of certain other species is soft, and soaking before cleaning is very beneficial. Compressed peat will soften on soaking and can be removed with less damage to toolmarks and other sensitive surfaces. The temporary holding tanks therefore serve a useful practical purpose. The wood is also readily available for photography and detailed examination; experience has shown that a depth of water helps support a long or fragile timber that might otherwise require elaborate and often damaging support, such as cradling and strapping, were it to be stored in any other way.

The holding tanks were constructed with wooden frames of builders' planks and posts, lined with polythene sheeting

41

Fig. 5.4 Temporary holding tank at Flag Fen, showing ultra-violet water circulation system. (Photo: Derek Rootes)

(Fig. 5.4)). A lining of cheap agricultural or builders' grade plastic (250-1000 gauge) lasts two or three years, and is easily replaced in due course. Tanks have been made in a variety of shapes and sizes to accomodate particular timbers but in general long, narrow ones are best. If a tank is so wide that timber cannot be reached from the side, it will have to be loaded and unloaded by people climbing in. This makes the work much colder, more dangerous because of the possibility of slipping, and boot abrasion may abruptly curtail the life of the liner.

Small pieces of wood are stored in a plastic stacking box system purchased from a discount warehouse. These boxes have been in constant use (and misuse) for nearly five years, indoors and out, and in a variety of weather conditions. They are only just beginning to show brittleness and other signs of age. They were an excellent investment. A stacking system makes it simple to check that water levels are maintained. If the tanks are also stacked near a water supply they can be serviced easily and wood is less likely to be lost by accidental drying-out.

Short-term storage of wood in holding tanks makes access for drawing and photography very simple but does not provide the solution for problems of long-term storage. Wood from trees of different species behaves differently when stored in water tanks; alder (*Alnus glutinosa*) sapwood and heartwood and oak sapwood, for example, tend

to deteriorate quite rapidly. Ideally the tanks should be shaded to inhibit algal growth. Some of the tanks at Flag Fen are also fitted with a system in which water is pumped through a powerful ultra-violet light which acts as a biocide. The system is in widespread use by retailers and breeders of ornamental fish, as it is particularly effective against fungal infection. Unlike chemical agents, water treated by the ultra-violet light system has no effect on human skin. Unless the growth is particularly severe, algae do not seem to cause obvious damage to the wood itself, but they can obscure surface detail, they are unsightly and, most importantly, often cannot be removed without causing damage. Insect larvae are a far more destructive problem, sometimes boring extensively into timber. At Flag Fen the wood of alder is very prone to this kind of attack whilst stored in water tanks. It is also probable that algae on the surface of the wood attract certain insects or larvae, and damage to the wood is done incidentally whilst 'grazing'.

Although it is preferable that archaeologically significant timber and wood should be stored in water tanks, a system of storing identification or dendrochronological samples by wrapping them in thin plastic or cling-film has been developed. It was observed some years ago that wood packed when very wet, well sealed, and with a minimum of air would quite quickly 'shrink-wrap' itself. Investigation suggested that bacteria naturally present in the waterlogged wood were continuing to be active while there was still some air available but would die once the air supply had been exhausted. Trial-and-error has shown that the most efficient method of packing the samples is closely to wrap the wet wood in cling-film and then double wrap in polythene. There are two main drawbacks to this method. First, cling-film or thin polythene soon becomes brittle if exposed to direct sunlight; second, the cling-film can be drawn so taught that it punctures easily and can compress delicate surfaces, such as toolmarks. This system is only used on samples where the loss of surface detail does not matter.

PRELIMINARY RESULTS OF THE FLAG FEN DENDROCHRONOLOGY PROJECT
(by Janet Neve)

Due to the large amounts of suitable wood at Flag Fen, it was decided that the dendrochronology would be carried out 'in house'. The apparatus for measuring and recording tree-rings (the dendrometer) was built by students at Peterborough Regional College; supervision and guidance of the subsequent tree-ring research has kindly been provided by staff at the English Heritage Dendrochronology Laboratory, Sheffield University. This work is still in its early stages, but the initial results are encouraging; they are outlined below.

The first priority was, and still is, chronology-building using oak samples with as many annual rings as possible, preferably 100 or more (Baillie 1982). By visual and statistical cross-matching of timbers using the Belfast Tree-ring Programs, it was hoped to establish a long chronology or master curve for the site. Two areas were selected for study: the area of the platform under excavation at Flag Fen, and a 20 m transect across the Fengate Power Station post alignment. The majority of the samples measured so far are vertical posts, although at Flag Fen a few horizontal timbers have also been measured.

To date, three separate floating master curves have been constructed using samples from Flag Fen. The first and largest, FFMEAN1, spans 206 years; the second and third span 108 and 148 years respectively. At present there appears to be no link between any of the three curves, but hopefully as work continues samples which bridge the gaps will be found. At the Power Station site, Fengate, two master curves of 180 and 92 years have been constructed. These have been compared with the Flag Fen master curves, and the larger Fengate curve matches well against the main Flag Fen curve, FFMEAN1. The second curves from each site also show good agreement, and there is a single timber match between a Fengate sample and the third Flag Fen mean.

The curves so far produced cannot be precisely dated at present. However, samples of two large vertical posts, spanning 200 years of the Flag Fen curve FFMEAN1, have been selected for 'wiggle-matching' at the Radiocarbon Laboratory in Belfast, which may accurately date the time-span of FFMEAN1 to within 10 calendar years.

The results outlined above seem to indicate that both sites are broadly contemporary, although at this stage nothing can be said regarding finer detail such as felling and construction or rebuilding phases. This will only emerge as work continues.
[See addendum below, p.46. *Ed.*]

DISCUSSION

The Post Alignment

Trial trenches have shown that the post-alignment runs in a straight line across Flag Fen (Fig. 5.2). Its posts can sometimes be seen to run in not-very-straight lines but these patterns are never very distinct and there are always many posts seemingly placed at random within the 10-12 m width of the alignment. Posts may be of roundwood or split timber and carry long pencil-like sharpened tips that were driven into the clay and gravel subsoil; an important exception to this was at the extreme western edge of the wetland at Fengate, where the highest and driest posts had flat bases which were let into excavated post-holes.

With the exception of the trial trenches associated with the construction of the Platform-preserving lake, where conditions for observation were poor, wherever the post alignment has been encountered, horizontal timbers have also been revealed lying on or above the old land surface. In many instances these had been pegged into position. Towards the centre of the alignment, perhaps 300 metres east of the Fengate 'shore', more than one layer of horizontal timbers was encountered. Most of the trial trenches were too small or shallow to reveal non-wooden finds, but the single trench located on the south-east side of the Mustdyke produced a fragment of hollow bronze bracelet of probable Wilburton type (D.G.Coombs, pers. comm.) even though only a very small part of this trench was excavated down to horizontal timber, due to the hot weather of 1990.

The alignment, running across Flag Fen from dryland at Fengate to dryland at Northey, crossed about a kilometre of open water or fen. At present it may best be interpreted as a boundary, that has its roots in the landscape divisions of later neolithic Fengate (Pryor 1978, ditches 8 and 9). The alignment may also be seen as a formalisation of the distinction between the dryland of the south-west and the open fen to the north-east. This interpretation follows survey work in the 'basin' land around the Fengate fen-edge to the south-west. Here the confidently expected wet 'basin' was found to be less low-lying and waterlogged than anticipated; instead, a flat plain was revealed with a preserved palaeosol indicative of a seaonally flooded, natural water-meadow type of environment (C.French, pers. comm.). In wet seasons in the later Bronze Age this land would undoubtedly have been flooded, but in drier summers it could have provided rich grazing. In this instance the distinction between wetland and dryland is difficult to make with any precision. The precise nature of the changing environment and land-use of the Fengate and Flag Fen dryland/wetland interface will be one of the principal research objectives of a new project to be funded by English Heritage: the Flag Fen Environs Project.

When first revealed, the post alignment clearly ran straight towards the main Flag Fen excavations, where there were also posts that had been interpreted as the remains of a domestic building (Pryor *et al* 1986) but now this seems less certain. The discovery in 1986 of a bronze dagger deeply buried within the posts and horizontal timbers of the supposed domestic structure also cast doubt on the straightforward domestic interpretation.

The Platform

The original exposure of the platform in 1982 was along one side of the Mustdyke and it revealed over 500 timbers, many of which had been pegged into place. The posts of the alignment in the dykeside exposure were located to one side of the platform and were by no means at its thickest part (which was about 20 m to the north). We have also noted that the platform's edge revetment was revealed at two locations to the north and south of the post alignment, within the dyke exposure. Excavation in 1987 revealed that a substantial alder post had been pulled from the earth (distinctive clay was still attached to its pencil-like sharpened tip) and laid on the ground alongside its post-hole; the make-up timbers of the southern revetment were then placed above it. The post in question (A6256) survived 2.27 m long, and was 135 mm in diameter. Perhaps originally, when the area was not fully waterlogged, this post marked the edge of a defined area that was later to become the platform, and it was removed from the ground to form part of the revetment as the waters continued to rise. This is important because it indicates that the area later to be covered by a platform, whose role was probably mainly ritual, was already significant in drier times, before the timbers were laid in place.

The structure of the platform can best be described in the order in which it was deposited. The lowest level consists of large timbers, laid directly on the soft organic mud that overlies the clay and terrace gravel subsoil (Pryor *et al* 1986, fig.3). These large timbers were mostly felled trees , but there are also large branches and re-used timber from earlier structures. Above these large timbers was laid a layer of smaller branches and occasionally bundles of coppiced material. In and around the posts of the 'building' and the post alignment the second layer was overlain by further layers of woodchips and woodworking debris mixed with sand and fine gravel. This is interpreted as a floor. The posts were hammered into the ground at various stages. Some seem to have been hammered in when very little horizontal material was in place. Others were put in later, some much later, piercing horizontals that were already waterlogged and which broke in a characteristic manner.

The felled trees of the lowest level are very distinctive and are often a source of clear toolmarks (Fig. 5.5). They were felled and very soon afterwards thrown into the water

0   15cm

Fig. 5.5 Felled butt of alder showing the distinctive angle and stepped pattern of cut. (Photo: Derek Rootes)

and wet mud. The tool marks are so sharply defined that they could not have had time to weather. Most of the felled trees examined in detail to date appear to have been alders with a diameter of 250-300 mm. A great deal of the material in the lower levels is branch wood, which differs from the wood of the trunk because of the effect of gravity on its growth. The branch lays down extra wood to support its own weight, and in deciduous trees this occurs on the upper side of the branch and is known as 'tension wood' (Wilson and White 1986). It produces a disinctive, eccentric pattern in the growth rings which allows the identification of branch as opposed to trunk wood. The branch wood is rarely well enough preserved to show clear toolmarks but it is generally of alder with occasional willow or poplar (*Salix* sp. or *Populus* sp.) or oak.

In the lower levels of the platform some wood appears to show the distinctive eccentric growth pattern of branch wood when it has, in fact, been compressed. This is particularly noticeable in the basal levels where roundwood may be compressed nearly flat by the weight of material above.

The woodchips of the upper, 'floor' levels are often of oak and are characteristic of the debris created when trimming-up after the initial splitting or when shaping previously split wood. A high proportion are large, thin, radially aligned fragments. Work continues to characterise the wood-working debris from Flag Fen, which is by far the largest category of material from the site.

Characterisation of the posts must await the completion of the excavation and the results of the full dendrochronological study, but two observations can be made at this stage. Many of the smaller posts, usually alder, were probably not structural and often do not conform to the four rows identified in the first general report (Pryor *et al* 1986, fig. 4), but certain large slow grown oak timbers align both longitudinally (axially) and transversely, and could well have formed part of a building (Taylor and Pryor 1990).

THE RELATIONSHIP OF THE POST ALIGNMENT AND PLATFORM

A first point needs to be stressed: the timbers of the Fengate Power Station site and the timbers of the Flag Fen post alignment are part of one and the same monument. Apart from the obvious fact that the post alignment runs straight from Fengate via Flag Fen to Northey 'island', without, so far, any observed breaks or diversions, there are other reasons to believe that the posts are part of a unitary site.

Janet Neve has shown that the dendrochronological survey indicates a remarkable degree of overlap between the floating master chronologies of the Power Station site and the main Flag Fen excavation; this indicates that they are contemporary. Both sites have also revealed animal bone, pottery, broken shale bracelets, and a few flints of rather doubtful chronological significance. The single dagger from Flag Fen aside, the main archaeological aspect which once distinguished the two sites was the abundance of bronzes at the Power Station site and their rarity at Flag Fen.

Since the discovery of the small dagger just mentioned, the Flag Fen excavations have revealed two stick-pins of generalised Urnfield type, a La Tène fibula brooch (at a significantly higher level), a pegged and socketed spearhead and a chape with wooden scabbard fragments still *in situ*; the last two items are Wilburton types (D.G.Coombs, pers. comm.). It is quite probable, given the amount of wood still to be excavated, that the current main trench will produce another three or four metal artefacts. Three items found in the 1990 excavations (Fig. 5.3) had been damaged in antiquity: the pin had been bent and its tip broken off; the chape had been roughly broken off the scabbard, and its tip bashed off; the spearhead had been bent and its ashwood shaft had been broken inside the socket. This evidence, taken both with the finds from the Power Station site and the single bracelet fragment from the trial trench to the south-east of the Mustdyke, indicates that metalwork is probably to be expected along the entire length of the post alignment.

We have seen that metalwork was only found within and to one side of the posts at the Power Station site; so far metalwork has been found only on one side of the posts at Flag Fen, but the areas excavated to date have been too small to be very certain that the same distribution pattern is continued right across Flag Fen. It is just possible, however, to hazard a speculative estimate at the amount of metalwork that might have been deposited across Flag Fen in antiquity. We know from our excavations that metal items lie within the posts of the alignment and within a zone approximately 20 m wide to one side, say an average conservative band width of 25 m. About 800 m of the alignment is thought still to be in place; 800 x 25 = 20,000 sq. m. The present excavation at Flag Fen measures 7 x 9 m, or 63 sq. m, and it has so far yielded 7 items (including a fragment of bronze strip not mentioned above); this gives a concentration of approximately one find per 9 sq. m. With 20,000 sq. m one

might expect to find some 2222 bronzes; if the present excavation eventually yields ten bronzes, as would seem probable, the entire post alignment might contain over 3100 finds. Whatever the accuracy of this 'prediction' the quantities are quite extraordinary.

Many of the Flag Fen bronzes and particularly the dagger, one of the stick-pins, the spearhead and the chape, had been placed within the deep foundations of the putative building or within the basal platform timbers just outside. In the case of the spearhead, a felled alder log had been positioned directly over it. A few metres away, and within the posts of the south aisle of the 'building', a complete ceramic bowl had also been carefully placed beneath an alder log, which was then pegged into position by four pegs. The positioning of these and other items strongly suggests that they were placed in the water, and beneath the timbers, deliberately.

There is now an increasing body of evidence from Flag Fen to suggest that ritual, religion and ceremonial played a major role in the site's construction and use. It probably owed its location to the layout of the pre-Bronze Age landscape, and its very beginnings may well have been quite mundane, but as the waters around it rose so its *raison d'etre* became increasingly less domestic. This is not the place to speculate upon the nature of ritual at Flag Fen (Pryor 1990b; 1991) nor in the region as a whole (Pryor 1984b), but the sheer diversity of evidence, with complete structural timbers, pots whole or broken, animal bones, funerary remains, broken plain and inlaid shale bracelets or armlets, bronze pins, inlaid jewellery, knives, swords, daggers, parade armour etc., surely indicates that the site was used for a variety of ritual purposes. The most recent evidence of all, discovered in May 1991, suggests that some of the 're-used' alder timbers from the lowest layers had not actually been used in a purely functional sense, before being deposited at Flag Fen. Could this be an indication that buildings, or something symbolising them, were also deposited in the waters, together with the metalwork and other objects? The ethnographic parallels for the destruction of a person's house, caravan or boat upon death are many and varied; perhaps the extraordinarily preserved houses at Longbridge Deverill Cow Down, Wilts., could be a dryland archaeological example of the practice (Hawkes 1961).

There is evidence at Flag Fen for the destruction of ostentatious symbols of rank and power (Bradley 1990) and there is evidence, too, for humbler offerings made perhaps during rites of passage (especially at death), or indeed at less significant moments in life such as after a successful hunt. In ritual terms one could argue that all aspects of life are represented by the items deposited in the waters at Flag Fen. So the contrast of the current interpretation with that of the first overview (Pryor *et al* 1986) is not necessarily as striking as first impressions might suggest.

Acknowledgements

This report would not have been possible without the contributions of Janet Neve, Derek Rootes (photography) and Martin Redding (artwork). Charles French provided the initial location map and all thoughts on the environment (with the able assistance of Dr Rob Scaife); wood identifications are by Gwilda Holmes. Other members of the Flag Fen team include Norma Challands, Freddie Kramer, Paul Mitchell and Frank Rowley. Richard Bradley suggested the Longbridge Deverill parallel during one of many non-ritual phonecalls on matters religious and ceremonial.

BIBLIOGRAPHY

Baillie, M.G.L., 1982. *Tree-Ring Dating and Archaeology.* Chicago: University Press.

Binks, G., Dykes, J. and Dagnall, P. 1988. *Visitors Welcome.* London: English Heritage.

Bradley, R.J. 1990. *The Passage of Arms.* Cambridge: University Press.

French, C.A.I. 1990. Neolithic soils, middens and alluvium in the lower Welland valley. *Oxford Journal of Archaeology* 9, 305-312.

French, C.A.I. and Taylor, M. 1985. Desiccation and Destruction: the immediate effects of de-watering at Etton, Cambridgeshire. *Oxford Journal of Archaeology* 4, 139-56.

Hall, D.N. 1987. *The Fenland Project, No.2: Cambridgeshire survey, Peterborough to March.* Cambridge: East Anglian Archaeology Report 35.

Hall, D.N. and Chippindale, C. (eds) 1988. Special Section: Survey, Environment and Excavation in the English Fenland. *Antiquity* 62, 305-80.

Hall, D.N., Evans, C., Hodder, I.R. and Pryor, F.M.M. 1987. The Fenlands of East Anglia, England: Survey and Excavation. In J.M.Coles and A.J.Lawson (eds), *European Wetlands in Prehistory*, 169-202. Oxford: Clarendon Press.

Hawkes, S.C. 1961. Longbridge Deverill Cow Down, Wiltshire.Notes on Excavations, 1960. *Proceedings of the Prehistoric Society* 27, 346-47.

ICOM 1984. *Waterlogged Wood: Study and Conservation – proceedings of the 2nd ICOM waterlogged wood working group conference, Grenoble 28-31 August, 1984.* Grenoble: Centre d'Etude et de Traitment des Bois Gorgés d'Eau.

Pryor, F.M.M. 1974. *Excavation at Fengate, Peterborough, England: The first report.* Toronto: Royal Ontario Museum Archaeology Monograph 3.

Pryor, F.M.M. 1978. *Excavation at Fengate, Peterborough, England: The second report.* Toronto: Royal Ontario Museum Archaeology Monograph 5.

Pryor, F.M.M. 1980a. *Excavation at Fengate, Peterborough, England: The third report.* Toronto and Northampton: Royal Ontario Museum Archaeology Monograph 6 / Northamptonshire Archaeological Society Monograph 1.

Pryor, F.M.M. 1980b. Will it all come out in the Wash? Reflections at the end of eight years' digging. In J.C. Barrett and R.J.Bradley (eds), *The British Later Bronze Age*, 483-500. Oxford: British Archaeological Reports, British Series 83 (ii).

Pryor, F.M.M. 1984. *Excavation at Fengate, Peterborough,England: The fourth report.* Toronto and Northampton: Royal Ontario Museum Archaeology monograph 7/Northamptonshire Archaeological Society Monograph 2.

Pryor, F.M.M. 1988. Earlier Neolithic organised landscapes and ceremonial in lowland Britain. In J.C. Barrett and I.A. Kinnes (eds), *The Archaeology of context in the Neolithic and Bronze Age: recent trends*, 63-72. Sheffield: University Department of Archaeology and Prehistory.

Pryor, F.M.M. 1989. 'Look What We've Found' – a case-study in public archaeology. *Antiquity* 63, 51-61.

Pryor, F.M.M. 1990a. The Reluctant Greening of Archaeology. *Antiquity* 64, 147-150.

Pryor, F.M.M. 1990b. The many faces of Flag Fen. *Scottish Archaeological Review* 7, 114-24.

Pryor, F.M.M. 1991. *The English Heritage book of Flag Fen: prehistoric Fenland centre.* London: Batsford.

Pryor, F.M.M. in press. Flag Fen Excavations. Special section in *Antiquity*, June 1992.

Pryor, F.M.M.,French, C.A.I. and Taylor, M. 1985. An Interim Report on Excavations at Etton, Maxey, Cambridgeshire, 1982-1984. *Antiquaries Journal* 65, 275-311.

Pryor, F.M.M., French, C.A.I. and Taylor, M. 1986. Flag Fen, Fengate, Peterborough I: Discovery, Reconnaissance and Initial Excavation (1982-85). *Proceedings of the Prehistoric Society* 52, 1-24.

Pryor, F.M.M. and Kinnes, I.A. 1982. A Waterlogged Causewayed Enclosure in the Cambridgeshire Fens. *Antiquity* 56, 124-26.

R.C.H.M. 1969. *Peterborough New Town: a survey of the antiquities in the areas of development.* London: Royal Commission on Historical Monuments (England).

Taylor, M. and Pryor, F.M.M., 1990. Bronze Age building techniques at Flag Fen, Peterborough, England. *World Archaeology* 21, 425-434.

Tilley, C.Y. 1989. Excavation as Theatre. *Antiquity* 63, 275-80.

Vries-Zuiderbaan, L.H. de. 1979. *Conservation of Waterlogged Wood - international symposium on the conservation of large objects of waterlogged wood.* UNESCO Netherlands. The Hague: Government Printing and Publishing Office.

Wilson, K. and White, D.J.B. 1986. *The Anatomy of Wood: its diversity and variability.* London: Stobart and Son.

Addendum

Janet Neve has now established a 397 year chronology from the timbers of Flag Fen Platform and Post Alignment; this chronology spans the years 1363-967 BC. Felling phases have not yet been distinguished, but the chronology is built from three successive groups of timbers and there are indications that felling began perhaps *c* 1250 BC and continued until 967 BC at least.

6

RIVER VALLEY BOTTOMS AND ARCHAEOLOGY IN THE HOLOCENE

J.G. Evans

INTRODUCTION: THE SYSTEMIC AND ARCHAEOLOGICAL/ENVIRONMENTAL CONTEXTS

One of the main characteristics of human activity is its spatial variability in properties such as abundance, quality and diversity. Variation ranges in scale from the space of the individual through that of the site, the locality and region to the country. It may be static or be related to temporal variation at the individual, group or cultural level and from the diurnal through the intra-generational to the cultural-historical scales. In contrast, the evidence that comes down to us of this tempero-spatial variation in behaviour is only a partial record, partly because it is unilocational, and partly because of loss through erosion and decay. These two spheres - the past present, as it happened, and the present past, as it is preserved - are referred to as the systemic and the archaeological contexts respectively (Schiffer 1987). They can be applied to the biological and physical environmental worlds as well, so that a broader view than Schiffer's would refer to them as the systemic and archaeological/environmental contexts.

A main route to the systemic context is via settlement archaeology, the study of the spatial relationships of human remains and the activities they represent (Trigger 1989). Much of the practical framework is carried out with reference to major blocks of land types (e.g. upland, chalk downland, river gravels) which have particular environmental characteristics of topography, soils and land-use, as well as particular environmental and human histories. Another important characteristic of these land blocks is that they display particular states of archaeological preservation and visibility, with a major contrast between areas of thin deposits like chalk downland or gravel terraces, where there is good surface visibility and spatial resolution but poor time depth, and areas of deep deposits like blown sand or caves where there is poor surface visibility but good time depth. There are also differences in the physical and chemical environment which result in particular kinds of materials being preserved in particular circumstances.

These properties impose land blocks on us as study units, but we must not think that they had the same properties through the past or were equally applicable to human use, nor must we equate them with particular cultural or sociological groups. This is a criticism that has been levelled at wetland research, that it has concentrated on techniques of excavation, environmental sampling and dating, as well as on advertising the quality of the data by comparison with that of dryland archaeology, at the expense of interpretation of the data in terms of human behaviour (Evans 1990; Scarre 1989). "What wet sites share are preservation factors and similar environments. To divorce them from their (dry) regional cultural/chronological context necessarily pushes their interpretation towards functional universals and environmental determinism" (Evans 1990, 339).

HOLOCENE RIVER VALLEY BOTTOMS

A land block not widely recognised in archaeology as a locus for excavation until recently is the Holocene river valley *bottom*. This late recognition is surprising in view of the attention paid to river valleys *generally* in settlement archaeology from an early stage, e.g. Crawford (1924) on the different relationships of prehistoric and historic settlement to river valleys in southern England, and the focussing of research around river valleys generally (e.g. Willey 1953; MacNeish 1974). Even in the world of pure Quaternary research, the Holocene river valley bottom, and especially its biology, has fared badly by comparison with Pleistocene counterparts and other kinds of Holocene contexts such as peat bogs and lakes.

With regard to the relationship between humans and valley bottoms in the Holocene, some studies, such as Gladfelter (1985) and Gray (1984) in North America, have related archaeological site location at particular periods to particular topographical parts of river valley systems, and used such models predictively in site prospection. In Europe, and especially in countries around the Mediterranean, there has been work on the relationship of alluviation stages to human land-use and climate (Vita-Finzi 1969; Bintliff 1977; Bell 1982). In northern Europe, one of the earliest and best known investigations into valley bottom archaeology in which a predictive model of site location was established by surface survey and successfully tested by excavation was that of Rust (1943) at Stellmoor near the town of Ahrensburg, in north Germany. Impressed by the density of surface scatters of Upper Palaeolithic stone artefacts on the sandhills and moraines of the area, Rust excavated adjacent valley fills and located two archaeological horizons with organic materials and a sequence of biological assemblages which allowed the archaeology to be put into local and regional environmental frameworks. In northern Europe, too, there have been palaeoecological studies on Holocene river valley history, e.g. Becker and Schirmer (1977) using radiocarbon dating and dendrochronology in the River Main and Kozarski and Rotnicki (1983) on changing palaeochannel patterns in the north Polish plain, and for western Europe, Bell (1982) cites possible interrelationships between alluviation and human activities. (See also Lang and Schluchter 1988 for a number of studies, mostly of a palaeogeographical kind in which humans are mostly of incidental interest, if they are considered at all.)

In the British Isles there have been studies such as those of Lewin (1983) and Lewin *et al* (1983) in which humans are of only incidental concern, and those of Brown and Barber (1985) and Burrin and Scaife (1984) in which palynology and sedimentology are used to examine land-use changes in the river catchment and relate periods of alluviation to human activity and vegetational change. However, a research design in which spatio-temporal relationships between valley bottom history and human activities is explicit from the start is seen in very few studies, notable being those of Robinson and Lambrick (1984) in the upper Thames and of French (1990) in the East Anglian Fenland.

The main concern of this paper is not former human activity or environmental change but the archaeological/environmental context of the river valley bottom. If river valley bottom archaeology is not to be subject to the criticisms levelled at wetland archaeology, it needs a theoretical and methodological framework which incorporates past human behaviour, past environment, the present archaeological and environmental record, and present perceptions and study, especially an appreciation of the changing relationships of the first three through time.

To start with, a definition is crucial, but this depends on perspective. A river valley bottom is the area of a river valley that is, has been or may be flooded or influenced by ground water in a substantially different way from the ambient valley sides and plateaus. From the point of view of the present-day observer it is the area which displays land use, soils, vegetation and fauna that are strikingly different from those away from it. Archaeologically, river valley bottoms are areas of preservation, yet concealment, and there is also a contrast between the visible density of historic-age settlement in valley bottoms and of prehistoric settlement on the slopes. River valley bottoms may thus be defined from three points of view: (1) environment and specifically hydrology, (2) human use, and (3) archaeology, specifically with regard to preservation and visibility.

Three important questions must now be asked: (1) Are present-day visible archaeological differences between valley bottom and slopes/plateaus a reflection of past human behaviour or a result, partially or wholly, of taphonomic processes? (2) Have present-day environmental differences between valley bottom and slopes/plateaus always obtained throughout the Holocene? (3) How do archaeologists perceive and study river valley bottoms, especially the differences they present with the ambient slopes and plateaus?

PAST HUMAN USE OF RIVER VALLEY BOTTOMS

River valley bottoms can be defined and characterised from the point of view of past human perception and activity. There are three basic possibilities: (1) The valley bottom was the only area occupied. (2) It comprised a part of a larger range. (3) It was avoided. The second possibility is the most likely, and it is then a question of whether resources specific to the river valley bottom per se were being exploited, or whether the valley bottom was no different from, or no differently perceived than, the slopes and plateaus.

At a site and local scale, use of the valley bottom may be related to activities that are specific to water or its proximity – transport (waterfronts, boats), fishing, fowling, digging for monocotyledonous roots and tubers, and the extraction of peat. More broadly, the zone between the valley bottom and the valley slope may have been exploited for special purposes such as settlements connected with pastoralism (Lambrick and Robinson 1979), defence (Zvelebil 1987) or ritual (Hall *et al* 1987). Other sites are not special in regard to their exploitation of the unique wetland resources, either because the valley bottom was not a wetland or, if it was, in that dryland conditions were maintained and the wetland resources ignored.

On a regional and micro-regional scale, hunter-gatherer communities are unlikely to have exploited river valley bottoms in preference to high uplands at the natural/semi-natural forest edge, if there was a permanent water supply of lakes, ponds or springs in the uplands, and the valley bottom had no other attractive qualities. But in areas without permanent upland surface water, e.g. the chalklands, valley bottoms are likely to have been more intensively exploited. For farming communities, with their activities related to crop-ripening and, for cattle farmers, nearness to water, exploitation of the lower slopes and valley bottoms is more likely, although more settled life, by comparison with hunter-gatherers, with possibilities of water storage and the creation of dew ponds and wells in areas where there was no surface water potentially redresses this polarisation.

There are aspects like the degree of colonisation of an area – immigratory, established, dwindling, emigratory – with implications for competition for resources, and the significance of an area in terms of ritual or defence as opposed to more conventional settlement, which influence the response of humans to the river valley bottom. There is the question of environmental change, the rate of it, and the human perception and response to this. Change to wetter conditions usually results in adaptation, although that can mean different things and be done in different ways - people moving away from an area or exploiting the new conditions or maintaining the former dryland state, e.g. by the creation of pile dwellings, digging of deep drainage ditches and building settlement mounds.

So, human activity on the valley bottom can be viewed variously: (1) The wetland context was used for specific wetland properties and there was a contrast with activities on the valley sides and plateaus; the systemic and archaeological contexts are close - wetland activities preserved in wetland contexts. (2) Exploitation of a more nearly dryland character, e.g for pasture, but still with a contrast with valley side and plateau activities; sites of this type can be expected where a shift from dryland to wetland was beginning (e.g. French 1990). (3) Specific to the valley bottom, but not for wetland properties, or as part of the overall settlement of an area in which there is no contrast with valley side/plateau activities; the systemic and archaeological contexts are separate - dryland sites preserved by wetland.

Asymmetry of former human activity between valley bottoms and the slopes and plateaus is likely, with a concentration of human settlement in the valley bottom, and sometimes this was of a different quality from that of the valley sides and plateaus. But this was not always and everywhere the case. The valley bottom may have been no different from, or no differently perceived and used than, the slopes and plateaus. Or it may have been avoided. Uncritical acceptance of river valley bottoms as zones of high density and diversity of human settlement throughout the Holocene is unhelpful.

ENVIRONMENT

Equally, with environment, we cannot view valley bottoms as zones of high diversity and productivity everywhere and at all times. Valley bottom environments have changed through time in vegetational diversity and hydrology, particularly by contrast to the slopes and plateaus. Equally, spatial location is important, with the river valley concept often being better defined in the middle reaches than towards the source or mouth, or more important in areas such as the chalklands where there is a sharper contrast between wet valley bottom and dry plateau than in

other areas. Even the basic river valley concept is often used uncritically or undefined, being applied to the valley bottom only or to the valley bottom plus a part (usually unspecified) of the valley sides. Basically, everywhere in the British Isles and many other temperate areas is a part of a river valley, except for a few upland plateaus, especially in karst and chalk country, and extensive coastal plains, and even these exceptions are probably influenced by river valley hydrology.

Spatially, the valley bottom environment can be viewed in terms of (1) the distribution and abundance of valleys generally, (2) the long profile and (3) the cross profile, i.e. at decreasing scales.

The distribution and abundance of river valleys

The relationship between humans and an individual river valley may vary according to whether a region has abundant and densely concentrated valleys or few. Where rivers are few, as in chalklands and karst, the significance of the *individual river valley* may be greater than in areas where they are more abundant. On the other hand, viewing *regions as a whole*, those with abundant river valleys may be more distinctive in the response that humans make to them than those with few. This approach allows the possibility of characterising human communities in environmental terms as sociological unities – "people of the valleys" or "people of the hills or plains" for example – , river-valleyism as applying to human response being more or less valid according to circumstances rather than universally.

The long profile

Although the situation varies with geology and topography, as a generality the river valley concept is more relevant to human behaviour in the middle than towards the headwaters or the mouth. This is crucial because there has been too much uncritical application of the river-valley/slopes-and-plateau dichotomy in archaeology. For example, and especially, in chalkland headwater areas where there is a minimal floodplain and little distinction between the downs and the valley bottoms, the concept of the river valley hardly applies so I find it difficult to accept, with respect to his excellent overview, the conclusions of Smith (1984) concerning the distinction between valleys and uplands in the Avebury region. Equally in the estuaries of large rivers, the river valley concept is unlikely to apply, at least on a local scale, as there are extensive areas of flatlands with no topographical variation within the circumscription of human home ranges.

The cross profile

At the local scale, it is the degree of *contrast* between the slopes and plateaus and the river valley bottom that is of relevance. Generally there was a sharpening of this contrast as the Holocene progressed, although in terms of the relevance to humans, this was offset in some areas by an increase in habitat diversity generally.

With regard to the distribution of water on the valley bottom, some valleys had a more complicated system of channels - braided or anastomised - in the late-glacial and earlier Holocene which later gave way to a simpler pattern of meandering courses, e.g. Kozarski and Rotnicki (1983), Kozarski *et al* (1988).

With regard to soils and vegetation, in the earlier part of the Holocene uniform mixed deciduous woodland and brownearth soils blanketted the catena from plateau to river edge (Limbrey 1975; Thorley 1981). Under woodland, cycling of moisture and nutrients through the soil allowed free drainage and high fertility, on slopes and valley bottoms alike. The diversity of wetland vegetation and soils which is so characteristic of the valley bottom environments of today did not exist. These were brought about partly by natural processes such as ponding up due to sea-level rise, debris dams and beavers (Coles and Orme 1983), and partly by anthropogenic processes such as woodland clearance and agriculture, all of which altered the hydrology, leading to impedence of drainage, waterlogging, flooding and, ultimately, sedimentation (Bell 1982; Limbrey 1983). In the historic period, wetlands, such as fen, reedswamp and carr, were purposely created and managed (Tansley 1968, 242ff.). Changes on the slopes and plateaus, often to drier and more extreme soils in terms of high or low pH, wrought by forest clearance, cultivation and soil deterioration, exacerbated the differences with the valley bottoms. The environments of the two areas diverged.

Some examples

Observations in river valley bottoms in central southern England support the above proposals of environmental change and past human activity, although the routes to wetland and their chronology varied. As Burrin and Scaife (1988) have shown, the chronology of alluviation, and peat and tufa formation in Britain spanned the entire Holocene.

In the upper Thames, for example, there is a contrast between the archaeology of the gravel terraces, with extensive scatters of stone artefacts and cropmark traces of settlement, and the floodplain alluvium with a paucity of them (Benson and Miles 1974). Fieldwork has show that archaeology reflected by the cropmarks and other surface traces passes under the alluvium, where it is associated with contemporary soils and other environmental materials, and that the visible distribution of remains is not a real reflection of the situation in the past (Robinson and Lambrick 1984). Although earlier, probably localized, episodes are likely (e.g. Lambrick and Robinson 1979; Thomas *et al* 1986), the main period of alluviation was from the Middle Iron Age to the Roman period, so cropmark sites on the alluvium tend to be of later Iron Age, Roman and later date. The situation is not clear cut because there are sites under the alluvium which show up as cropmarks under favorable conditions, and in some areas the alluvium spreads onto the first gravel terrace. But the fact remains that there are many sites under the alluvium on the extant floodplain which date back to the Neolithic period.

Details of the morphological history of the floodplain and its soils are known through the work of Briggs and Gilbertson (1985), Robinson and Lambrick (1984) and Limbrey and Robinson (1988). The gravels of the first terrace and those under the alluvium are a single depositional unit, with the lowering and narrowing of the extant floodplain being a feature already of the Devensian period, continuing into the early Holocene. For several millennia there was practically no waterlogging, flooding or alluviation, or the development of wetlands except locally. The valley bottom was probably uniformly wooded "with a range of soils... which included brown earths of loamy texture in well drained situations close to the river" (Limbrey and Robinson 1988). This was the situation in the Neolithic, continuing into the earlier Bronze Age. But between then and the Middle Iron Age there was progressive waterlogging with the development of gleyed soils, followed by seasonal flooding and ultimately alluviation, so that by the later Iron Age the floodplain was unsuitable for settlement and exploitation other than for specialist activities like summer grazing.

In the upper valley of a Thames tributary, the Kennet, a similar situation obtains although here there were two main episodes of alluviation (Evans *et al* 1988), one between the Late Neolithic and Early Iron Age, the other in post-Medieval times. Prior to the earlier episode, there was woodland on the valley bottom which was cleared in the Neolithic to give way to grassland *as dry as that on the surrounding slopes*, and this extended right across the valley bottom; indeed it is questionable whether there was a stream at all at this time. The contemporary soil profile contained evidence of occupation from the later Mesolithic to the Early Iron Age, including massive sarsen stone structures which are similar to those visible as surface remains on the downs. Likewise in the Middle Ages there was settlement in the form of buildings right across the valley bottom in a dry ground environment, and these can be seen on the valley sides today as earthworks. Later on there was ploughing of the valley bottom, still in dry ground conditions. Only in post-Medieval times did alluviation resume and bury the valley bottom settlement.

A different situation obtains in the lower Welland valley in the East Anglian Fens (French 1990). Micromorphology of buried soils under archaeological sites and alluvium has shown that woodland, cleared in the Early Neolithic period, gave way to a landscape that soon became subject to seasonal alluviation. There was no dryland open-country Neolithic landscape. Instead the environment was trending towards wetland conditions at an early stage, with human use being of marshland resources in the lowest part of the floodplain and the building of ceremonial monuments along its edge. The permanent and long-lived domestic settlements were elsewhere.

In yet other cases, such as the lower Kennet at Thatcham (Limbrey 1983) and in the Test at Bossington, Hampshire (research in progress), dry ground environments with associated Mesolithic archaeology are sealed beneath and within peat and various tufaceous deposits (algal marl at That-cham) at an even earlier time in the Holocene,

The trend to wetlands can also be seen in pollen diagrams. In the Cuckmere in Sussex (Scaife and Burrin 1985) throughout 6 m of fine alluvium of probable post-Neolithic age there is evidence of cereal cultivation, and clearance of lime woodland, but it is only in the top 1.5 m that there is a significant increase in aquatic and marginal aquatic vegetation. In the Ripple Brook, a tributary of the lower Severn in the English West Midlands (Brown and Barber 1985), there was a stepwise development of wetlands, with alluviation, followed by alder carr and peat formation in the Bronze and Iron Ages, with clearance of lime woodlands on the valley sides during the later Bronze Age, followed by exploitation of the valley bottom alder woods in the same period but significantly later on. It was not however until the Iron Age that aquatic plants show a sustained increase. At Willow Garth, a carr in the Great Wold Valley of the Yorkshire Wolds, the increase of aquatics begins somewhat earlier, at *c* 6300 cal BC, but not until after a period of human activity which retarded woodland succession (Bush 1988). So while the valley bottoms were being exploited and various hydrological and sedimentological changes were taking place, the development of aquatic vegetation was confined to a narrow and often recent time bracket.

The river valley bottom environment varied spatially and temporally throughout the Holocene, particularly with regard to comparison with adjacent slopes and plateaus. In some cases there was a distinctive wetland landscape in the valley bottom with diverse vegetation, probably highly productive, certainly with all sorts of properties not present elsewhere. The contrast with the areas outside of the valley bottoms is particularly strong later on in the Holocene when the environments of the two areas were diverging in their hydrology, the valley bottoms becoming increasingly wet, the slopes and plateaus dry. In other cases there was practically no distinction at all between valley bottom and elsewhere, with dry land across the valley bottom and occupied by human communities for normal domestic purposes. In such instances, especially when there were no other draws towards the river edge, the concept of the valley bottom did not apply.

PRESERVATION AND VISIBILITY: THE ARCHAEOLOGICAL AND ENVIRONMENTAL RECORD

We can look at river valley bottoms in relationship to other major types of preservational context (e.g. Evans in Caseldine 1990), defined in terms primarily of topography and altitude, secondarily of past land-use, present land-use and hydrology, and tertiarily of pH.

A major contrast is between areas of preservation and areas of destruction. The latter include built-up areas and areas of intensive farming, concentrated in the lowlands and specifically in valleys, although only archaeology prior to

the latest building and enclosure is destroyed, so that in lowland valleys deserted Medieval villages and ridge and furrow are often visible. In land which has been marginal for arable farming since before the Middle Ages, including uplands like Dartmoor, much of the English chalk downlands, the coastal strip and offshore islands, preservation from earlier periods occurs as earthworks and stone structures. On gravel terraces of major rivers, extensive settlement traces occur only as cropmarks. In ploughsoils, surface scatters of artefacts give evidence of different kinds of activity such as settlement, rubbish dumping, manuring and manufacturing (e.g. Haselgrove *et al* 1985; Schofield 1987; Gaffney and Gaffney 1988). In all these types of preservation the archaeology is visible without excavation. There is good spatial resolution of dwellings, trackways, fields, stock enclosures and artefact distributions, so that, accepting contemporaneity, functional relationships can be assessed. But, because of the paucity of deposits, temporal resolution is poor and there are few opportunities for examining palaeoenvironmental context in long sequences. Furthermore, environmental information is likely to be site-specific and often related to non-domestic activities because archaeology which does not involve pits or earthworks – notably living floors and practically all pre-Neolithic archaeology – is lost, or incorporated into ploughsoil. Only particular types and ages of site are preserved, and these may have been located in selected areas and environments as well as bringing about their own special environments in features such as pits, ditches and wells. For the Neolithic period, this usually means burial, ritual/ceremonial and industrial sites, with domestic settlements unrepresented. Additionally, in these areas, soils and deposits are usually aerobic and biologically active so that the preservational record of organic materials is biassed towards bone and shell and away from uncarbonised plants and insects. The example of the Wilsford Shaft demonstrates how much natural history is usually lost in dry chalk sites (Ashbee *et al* 1989).

The other main type of preservation, archaeological invisibility, includes peat bogs – lowland basins and upland blanket peat – estuarine flats, lake edges, blown sand and valley bottoms, and, as was shown long ago by Rust (1943) for valleys and more recently by Bryony and John Coles (1986; 1989) for wetlands generally, there are long sequences of archaeology associated with environmental evidence and dating materials. Temporal resolution is often excellent, and so, potentially, is spatial resolution, but because of problems with removing large volumes of deposit, the latter is seldom realised. In river valley bottoms, there is potential for widespread sediments, the preservation of living floors and other activities not associated with earthwork building, and palaeosols whose location is not so closely tied to specific activities like defence or ritual. It is for the Mesolithic and Neolithic, where we have little evidence of their domestic settlements, which are likely to have been structures with no above-ground remains preservable in aerobic, non-depositional contexts, and when the river valley bottoms were still dry ground, that river valleys offer their greatest potential. Organic deposits, including uncharred plant remains and insects, are present in situations which have been permanently waterlogged since burial.

Asymmetries of former environment and human behaviour (the systemic context) between slopes/plateaus and valley bottoms are made more acute by asymmetries in the archaeological/environmental context.

CURRENT ARCHAEOLOGICAL ACTIVITY

There is a third asymmetry, that of current archaeological activity. This is related to prospection and discovery, the fine nature of the deposits, their thickness and the general absence of cultivation making them unsuitable for conventional means of archaeological prospecting. Furthermore they have not been subject to the same intensity of commercial exploitation as other Quaternary deposits, nor have they attracted attention from Quaternary geologists - with exceptions - largely because the deposits, even when peaty, are poor in or devoid of pollen. Even when sites are discovered

there are severe problems of excavation because of the watertable. Most seriously, most people have not theorised enough about the potential of river valley bottoms as an archaeological resource and even if they have, they have not put theory into practice.

So the valley bottoms have been ignored, the slopes and plateaus concentrated upon, with the result that only a part of the evidence of former human activities and environments, especially those related to non-domestic settlement, has been obtained. In situations where the river valley bottoms were more generally or uniquely exploited, entire segments of information, especially related to domestic settlement, are missing. The asymmetry of past human behaviour towards the river valley bottom by comparison with that on the valley sides, the asymmetry of invisibility in the valley bottoms and the asymmetry of current archaeological activity, have reinforced each other to give us an atypical record of the past.

BIBLIOGRAPHY

Ashbee, P., Bell, M. and Proudfoot, E. 1989. *Wilsford Shaft: Excavations 1960 - 62.* London: Historic Buildings & Monuments Commission for England.

Becker, B. and Schirmer, W. 1977. Palaeoecological study on the Holocene valley development of the River Main, southern Germany. *Boreas 6,* 303-21.

Bell, M. 1982. The effects of land-use and climate on valley sedimentation. In A.F. Harding (ed.), *Climatic Change in Later Prehistory,* 127 - 42. Edinburgh: Edinburgh University Press.

Benson, D.G. and Miles, D. 1974. *The Upper Thames Valley: An Archaeological Survey of the River Gravels.* Oxford: Oxford Archaeological Unit.

Bintliff, J. 1977. *Natural Environment and Human Settlement in Prehistoric Greece.* Oxford: British Archaeological Reports,Supplementary Series 28.

Briggs, D.A., Coope, G.R. and Gilbertson, D.D. 1985. *The Chronology and Environmental Framework of Early Man in the Upper Thames Valley: A New Model.* Oxford: British Archaeological Reports, British Series 137.

Brown, A.G. and Barber, K.E. 1985. Late Holocene paleoecology and sedimentary history of a small lowland catchment in central England. *Quaternary Research 24,* 87-102.

Burrin, P.J. and Scaife, R.G. 1984. Aspects of Holocene valley sedimentation and floodplain development in southern England. *Proceedings of the Geologists' Association 95,* 81-96.

Burrin, P.J. and Scaife, R.G. 1988. Environmental thresholds, catastrophe theory and landscape sensitivity: the relevance to the impact of man on valley alluviations. In J.L. Bintliff, D.A. Davidson and E.G. Grant (eds), *Conceptual Issues in Environmental Archaeology,* 211 - 32. Edinburgh: Edinburgh University Press.

Bush, M.B. 1988. Early Mesolithic disturbance: a force on the landscape. *Journal of Archaeological Science 152,* 453 - 62.

Caseldine, A. 1990. *Environmental Archaeology in Wales.* Lampeter: Department of Archaeology, St David's University College.

Coles, B. and Coles, J. 1986. *Sweet Track to Glastonbury.* London: Thames & Hudson.

Coles, B. and Coles, J. 1989. *People of the Wetlands: Bogs, Bodies and Lake-dwellers.* London: Thames & Hudson.

Coles, J.M. and Lawson, A.J. (eds) 1987. *European Wetlands in Prehistory.* Oxford: Clarendon Press.

Coles, J.M. and Orme, B.J. 1983. *Homo sapiens* or *Castor fiber? Antiquity 57,* 95 - 102.

Crawford, O.G.S. 1924. *Air Survey and Archaeology.* London: HMSO.

Evans, C. 1990. Review of "B.A. Purdy (ed.) 1988, Wet Site Archaeology. Caldwell, New Jersey: The Telford Press". *Proceedings of the Prehistoric Society 56,* 339 - 40.

Evans, J.G., Limbrey, S., Máté, I. and Mount, R. 1988. Environmental change and land-use history in a Wiltshire river valley in the last 14,000 years. In J.C. Barrett, and I.A. Kinnes (eds), *The Archaeology of Context in the Neolithic and Bronze Age: Recent Trends,* 97 - 103. Sheffield: Department of Archaeology and Prehistory, University of Sheffield.

French, C.A.I. 1990. Neolithic soils, middens and alluvium in the lower Welland valley. *Oxford Journal of Archaeology 9,* 305-11.

Gaffney, C.F. and Gaffney, V.L. 1988. Some quantitative approaches to site territory and land use from the surface record. In J.L. Bintliff, D.A. Davidson and E.G. Grant (eds), *Conceptual Issues in Environmental Archaeology,* 82 - 90. Edinburgh: Edinburgh University Press.

Gladfelter, B.G. 1985. On the interpretation of archaeological sites in alluvial settings. In J.K. Stein and W.R. Farrand (eds), *Archaeological Sediments in Context*, 41 - 52. Maine: Orono.

Gray, H.H. 1984. Archaeological sedimentology of overbank silt deposits on the floodplain of the Ohio River near Louisville, Kentucky. *Journal of Archaeological Science 11*, 421 - 32.

Hall, D., Evans, C., Hodder, I. and Pryor, F. 1987. The Fenlands of East Anglia, England: survey and excavation. In J.M. Coles and A.J. Lawson (eds), *European Wetlands in Prehistory*, 169 - 201. Oxford: Clarendon Press.

Haselgrove, C., Millett, M. and Smith, I. (eds) 1985. *Archaeology from the Ploughsoil*. Sheffield: Sheffield University, Department of Prehistory.

Kozarski, S. and Rotnicki, K. 1983. Changes of river channel patterns and the mechanism of valley-floor construction in the North-Polish Plain during the Late Weichsel and Holocene. In D.J. Briggs and R.S. Waters (eds), *Studies in Quaternary Geomorphology*, 31-48. Norwich: Geo Books.

Kozarski, S., Gonera, P. and Antczak, B. 1988. Valley floor development and paleohydrological changes: The Late Vistulian and Holocene history of the Warta River (Poland). In G. Lang and C. Schluchter (eds), *Lake, Mire and River Environments during the last 15,000 Years*, 185 - 203. Rotterdam & Brookfield: A.A. Balkema.

Lambrick, G. and Robinson, M. 1979. *Iron Age and Roman riverside settlements at Farmoor, Oxfordshire*. London: Oxfordshire Archaeological Unit/Council for British Archaeology.

Lang, G. and Schluchter, C. (eds), 1988. *Lake, Mire and River Environments during the last 15,000 Years*. Rotterdam: A.A. Balkema.

Lewin, J. 1983. Changes of channel patterns and floodplains. In K.J. Gregory (ed), *Background to Palaeohydrology*, 304 - 19. London: John Wiley & Sons.

Lewin, J., Bradley, S.B. and Macklin, M.G. 1983. Historical alluviation in mid-Wales. *Geological Journal 18*, 331-50.

Limbrey, S. 1975. *Soil Science and Archaeology*. London: Academic Press.

Limbrey, S. 1983. Archaeology and palaeohydrology. In K.J. Gregory (ed.), *Background to Palaeohydrology*, 189 - 212. London: John Wiley & Sons.

Limbrey, S. and Robinson, S. 1988. Dry land to wet land: soil resources in the upper Thames valley. In P. Murphy and C. French (eds), *The Exploitation of Wetlands*, 129 - 44.

Oxford: British Archaeological Reports British Series 186.

MacNeish, R.S. 1974. Reflections on my search for the beginnings of agriculture in Mexico. In G.R. Willey, (ed.), *Archaeological Researches in Retrospect*, 205 - 34. Cambridge: Winthrop.

Robinson, M.A. and Lambrick, G.H. 1984. Holocene alluviation and hydrology in the upper Thames basin. *Nature 308*, 809 - 14.

Rust, A. 1943. *Die alt- und mittelsteinzeitlichen Funde von Stellmoor*. Neumünster: Karl Wachholtz Verlag.

Scaife, R.G. and Burrin, P.J.1985. The environmental impact of prehistoric man as recorded in the upper Cuckmere valley at Stream Farm, Chiddingly. *Sussex Archaeological Collections 123*, 27-34.

Scarre, C. 1989. Review of "J.M. Coles and A.J. Lawson (eds) 1987. *European Wetlands in Prehistory*. Oxford: Clarendon Press". *Proceedings of the Prehistoric Society 55*, 274-75.

Schiffer, M.B. 1987. *Formation Processes of the Archaeological Record*. Albuquerque: University of New Mexico Press.

Schofield, A.J. 1987. The role of palaeoecology in understanding variations in regional survey data. *Circaea 5*, 33-42.

Smith, R.W. 1984. The ecology of Neolithic farming systems as exemplified by the Avebury region of Wiltshire. *Proceedings of the Prehistoric Society 50*, 99-120.

Tansley, A.G. 1968 (2nd edition). *Britain's Green Mantle, Past, Present and Future*. London: George Allen and Unwin Ltd.

Thomas, R., Robinson, M., Barrett, J. and Wilson, B. 1986. A Late Bronze Age riverside settlement at Wallingford, Oxfordshire. *Archaeological Journal 143*, 174-200.

Trigger, B.G. 1989. *A History of Archaeological Thought*. Cambridge: Cambridge University Press.

Vita-Finzi, C. 1969. *The Mediterranean Valleys: Geological Changes in Historical Times*. Cambridge: Cambridge University Press.

Willey, G.R. 1953. *Prehistoric Settlement Patterns in the Viru Valley, Peru*. Washington: Bureau of American Ethnology.

Zvelebil, M. 1987. Wetland settlement of Eastern Europe. In J.M. Coles and A.J. Lawson (eds), *European Wetlands in Prehistory*, 94 - 116. Oxford: Clarendon Press.

7

NOYEN-SUR-SEINE: A MESOLITHIC WATERSIDE SETTLEMENT

Daniel Mordant and Claude Mordant

SYNOPSIS

The site consists of series of boreal water-meadows. Detrital mesolithic material is included in peat and gravel levels on the edge of the river Seine ; no domestic structures have been recognized. Faunal remains are very common: red deer, roe deer, wild-boar, aurochs, wolf, some aquatic birds were hunted; pike and eel were fished. The flint industry is mainly composed of scrapers, notched scrapers, cores and retouched flakes; only 2 points have been discovered and no microliths. Wood and organic remains are well preserved and some fish-traps, one basket and a dugout canoe (pine tree) are considered as major discoveries for the French Mesolithic. The material is dated c 8000 uncal BP .

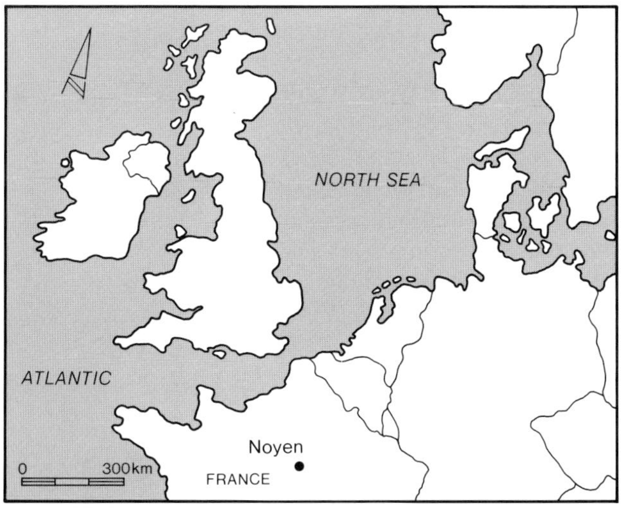

ries. In fact, investigations were realised principally on alluvial gravel "islands" (dry lands) which represented only a part of the bottom of the valleys. For a long time, wetlands have been overlooked but the industrial practice by the quarries of lowering the water table has given the opportunity , since the 1980s, of new research in ancient river channels totally filled up with gravel, silt and peat.

The Mesolithic of the Paris Basin is well known since Hinout and Rozoy's studies (Hinout 1984; Rozoy 1978). The open sites located in sandy regions (Fontainebleau Forest, Tardenois region) belong to the Tardenoisien Culture to the north, and Sauveterrien to the south of the river Seine (Fig. 7.1-7.2). Valley bottom settlements are still rare

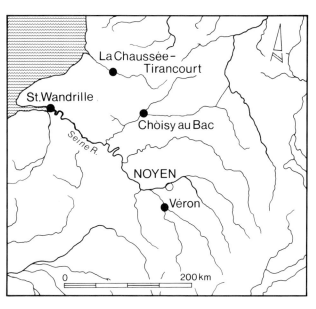

Fig. 7.1 Location Map

The development of prehistoric archaeology in the Paris Basin is mostly linked to research in the main alluvial valleys: Aisne, Oise, Upper Seine, Yonne. The work is mainly prospection and rescue excavation in gravel quar-

Fig. 7.2 Noyen-sur-Seine and contemporary valley bottom settlements

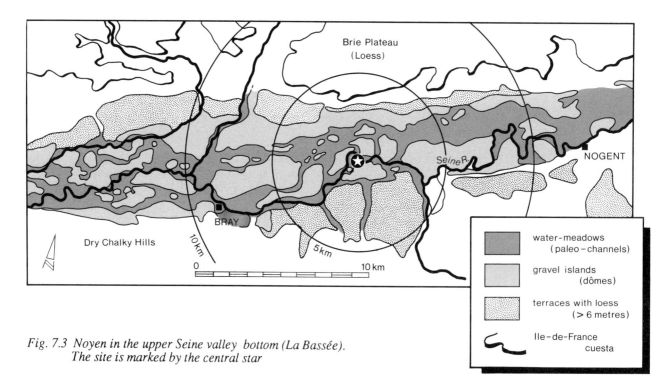

*Fig. 7.3 Noyen in the upper Seine valley bottom (La Bassée).
The site is marked by the central star*

apart from a few new sites such as Véron, Yonne valley
(Carré 1991); St-Wandrille, lower Seine valley (Chancerel
and Paulet-Locard 1991), Choisy-au-Bac, Oise-Aisne confluence, (Valentin 1991), La Chaussée-Tirancourt, Somme
valley (Ducrocq, 1991; Fagnard, 1991) (Fig. 7.2). This
present rarity is due only to a lack of research on the valley
wetlands. But the Noyen sequence appears to be exceptional for its record of the Upper Seine environment from
Preboreal to Atlantic periods and for its mesolithic remains.

SITUATION

The Seine-Yonne region

The country around Noyen (50 km radius) includes an
important alluvial area of about 1000 sq.km. The Seine
valley contains the greater part of it (85%) then the Yonne
(10%) and Loing (5%). These low lands are surrounded by
3 plateaux: Brie, Southern Champagne (Sénonais), and
Gâtinais (Fig. 7.3). In the north, the Brie plateau bordered
by the Ile-de-France *cuesta* is composed of tertiary calcareous layers covered by loess. The Sénonais hills in the south
have chalky dry soils and the Gâtinais ones in the West are
more clayey. Three vegetation zones can be identified: the
Quercus pedunculata series on deep and rich soils (Brie),
Quercus sessiliflora and *pubescens* series on rendzina
(Sénonais chalky lands) and other soils of the Gâtinais
plateau, and the wide and flat Seine valley (La Bassée) is
occupied by *Alnus* series.

Noyen and the Bassée

In the eastern part of the Bassée, peaty alluviums predominate but in the west they are in equal proportion with
gravel deposits; these sediments are more common in the
Yonne valley and in the confluence. Terraces with loess

cover develop along the Seine valley and expand in the
Orvain region, in the south of Noyen. As a result, within a
5 km radius around Noyen, we can find plateaux and
terraces with loess, chalky dry hills, wetlands and the river
(Fig. 7.3).

The site is limited by ancient meanders of the Seine and
during neolithic times (Middle Neolithic II), several enclosures were built inside, on the top of this gravelly flat island.
The first system consisted of a long palisade which closed
the meander at its base; it was rebuilt four times. In a second
phase, a causewayed-camp was set up along the north bank.
Neolithic settlements connected with the first system have
been explored inside the meander over more than 10,000
sq.m (Mordant D., 1977 ; Mordant C. et D., 1988).

The neolithic site is only a "dry site" and it was the search
for contemporary organic material that led to the discovery
of the mesolithic levels and their various remains (Fig. 7.4).
Secondly, the quarry exploitation and the lowering of the
water table allowed the exploration of the deepest levels. In
1983 the first fish-trap was found, and in 1984 radiocarbon
dates proved the mesolithic nature of all the material.
Noyen was the first wetland mesolithic site discovered in
France (Mordant D. ,1985 ; Mordant C.et D.,1989).

POST-GLACIAL SEQUENCE

Excavations took place from 1983 to 1988 during the
summer (Fig. 7.5). The environmental research programme, partly funded by the Centre National de la Recher-
che Scientifique, was set up in 1985 and brought together
21 specialists (Noyen C.N.R.S. project)[1]

Sedimentology (Fig. 7.6. Studied by V. Krier) During
Tardi-glacial times, many wide overlapping channels

Fig. 7.4 Noyen: the site in relation to the river

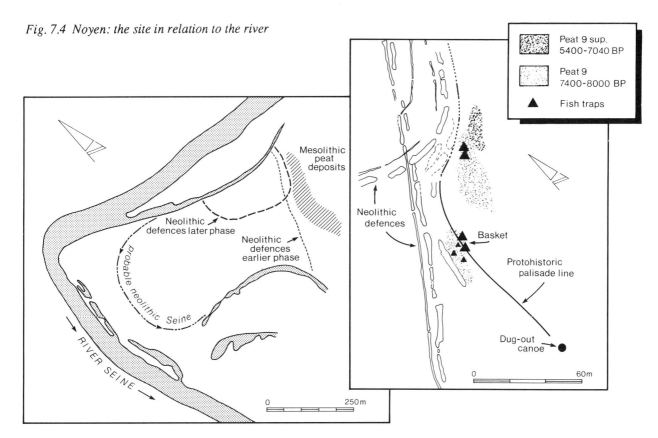

flowed all over the valley, and there was a succession of contrasted floods and subsidences. The river was able to dig its bed into the chalk substratum and to remove gravel deposits.The model changes during the *Pre-boreal* to wide slow channels. They filled up with gravels but also with organic silts which indicate running water with a light flow. Some phases of high activity and erosion stopped this phase of calm dynamics. The *Boreal* period saw 2 types of river activity. First, the same overload process known since the Pre-boreal continued and more compact organic silts per-

sisted after an erosion phase, proof of the same running water and a light flow. Secondly, in other parts of the site, many little active and tangled channels filled with gravels during rapid overflow. Some organic levels made by floated plant remains piled up by the current are included at the bottom of these stratigraphies; some fish-traps lie in these deposits (Fig. 7.5). After this episode, a wide river bed quite independent of the main channel appeared and progressively filled with organic silts, wood and vegetal debris. It was now still water. During the *Atlantic* period the same phe-

Fig. 7.5 Noyen: stratigraphy of the main channel; 1-2, fish-traps

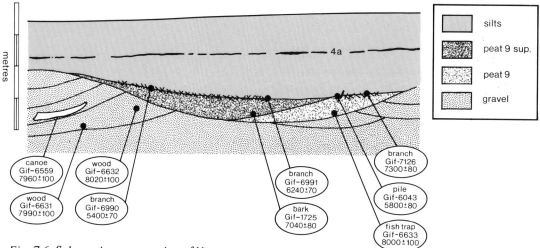

Fig. 7.6 Schematic cross-section of Noyen

nomenon continued and the thick organic deposits completed the filling up of the channel which became a pond with swampy banks. In the late part of the period, the completion of a long process transformed all this paleo-channel into marshy grassland. From Atlantic to *Sub-boreal* all this part of the site was a wet grassland crossed now and then by a sporadic flow of water. So an evolution of 8 thousand years permits the passage from active river channels to marshy grassland. The present main bed of the river Seine dates probably from the Early Bronze Age, and it was partly canalized in the XIXth century.

Radiocarbon dates realized on wood (Pre-boreal to Atlantic) range between 9000 and 5000 uncal BP (Fig. 7.6-7.7 and Appendix). Mesolithic remains found in gravel or in peaty levels date from 8000 to 6500 uncal BP.

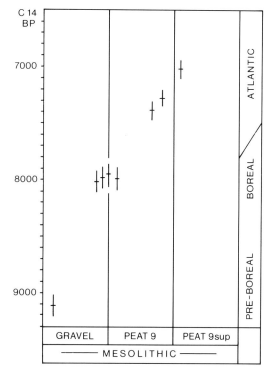

Fig. 7.7 Radiocarbon dates from the mesolithic levels at Noyen

Palynology (studied by C. Leroyer) The tree pollen diagram based on the study of 7 sequences picked up in different channels (Fig. 7.8) shows a classic development. During the *Pre-boreal*, pine dominates other trees like oak and hazel. Later, in the *Boreal* period, hazel, oak and elm increase whereas pine declines. The *Early Atlantic* phase is marked by oak and elm always important, hazel in decrease and a slight increase in pine. During the *Late Atlantic* hazel, oak and elm decrease but lime reaches its upper limit while alder increases markedly. Throughout the *Sub-boreal* alder dominates and masks the deciduous forest. The nearby environment seems to be lightly influenced by human presence. The first deforestation occurs during the Late Neolithic. This observation conflicts with Middle Neolithic archaeological evidence. Many fences, probably 3km long in total, and houses were erected and all these wooden constructions probably cleared the neighbouring forest. However it is only in the latest silty levels of the main channel fill that we can observe clear bush fires of deforestation dating from the Late Neolithic or Early Bronze Age.

So, as long ago as mesolithic times, the Seine valley offered a contrasted landscape with gravelly islands covered with grass and bushes, swamps and river channels bordered by alder, and wooded loess terraces. All these ecosystems were rationally exploited by mesolithic people.

Distribution of Remains

Mesolithic remains were concentrated in 4 main areas on the edges of channels or peaty ponds (Fig. 7.4). One thousand sq. m have been dug 0.1 m to 1 m deep. No trace of domestic structures has been revealed and the evidence consists of rubbish deposits coming from the real settlements set up on the top of the gravel banks and totally destroyed by erosion. The remains are composed of 7500 bones, 1000 flints, some 100 bone tools and rare wooden artefacts (dug-out canoe, fish-traps, basket). Most of them lie in the bottom of the swampy channels but some have probably been moved by the water and redeposited with alluviums. The pine canoe, filled up with gravel, was probably washed away with some branches during a flood.

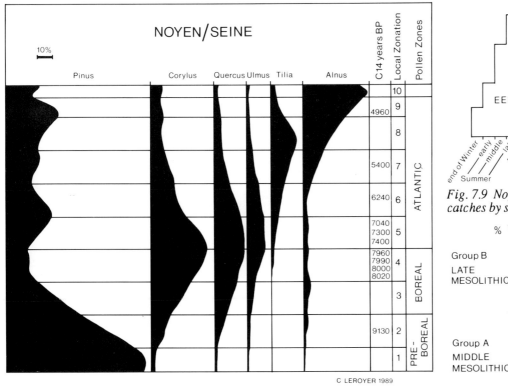

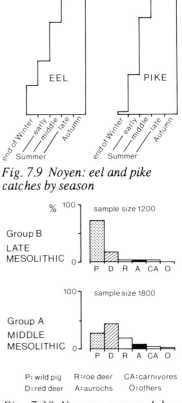

Fig. 7.9 Noyen: eel and pike catches by season

P: wild pig   R: roe deer   CA: carnivores
D: red deer   A: aurochs   O: others

Fig. 7.10 Noyen: mammal bone identifications, middle and late mesolithic

Fig. 7.8 Noyen: tree-pollen diagram (after Leroyer 1989)

Two major levels are observed principally within peaty deposits (peat 9 and 9 *sup*) but they are separated by roughly a millennium in radiocarbon years (Fig. 7.7). In fact, these layers mark more than 2 occupations of the site and it is quite impossible to estimate in detail the periodicity of the presence of mesolithic fishers and hunters from 8000 to 6500 uncal BP.

Erosion easily explains the lack of well preserved settlement patterns, but the absence of flint hunting artefacts is unexplained and evidence for plant consumption is not attested, although it too could be expected in the water-logged context at Noyen.

HUMAN ACTIVITIES

Fishing (studied by C . Dauphin) Fishing was mainly based on eel and pike. In the oldest peat (layer 9, group A), eels dominate all the other species but later (layer 9 *sup*, group B) mainly pike were fished. Fishing took place throughout the year but was practised more during the summer (Fig. 7.9). Eel vertebrae show many traces of burning which may result from smoke curing over a fire place. Fish-traps, frequent in the first period, were probably used for catching eels; the straight fish hooks come from the later levels where pike remains are common. Throughout mesolithic times fishing appears to have been a major activity but the techniques changed (Dauphin 1989).

Hunting (Figs. 7.10, 7.12. Studied by J.D.Vigne and M.C. Marinval-Vigne) Faunal remains are abundant and very well preserved. Most are mammalian bones, but aquatic birds and turtles are also present. Two groups have been identified and studied in connection with the stratigraphy: group A, peat 9 – about 1800 identified bones; group B, peat 9 *sup* – about 1200 determined bones (Vigne *in* Marinval-Vigne 1987, 1990; Marinval-Vigne *et al* 1991).

Group A: Middle Mesolithic. The frequency of the parts of the skeleton suggests that Noyen was a base camp at this period. The killing season spans spring to autumn. Animal carcasses were butchered at the hunting places and then brought back to the camp, probably in one part for roe deer, and in quarters for wild pig, aurochs and red-deer. The same butchery practices were regularly used, meat was commonly grilled and bone-marrow always taken out. Three ecosystems were exploited: the river itself, identified by the hunting of beaver, otter and the collecting of many aquatic turtles (*Emys* – some carapaces are probably used as vessels); the forest edge and some clearances, revealed by the presence of wolf, fox, aurochs, roe deer; but the forest was the main ecosystem exploited, where they hunted red deer, wild-pig, and lynx or *Felis*. Red deer was the most abundant quarry (49 % of the N.I.S.P.), hunted between 6 and 9 years old; wild-pig came in second place (27 % of the N.I.S.P.), hunted between 2 and 3 years old.

59

Fig. 7.11 Noyen: fish-trap on bottom of peat 9 (0.86 m length)

Fig. 7.12 Noyen: wild pig bones in peat 9 sup

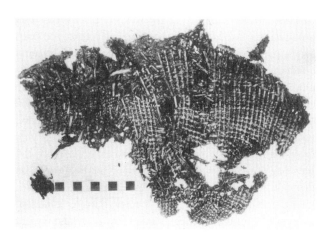

Fig. 7.13 Noyen: basket on bottom of peat

Fig. 7.14 Noyen: dug-out canoe, pine tree; preserved length 4 m.

Group B: Late Mesolithic. Base camps were now occupied for a shorter season but there were still the same three ecosystems exploited by the hunters. Eating habits had changed: wild-pig came first (70 % of the N.I.S.P.) and it was killed at 7-8 months and after 10-12 months, a pattern probably due only to opportunistic hunting at the very moment of the year when these age classes are present, that is the end of the summer and beginning of autumn. Butchery changed too and was carried out at the camp site for the young boars. Although this human group remained at a mesolithic stage in social – economic terms, without sheep (or other domestic animals), they were probably contemporary with the first neolithic farmers of the Seine valley, as shown by the presence of a very few bones of domestic pig and cattle in the mesolithic layers. The dog is missing in Noyen but it is present at Star Carr (Clark 1954) and other mesolithic sites of the same period. Three wolf skulls have been studied in detail by J.D. Vigne (Vigne and Marinval-Vigne 1987) and they seem to be a bit different from real wild specimens. They can be compared to modern zoo animal skulls, and if it is impossible to conclude that a real proto-domestication of wolf had taken place, we can still assume a possible use of the animal for hunting.

Plant artefacts These all date from 8000 uncal BP and belong to Group A remains.

Basketry The same technology was used for all the basketry objects: 2 stems of willow (or other species) were twisted together. It is one of the simplest and oldest methods of basketry.

Six fragments of fish-traps (Fig. 7.11) have been discovered in the deepest levels on the edge of the channel. They have a simple cone shape, 0.85 m long and perhaps 0.3-0.4 m diameter, and they look similar to northern European types of fishtrap (Brinkhuizen 1983). They were probably used for eel fishing.

A piece of probable hurdle, about 1 sq.m, was found that had floated onto the edge of the channel. The thin juxtaposed woods are only held by 2 straight rods without linkage. Several interpretations can be made: an element of a light shelter, or a part of a barrier for fishing. Maybe some bundles of little branches (1 m long) could also be considered as eel or crayfish traps.

The basket (Fig. 7.13) probably had a cylindrical shape, 0.2 m high and 0.25 m diameter; the bottom is missing. It was made of wicker of different colours and *Ligustrum* for the top shoot. It is surely one of the oldest baskets known in Europe at present (Egloff 1985).

The dug-out canoe (Fig. 7.14) was run aground at the bottom of an ancient channel filled up by gravel (group A system- Fig. 7.6). It was made from a pine trunk and it had been hollowed out using fire. Some cut marks from tranchet tools have been seen on the bottom, but no flint tranchet axes have been found on the site. An unexplained little step exists near the preserved extremity, and may be the poop.

The canoe was 5m long at least; 0.5 - 0.55 m wide; 0.20 m deep; thickness of the bottom, 7 cm. The date is 7960 ± 100 uncal BP (Gif 6559). It is one of the oldest canoes known in Europe, along with the one from Pesse in the Netherlands also made in pine (Arnold 1976), and the oak canoe from Estavayer in Switzerland (Ramseyer *et al* 1989). The Noyen dugout proves a high technology for wood use and a regular practice of navigation on the river Seine. We are convinced that Noyen mesolithic hunters and fishers adjusted well to this environment.

Flint industry (Fig. 7.15. Studied by A. Augereau) Less than one thousand flint artefacts have been found with only 10% tools and absolutely no microliths (Augereau 1989).

Group A There was a major flake production on black or brownish flint from cretaceous chalk. Nodules could be collected on the riverbank or on chalky lands 3 km to the north or 5 km to the south. The brownish flint appears in the region of the Seine-Yonne confluence, 30 km from Noyen. A high rate of scrapers and notched scrapers (60%) characterizes this oldest industry; only one Tardenoisien point is present.

Group B The industry changes a little with more blades (nearly Montbani type) but scrapers still dominate. Only one Sonchamp point has been found, near a young red deer scapula.

This flint industry is composed of common tools, and all the potentially diagnostic microliths and points are missing so it is quite impossible to compare Noyen to the "dry" sandy mesolithic sites of the Paris Basin.

Bone and antler products The age of the antlers used as tools appears to be different from those of the hunted red deer. This observation suggests that the mesolithic people collected shed antlers or brought into Noyen lots of tools and antlers from other base camps (Marinval-Vigne *et al* 1991). Roe deer antlers were never used. Several specimens of tools have edge polish of the sort commonly attributed to leather working; a sort of antler adze may have held a flint blade, like artefacts from Schötz 7 in the Wauwil swamp (Wyss 1979, 55-56). Groove and splinter technique is attested on red deer and aurochs long bones. A bone stick with oblique scores is quite similar to a Téviec pattern and there is a fragment of antler rod with a penis-shaped end. It is not possible to distinguish important differences between the 2 main levels, with the exception of 2 straight hooks found in the later one.

Human bones (studied by G. Auboire) These were found mixed with detritic remains: 4 incomplete skulls, one mandible, and several long bones (femur, ulna, radius, humerus). They belong to at least 4 individuals. Human remains of this period are rare in Northern France, only 2 skull fragments in Larchant cave (Fontainebleau Forest, excavations of J. Hinout). The Noyen people look like mesolithic Bretons but they can also be compared to the later neolithic population of the Bassée region (Auboire 1991). Many cut

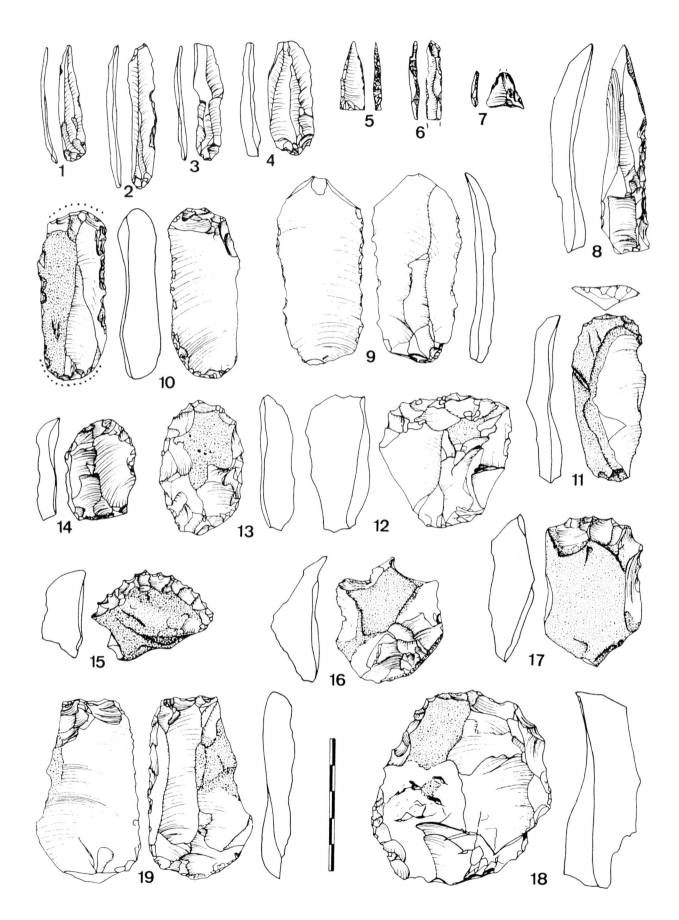

Fig. 7.15 Noyen flint industry (after Augereau 1989). Late Mesolithic, peat 9 sup.: 1-4 and 6-10.
Middle Mesolithic, peat 9: 5 and 11-18

marks can be seen on mandible, elbow and hip, and a femur head with burnt spots should be noted.

CONCLUSION

The Noyen site provides lots of information owing to its waterlogged position, but we have only explored the rubbish edge of the main settlement set up on the "dry" slope of a gravel island. It is the first mesolithic site of this kind discovered in the north of France. The complete stratigraphy (nearly 4 m high) clarifies the whole environmental sequence from Pre-boreal to Sub-boreal. Some wooden artefacts (fish-traps, basket, dugout) are really remarkable for France and the Mesolithic.

All the archaeological remains indicate a systematic exploitation of and a good adaptation to the river ecosystem by the mesolithic hunters and fishers. They fished and hunted during summer and they were probably not very far from their winter base camps which were perhaps 5 km to the south on the low terraces of the Orvain valley. The deep silty soils of this region were propitious for the growth of deciduous forest, and abundant game would provide subsistence for the group during winter. If so, the seasonal movements of the population were very restricted. The Seine valley, its banks and neighbouring plateaus offered various associations of different ecosystems: river and ponds, marshy lands, grassland, and forest of different kinds whether dense on the heavy soils of Brie or more open forest elsewhere on the rendzina. As the mesolithic people walked through these diverse environments, so they took advantage of them.

Note

1. Preliminary results of this research programme directed by D. Mordant and M.C. Marinval-Vigne have been presented during the Paris congress organized by the Société Préhistorique Française and G.M.P.C.A. research group in November 1989. The paper is ready for press, see Marinval-Vigne *et al* in press. Results from different specialists have been summarised here.

APPENDIX (see also Fig. 7.6) Noyen-sur-Seine Radiocarbon Dates

Level	Sample	Result	Lab. No.
23 inf	bark	9130 ±100 uncal BP	GIF - 7286
13-14	wood	8020 ± 100 uncalBP	GIF - 6632
9	fish-trap	8000 ± 100 uncalBP	GIF - 6633
12-13	wood	7990 ± 100 uncalBP	GIF - 6631
Gravel	canoe	7960 ± 100 uncalBP	GIF - 6559
9	board ?	7400 ± 80 uncalBP	GIF - 6989
9	wood	7300 ± 80 uncalBP	GIF - 7126
9 sup	b ark	7040 ± 80 uncalBP	GIF - 7125
9 sup	wood	6240 ± 70 uncal BP	GIF - 6991
St XVI 160	pile ?	5800 ± 80 uncalBP	GIF - 6043
9 sup	wood	5400 ± 70 uncal BP	GIF - 6990

BIBLIOGRAPHY

Arnold, B. 1976. La pirogue d'Auvernier Nord (Bronze final). Contribution à la technologie des pirogues monoxyles préhistoriques. *Cahiers d'Archéologie subaquatique* V, 75-84.

Auboire, G. 1991. *Apport de l'anthropologie physique à la connaissance du Mésolithique et du Néolithique dans le Nord et l'Ouest de la France.* Thèse de doctorat, Museum national d'Histoire naturelle, unpublished thesis.

Augereau, A. 1989. L'industrie lithique de Noyen-sur-Seine: présentation de l'outillage. In *l'Homme et l'Eau au temps de la Préhistoire*, 191-202. Congrès des Sociétés savantes de Lyon 1987. Paris: Comité des Travaux historiques et scientifiques.

Brinkhuizen, D. C. 1983 . Some notes on recent and protohistoric fishing gear from north western Europe. *Palaeohistoria* 25, 7-53.

Carré, H. 1991. Le Mésolithique dans l'Yonne. In *Mésolithique et néolithisation en France et dans les régions limitrophes*, 389-401. Congrès des Sociétés savantes de Strasbourg 1988. Paris: Comité des Travaux historiques et scientifiques.

Chancerel, A. et Paulet-Locard, M.A. 1991 . Le Mésolithique en Normandie. In *Mésolithique et néolithisation en France et dans les régions limitrophes*, 213-229. Congrès des Sociétés savantes de Strasbourg 1988. Paris: Comité des Travaux historiques et scientifiques.

Clark, J.G.D. 1954. Excavations at Star Carr. Cambridge: University Press.

Dauphin, C. 1989. L'ichtyofaune de Noyen-sur-Seine. In *L'Homme et l'Eau au temps de la Préhistoire*, 11-32. Congrès des Sociétés savantes de Lyon 1987. Paris: Comité des Travaux historiques et scientifiques.

Ducrocq, T. 1991. Les armatures du Mésolithique final et du Néolithique ancien en Picardie: héritage ou convergence? In *Mésolithique et néolithisation en France et dans les régions limitrophes*, 425-426. Congrès des Sociétés savantes de Strasbourg 1988. Paris: Comité des Travaux historiques et scientifiques.

Egloff, M. 1985. Le panier du cueilleur. Etapes de la vannerie préhistorique en Europe. *Jahrbuch des bernischen historichen Museums*, 63-64, 81-87.

Fagnard, J.P. 1991. La fin du Mésolithique dans le Nord de la France. In *Mésolithique et néolithisation en France et dans les régions limitrophes*, 437-452. Congrès des Sociétés savantes de Strasbourg 1988. Paris: Comité des Travaux historiques et scientifiques.

Hinout, J. 1984. Les outils et armatures standarts mésolithiques dans le Bassin parisien par l'analyse des données. *Revue archéologique de Picardie* 1-2, 9-30.

Marinval-Vigne, M.C., Mordant, D., Auboire, G., Augereau, A., Bailon, S., Dauphin, C., Delibrias, G., Krier, V. , Leclerc, A.S. , Leroyer, C., Marinval, P., Mordant, C., Rodriguez, P., Vigne, J.D. and Vilette, P. In press. Noyen-sur-Seine, site stratifié en milieu fluviatile: une étude multidisciplinaire intégrée. In J.D. Vigne, M. Menu, C. Perlès and H. Valladas (eds), *Du terrain au laboratoire: pour un meilleur dialogue en archéologie*, Congrès préhistorique de France de Paris 1989, *Bulletin de la Société préhistorique française* 86, 370-379.

Mordant, C. and D. 1988 . Les enceintes néolithiques de la haute vallée de la Seine. In C. Burgess, P. Topping, C. Mordant and M. Maddison (eds), *Enclosures and defences in the Neolithic of Western Europe*, 231-254. Oxford: British Archaeological Reports, International Series, 403.

Mordant, C. and D. 1989 . Noyen-sur-Seine, site mésolithique en milieu humide fluviatile. In *L'Homme et l'Eau au temps de la préhistoric*, 33-52. Congrès des Sociétés savantes de Lyon 1987, Comité des Travaux historiques et scientifiques , Paris.

Mordant, D. 1977. Noyen-sur-Seine, habitat néolithique de fond de vallée alluviale. *Gallia-Préhistoire* 20(1), 229-269.

Mordant, D. 1985. Pour l'archéologie en milieu fluvial. *Bulletin de la Société préhistorique française* 82, 70-72.

Ramseyer, D., Reinhard, J. , Pillonel, D. 1989. La pirogue monoxyle mésolithique d'Estavayer-le-Lac. *Archéologie suisse* 12, 91-93.

Rozoy, J.G. 1978. *Les derniers chasseurs. Essai de synthèse sur l'Epipaléolithique en France et en Belgique*. Société archéologique champenoise .

Valentin, B. 1991. Le site tardenoisien de "la Bouche d'Oise" à Choisy-au-Bac. In *Archéologie de la vallée de l'Oise*, 41-42. Compiègne: Centre de recherches archéologiques de la vallée de l'Oise.

Vigne, J.D. and Marinval-Vigne, M.C. 1987. Quelques reflexions préliminaires sur les canidés mésolithiques de Noyen-sur-Seine et sur la domestication du chien en Europe occidentale. 5è International Conference, International Council for Archaeozoology, Bordeaux 1986. *Archaeozoologica* 2, 153-164.

Vigne, J.D. and Marinval-Vigne, M.C. 1990. First experiments of domestication in a mesolithic hunters' society contemporaneous of early Neolithic: zooarchaeology of Noyen-sur-Seine. 6th International Conference, International Council for Archaeology, Washington. Unpublished conference paper.

Wyss, R. 1979. *Das mittelsteinzeitliche Hirschjägerlager von Schötz 7 im Wauwilermoos*. Zürich: Schweizerischen Landesmuseum.

8

FRIESACK MESOLITHIC WETLANDS

Bernhard Gramsch

SYNOPSIS

Friesack 4 and Friesack 27 are Mesolithic marshland sites in Northern Germany, about 60 km northwest of Berlin. The sites lie in the most western part of the Warsaw-Berlin ice-marginal valley which in this area is filled with fluvioglacial sand and has extensive peat cover. At the time of Mesolithic occupation the sands formed a topography of low hills with lakes and ponds in process of peat formation. At Friesack 4, the excavations were undertaken from 1977 to 1989 mainly in the refuse area of the site in the sublittoral zone of a former lake adjacent to the settlement area. A multi-stratified sequence of sediments, consisting of sands, humose sands and peat muds, indicated many Mesolithic occupations from the middle Pre-boreal (around 9700 uncal BP) to the middle Atlantic (around 6600 uncal BP), except the younger Pre-boreal, according to 74 radiocarbon dates and to extensive palynological research. Owing to the chemical neutrality of the sediments, organic materials are well preserved. The finds comprise artefacts - besides flint and stone - of bone, antler, teeth, wood, and bark as well as bast including fragments of nets, strings and ropes. The environmental and archaeological data in their chronological contexts add considerably to the knowledge of the development of ecology, technology, subsistence and settlement pattern in the southern marginal zone of the west Baltic Mesolithic. Sites like Friesack may well be confined to the lower-lying areas of the ice-marginal valleys between the Elbe and Oder. The other site of this type, which has been partly excavated, is Friesack 27; it was discovered at a distance of only 500 m, and we expect many more in the area.

In the Marchia of Brandenbourg, there is a special type of wetland: the so-called *Luchs* (Havel-Luch, Upper and Lower Rhin-Luch). *Luch* is a term of the Slavonic tribes of the Middle Ages who settled in Brandenbourg in the 7th century AD, and it means 'swampy meadows'.

The *Luchs* are connected with the westernmost and lowest part of the Warsaw-Berlin and Torun-Eberswalde ice-marginal valleys of the last glaciation, not far from their junction with the lower Elbe valley. Up to the 18th century the *Luchs* were described as swampy wildernesses, not to be crossed by man and horse. But in the 1770s the Prussian king Frederick II decided to cultivate these lands which had been the property of the dynasty since ancient times, in order to raise the income of the Prussian state.

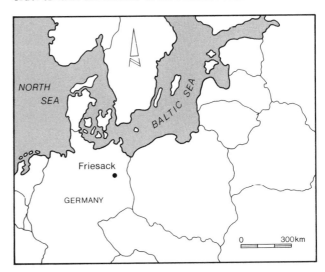

Fig. 8.1 Location Map

The region where we excavated is the Lower Rhin-luch near to the small town of Friesack, about 60 km northwest of Berlin (Fig. 8.1). For that region we can now give estimates about the results of the cultivation of the 18th century. For many years we were very cautious in estimating the lowering of the ground water table since the 1780s. From our excavations at the site of Friesack 4 we estimated not more than 1.5 m, but since last year, when we had to undertake salvage excavations in Friesack itself, we know that the ground water level fell by 3-3.5 m since the 1780s! This can be derived from a swamp peat layer inside the

Fig. 8.2 Friesack, site 4. A view of the excavation from the east, showing the general location of the site

town, on which the medieval wooden houses were built and wooden roads were constructed.

Lowering of the ground water and the subsequent fall of the surface of the swampy wetlands due to humification and mineralization of organic substances, exposed many Stone Age sites of this wetland to the air. Sand hills and ridges and low plateaux, which had been partly occupied by Mesolithic and Neolithic man and then covered by growing swamp peat in the later Sub-boreal and Sub-atlantic times, are now visible and they form the only morphological elements to break the monotonous landscape of meadows.

THE SITES OF FRIESACK AND THEIR ENVIRONMENT

Site Friesack 4 was excavated by the author for the Museum für Ur- und Frühgeschichte Potsdam between 1977 and 1989 (Gramsch 1979, 1981a, 1985, 1987, 1989). The site has been known since 1910, and there had been two excavations, from 1916 to 1925 (Schneider 1932) and in 1940 by Reinerth (unpublished). From these excavations we knew that there were undisturbed layers with preservation of organic archaeological materials. Our excavations were caused by a new amelioration project connected with lowering of the ground water table for a further 0.5 m, which would expose more organic materials to be destroyed. The other site Friesack 27, lying 500 m northeast of Friesack 4, was partly excavated in 1980, 1984 and 1989 alongside the excavations at site 4.

Both sites are situated in the central part of the Lower Rhin-luch which is about 4 km wide in this area. North and south of the Luch-valley there are ground moraines and end

moraines. According to borings and palynological investigations carried out by Kloss (1987a, 1987b), at the beginning of the Holocene the topography of the valley differed somewhat from today. The organic sediments – peats, muds and swamp peats – have grown from Pre-boreal to Sub-atlantic times. At the beginning of the Pre-boreal the valley showed only plains, hills and ridges of fluvioglacial sands as well as depressions and channels filled by water and thus forming small lakes, ponds and beds for running water. Open waters had a table of around 0.5 m above the present surface of the meadows.

The Mesolithic sites Friesack 4 and Friesack 27 are on low sandhills, now about 1.5 m above the surrounding meadows. In Pre-boreal and Boreal times, an extensive lake -maximum depth 6 m- lapped the southern and southeastern edges of Friesack 4, while Friesack 27 was beside a pond, only about 100 m in diameter and up to 3 m deep. Organic production of the waters started in the Pre-boreal, and at the end of the Boreal most of the waters were filled up by peat and muds, so that the pond at Friesack 27 did not exist any longer. Mesolithic man ceased visiting this site in the middle of the Boreal period. At Friesack 4 open water remained longer, because of the extent and the depth of the adjacent lake, and the site was frequented up to middle Atlantic times.

FRIESACK 4

At Friesack 4, nearly 300 sq.m of the shore zone of the former lake, corresponding to the sublittoral refuse area of the Mesolithic habitation site, have been excavated (Figs. 8.2-8.3). In the first three years of the excavation the 2-3.5 m deep trenches were kept dry by pumping, but because

Fig. 8.3 Friesack, site 4. Section of trench C, showing the multilayered stratigraphy of covering peat, layered sands, humose sands, sandy muds and coarse mud overlying the late Weichselian sands

of the problems caused by the sandy layers and by the sand in the ground, later the water table was lowered artificially by filter-wells. On account of the multi-stratified sequence of organic and clastic sediments, excavation methods were similar to a cave excavation: a row of square metres was investigated one after the other while the layers were permanently controlled on the profiles (sections).

Stratigraphy and chronology

As to the geological and stratigraphical situation, we were somewhat surprised at the beginning of the excavation. Below humified peat and peat layers, containing two Neolithic horizons, there was found an unusual sequence of sand layers, humose sands, sandy organic muds and coarse peat muds. The majority of these sediment-layers yielded Mesolithic artefacts: flint and pebble artefacts as well as objects made of bone, antler, teeth, wood, bark and plant fibres, and these in a well-stratified sequence of nearly 3000 radiocarbon years of the Mesolithic Age.

Sedimentological and palynological research allows the following interpretation of the formation of the body of sediments: the muds and the coarse peat muds resulted from the natural process of organic sedimentation in the lake, but in the shore zone this process was interrupted over and over again by sand intrusions from the sand hill where Mesolithic people settled many times. The sands may have been brought partly by water level changes and displacement of the shore, partly by wind erosion. But both processes seem to have been supported by the presence of Mesolithic people on the site, by destruction of the ground vegetation and by activities on the shore. The distribution of sands along the former shore is not regular, but occurs as cones at different places along the shore. This phenomenon is explained by the supposition that people had favoured certain paths in going to the shore, and that they changed their access from time to time.

The sand complexes, which are up to 0.8 m high and 12 m wide, are built up as changing layers of pure sand and humose sand. According to radiocarbon dates each of them was sedimented within only about 200 to 300 radiocarbon years. These characteristics again attest that they were built up not only naturally but also anthropogenically. This interpretation is supported by quantitative palynological tests. The pollen contents of pure sand layers of 5-10 cm thickness point to a sedimentation-rate of less than one year, while the intermediate humose sand-layers of 2-4 cm thickness seem to have been sedimented within 5 to 25 years.

Chronology at Friesack 4 is based on palynology and on 74 radiocarbon dates. From pollen analysis it is clear that the Mesolithic layers span the pollen zones from the middle Pre-boreal period to the middle Atlantic period, except the younger Boreal. The radiocarbon dates indicate four main periods of Mesolithic occupation:

I	9700-9500 uncal BP
II	9400-9200 uncal BP
III	9100-8800 uncal BP
IV	8200-7000 uncal BP

The archaeological materials

In the sublittoral refuse area of Friesack 4 have been unearthed up to now:
- about 150,000 flint and stone artefacts

- about 25,000 animal bones and fragments
- about 800 artefacts of bone, antler and animal teeth
- about 100 artefacts of wood and bark
- many remains of nets, ropes and strings and thousands of fragments of twisted yarn

For Mesolithic research in the West Baltic marginal zone it is very important to have a site where the development of technology and equipment can be traced through three stages of the Earlier Mesolithic, starting with a very early stage in the Pre-boreal around 9700 uncal BP, then for the earlier Late Mesolithic from the transition Boreal/Atlantic to the middle of the Atlantic times around 7000 uncal BP.

It is impossible in this paper to give an account of all finds. I will concentrate on the artefacts made of organic materials, which are well preserved in all layers below the ground water table, as well as the bone and antler objects from above the water level which was lowered only in the last 200 years.

Bone and Antler artefacts Nearly 400 bone points and fragments were excavated. These are, with few exceptions, manufactured from cervid limb bones. Only five points are of red deer antler. Particular mention should be made of three simple bone points still attached to their broken shafts

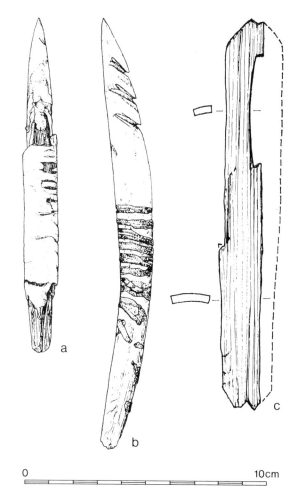

Fig. 8.4 a. Bone point with wooden shaft and pitch. b. Bone point with bast binding. c. Wooden board for winding

by means of bast binding and pitch (Fig. 8.4a). A further 34 bone points with smaller or larger traces of pitch must have been hafted in a similar fashion. Five other points had been hafted by binding with narrow strips of bast, without use of pitch (Fig. 8.4b), similar to the well-known point fixed to the shaft with bast cord from Ulkestrup Lyng, Denmark (Andersen *et al* 1982, fig. 68). All other bone and antler artefacts belong to the range of the Pre-boreal Mesolithic as represented by Star Carr (Clark 1954) and of the late Pre-boreal and Boreal Maglemosian (Clark 1975, 105). They include awls, chisel-like tools, axe blades of deer and elk antler, perforated antler adzes, axes and sockets (three with wooden shafts), unperforated tool mounts, deer antler points with blunt or obliquely cut ends, a bone 'needle' perforated at one end, perhaps for making nets, a fragment of perforated bone mattock made from an aurochs ulna. Further information is given in earlier publications (Gramsch 1987, 1989, 1990).

Ornaments and ornamented bone and antler objects The ornaments include 34 perforated teeth from all periods, among them teeth of deer, roe deer, aurochs, wild pig, wild horse, bear, wolf, fox, wild cat, otter, beaver, and also two human teeth. There were also small perforated bone plates, one perforated tubular bird bone, and one perforated pendant made from a piece of wild boar tusk.

Thirteen decorated antler and bone pieces have been found. Most of them are fragmented, some unfortunately heavily. Fragments of eight perforated red deer antlers with decoration like 'bâtons de commandement' (Fig. 8.5) derive from late Pre-boreal, early Boreal and from early Atlantic periods. The one from the late Pre-boreal around 9300 uncal BP is the oldest in the West Baltic region up to now. But its ornamentation is very similar in technique and type to a specimen from the early Atlantic period. Another outstanding decorated object is a dorsal tortoise-shell, dated to the turn of Boreal to Atlantic times.

Artefacts of wood and bark In general, wooden artefacts are preserved, but the condition and fragmentation of many objects does not allow much to be said about function. They include fragments of spears and arrows, blunted arrows for shooting small furred animals, two possible digging-sticks, two paddles, fragments of a dug-out canoe, pointed sticks and worked fragments of unknown use. Two small boards with opposed notches (Fig. 8.4c) seem to have been used for winding bast cord. One net-float was made of birch-bark, while four axe hafts had been made of alder roots. The high level of wood-working in the early Boreal times is emphasized by a fragment of a carefully worked pointed-ended trough like the Australian aboriginal 'koolamon'. There is also a handle, made of twisted rods, for a basket or carrying net. Most of the objects are made of pine wood, then rowan, alder, hazel and poplar.

An outstanding find is a birch bark container (Fig. 8.6) which had been excavated not in the former sublittoral zone but in a deep pit on the habitation site itself. The pit seems to have been an artificial water hole or well. The birch bark

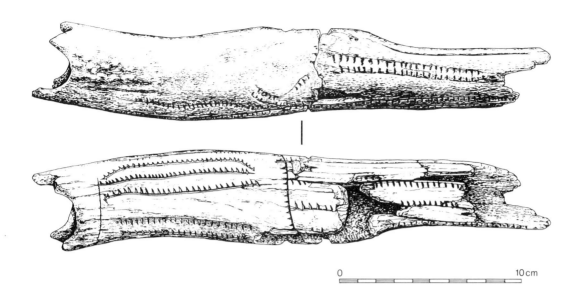

Fig. 8.5 Fragment of perforated red deer antler with ornamentation

container is dated to 8950±110 uncal BP (OxA-600. Hedges *et al* 1987, 294). Thus it is now the oldest bark vessel known from Europe.

The use of pitch or resin for hafting implements is indicated by the bone points mentioned above. Lumps and flat pieces of pitch have been found in many layers, teeth marks suggesting that some of these had been chewed. Even if it is not yet sure that the pitch was produced from birch bark, it seems to be possible that the many birch bark rolls unearthed from the layers were intentionally collected for pitch production.

Use of bast In addition to the binding of bone points, there is more proof for the use of bast. Outstanding are numerous fragments of nets, twine, cord and rope which were found in nearly all layers of the Pre-boreal and Boreal periods. Two types of net are proved: the knotless net (Fig. 8.7) and the knotted net. Net making was based on production of twisted yarn, which is also found in innumerable fragments (Kernchen and Gramsch 1989). Ropes were made in the techniques of twisting (Fig. 8.8) and of plaiting. The bast products found at Friesack in the layers of the middle Pre-boreal around 9700 uncal BP are now the earliest in Europe. The developed techniques suggest that the manufacturing of bast had already a long history, including making of knotted nets, fragments of which date from the late Pre-boreal (*c* 9300 uncal BP) at Friesack 4.

Faunal remains Only a few remarks on the faunal remains, which were very abundant in all layers. According to the analysis of Teichert (unpublished) there are represented nearly all species of mammals of the temperate climatic zone. The main animals hunted were red deer, roe deer and wild pig, but there are also significant quantities of beaver, tortoise (*Emys orbicularis*) and large species of birds of the water regions. Fish are not numerous. Finally, there is clear evidence for the wild horse as a hunted animal in the Pre-boreal and in the early Boreal, and the domesticated dog has been found in layers of all four main habitation periods.

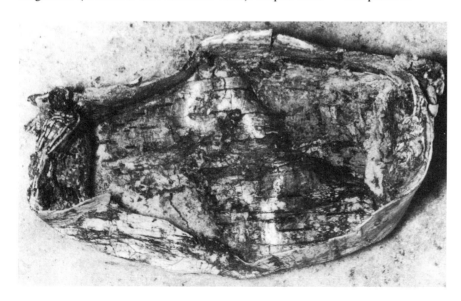

Fig. 8.6 Friesack, site 4. Birch bark container; c 200 mm wide

69

Fig. 8.7 Friesack, site 4. Fragment of a knot-less net made of bast; c 280 mm at widest point

The habitation site at Friesack 4

Outside the waterlogged area, on the habitation site itself, we have excavated only two dozen square metres up to now. Up to the second half of the 18th century, the low hill with the habitation site was covered with swamp mud and was below the ground water table. Two hundred years after cultivation and lowering of the water table, bones are fairly well preserved to within a few centimetres of the surface, but not any wood or plant remains. Mesolithic structures are well preserved too in that the contours and the stratification of artificial pits were easily visible. Three deep pits were found and excavated, and in each of them remarkable features and finds could be observed and removed. The stratification showed clearly that they had been dug below the ground water table of Mesolithic times, and the objects from the base of the pits were as follows: Pit 1 – a birch bark container mentioned above, Pit 2 – a dorsal tortoise shell with cutting marks, Pit 3 – one artificially-cut piece of wood, one piece of birch bark, which seems to have been another kind of container (cup-like?), four beaver canines. I am convinced that these pits were intentionally dug water holes for wells for getting drinking water, and the objects could have been scoops and/or cultic offerings (Gramsch in press).

All the objects mentioned above were found at a level higher than the present ground water table, i.e. the table since 1980 when the last amelioration lowered it for about half a metre. Up to 1980 the objects were below the water table. The pits were excavated in 1984 and 1987, and both the wooden and the bark objects were preserved up to this time because of being in the capillaric water horizon above

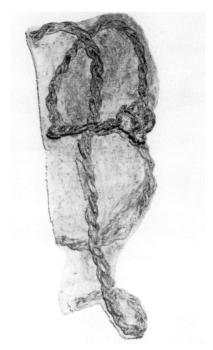

Fig. 8.8 Friesack, site 4. Fragment of a twisted rope made of bast; c 475 mm top to bottom

the ground water level. But what will happen in the next few years and later? I fear that at this site and at others known and unknown in the region many 'usual' and outstanding structures and objects will rot, if the sites are not excavated within the next 20 to 30 years. Cultivation and amelioration of wetland areas on a large scale is - as everywhere - the greatest danger for many of our last extraordinary sources of knowledge about life and culture in the Stone Age and in later periods.

General results and conclusions

Habitation frequencies According to the number of sand layers in the sublittoral zone of the site, Mesolithic people were present at the site about 50 or 60 times:

I   In the middle Pre-boreal period about 20 times within about 200 radiocarbon years; 9700-9500 uncal BP

II In the late Pre-boreal period about 10 times within about 200 radiocarbon years; 9400-9200 uncal BP

II In the earlier Boreal period about 20 times within about 300 radiocarbon years; 9100-8800 uncal BP

IV In the early Atlantic period about 10-15 times within about 1000 radiocarbon years with longer breaks; 8200-7000 uncal BP

These estimates show that people came to the site not every year, but it seems possible that they settled in the intermediate phases at places not far from Friesack 4 in the same area. For example, the other site excavated by us, Friesack 27, is situated only 500 m from the Friesack 4 site, and there are cultural layers of the Pre-boreal and early Boreal periods too. And in all the region inside the Warsaw-Berlin ice-marginal valley we now know about 20 sites of the Earlier Mesolithic.

Seasonality For Friesack 4, the seasons of habitation can be estimated up to now only by red deer and roe deer antler growth stages, but the present state of research on the age structure of mammals and birds supports that:

– in all Pre-boreal and early Boreal times the site was visited in spring, perhaps from March to May

– in early Atlantic times habitation time was late summer and beginning autumn

Ethnical interpretations There seem to be indications for the recognition of ethnically different groups on the site for the settlement periods I,II and III (see above). Indicators are as follows:

– In periods I and III there was the knotless net and plaited rope, and the bone points were fixed to the shafts by use of pitch.

– For period II we found no knotless net and no plaited rope but only some fragments of knotted net and of twisted rope. In no case was pitch used for hafting bone points, but there are the only examples of hafting bone points by using narrow bast strips. Moreover, a new type of bone point was introduced in this period, with barbs in the terminal part of the point. For several simple bone points there was also a technical-functional attribute, found only for points in this period, in that they were cut flat in the basal part, perhaps in connection with a special method of hafting them.

These technological and typological differences of artefacts of Mesolithic units, with time differences in the range of about 100 years, seem to be so striking that they probably represent different technological traditions on the level of ethnic units. This would mean that in period II groups from an ethnically distinct area came to the site.

Cultural observations Friesack 4 is the first Mesolithic site in Northern Germany with a long stratigraphy and with reliable dates. The following deductions seem to be justifiable:

– Most of the isolated finds of organic artefact types from Northern Germany belong earlier, in the Pre-boreal, than supposed up to now by comparison with the Danish Mesolithic. For example, the cultural set of the classical Maglemosian started at Friesack in the late Pre-boreal around 9300 uncal BP, some hundred years earlier than in Denmark. Does that mean that the Maglemosian technology was developed in Central Europe, or is there simply a lack of evidence in Denmark where up to now Pre-boreal sites with preservation of organic artefacts are under-represented compared with sites of Boreal times?

– In the middle Pre-boreal around 9600 uncal BP, according to only a very few sites and dated single finds of course, technology and types of bone and antler artefacts seem to be somewhat similar in northern Europe, from England to Denmark and Northern Germany and perhaps to the North-east Baltic region too. Simple bone points, finely toothed bone points and bone points with spaced barbs are common, supplemented by antler adzes, big chisel-like instruments made of tubular bones, and awls. At Friesack there are also finely notched bone points and antler hafts.

– Cultural differentation within the whole area seems to have started in the late Pre-boreal with some introductions in Northern Germany. Perhaps that could be explained by the arrival of new hunter-gatherer groups in the region, possibly in connection with the full establishment of temperate ecological conditions in Northern Europe in the course of the Pre-boreal.

Influence of man on nature According to the results of palynological research and to the evidence for extensive wood-use at Friesack 4, people influenced the vegetation in all periods of their presence on the site. Pine seems to have been cut on the site itself and in the neighbourhood continuously, and it could not have fully regenerated thereafter. The variations in the curves for pine and birch in the diagrams seem to reflect this. The ground vegetation on the site was surely mainly disturbed when people were present, and because of habitation nitrophilous plant taxa extended their area. Last but not least, the people caused considerable changes in the morphology of the sandhill. Indirectly aided by the inhabitants it is estimated that about 1000-1500 sq. m of sand drifted to the sublittoral zone of the lake at the site. Thus Mesolithic people directly and indirectly influenced the character of the landscape, even if no significant changes resulted.

THE SITE OF FRIESACK 27

Some remarks on the result of the excavation at Friesack, site 27 (Gramsch 1991). There have been excavated 40 sq. m in a trench of 10 m length in the sublittoral zone immediately on the edge of the inhabited sandhill. The stratigraphy differed to some degree from the site at Friesack 4. The former small lake was on the windward side of the low hill, and therefore only low quantities of sand were transported into the shore region. Muds and peat have grown since the earlier stage of the Pre-boreal, and only thin layers and lenses of sand were connected with artefact horizons. On the other hand, the relation between sand horizons and artefact layers was so clear that the sand intrusions to the organic sediments can only be explained by the activity of man in the shore zone as at Friesack 4.

Many artefacts made of flint, bone, antler and wood were found. Remains of nets and string made of tree-bast were not detected, despite a very careful search for them. The finds that were made parallel very well those from Friesack 4, and therefore information will not be given here, except the following. At the base of organic sediments there was a layer which is dated by palynology and radiocarbon dates to the very beginning of the Holocene (9900 uncal BP). The archaeological objects from this layer represent therefore the earliest mesolithic of Northern Central Europe known up till now. The set of artefacts and the technology are really

Mesolithic, not of transitional character from the late Palae-olithic to Mesolithic. There are 'normal' microliths as points and one broad scalene triangle, one flake axe, and scrapers, burins and flakes with retouched edge(s). The bone and antler industry includes simple bone points, finely as well as deeply notched bone points, one chisel-like bone tool of the Star Carr type, one awl made from a bone splinter, and one red deer antler with cut tines and with unfinished perforation which seems to be a semi-manufac-tured 'bâton de commandement'. The fauna of the initial Pre-boreal layer includes only genera of the temperate climatic zone, and not reindeer or other elements of the Late-glacial 'cold' fauna. The domesticated dog is proved by a well preserved skull.

Altogether by these facts the author feels confirmed in his hypothesis (Gramsch 1981b, 64), that Mesolithic people were immigrants to Northern Central Europe, coming with already developed 'Mesolithic' techniques and equipment, contrary to the hypothesis that the Mesolithic of the North-ern plain had its roots in the Late-glacial Ahrensburgian of reindeer hunters. For solving the problem of the genesis of the Mesolithic technology we should rather look to the Late-glacial descendants of the Magdalenians living under nearly Post-glacial climatic conditions and in forested land-scapes in Southern Central Europe and Western Europe since the Allerød warm phase. But this problem is beyond the subject of this paper and cannot be followed further.

BIBLIOGRAPHY

Andersen, K., Jørgensen, S. and Richter, J. 1982. *Maglemose hytterne ved Ulkestrup Lyng*. Copenhagen: Det kongelige Nordiske Oldskriftselskab.

Clark, J.G.D. 1954. *Excavations at Star Carr*. Cambridge: Cambridge University Press.

Clark, G. 1975. *The Earlier Stone Age Settlement of Scandi-navia*. Cambridge: Cambridge University Press.

Gramsch, B. 1979. Neue Ausgrabungen auf dem mesolithisch-neolithischen Fundplatz Friesack, Kr.Nauen. *Ausgrabun-gen und Funde* 24, 56-61.

Gramsch, B. 1981a. Der mesolithisch-neolithische Moorfund-platz bei Friesack, Kr. Nauen,2. Vorbericht. *Ausgrabun-gen und Funde* 26, 65-72.

Gramsch, B. 1981b. Spätpaläolithikum und Frühmesolithikum im nördlichen Mitteleuropa. *Veröffentlichungen des Mu-seums für Ur- und Frühgeschichte Potsdam* 14-15, 63-65.

Gramsch, B. 1985. Der mesolithisch-neolithische Moorfund-platz bei Friesack, Kr. Nauen, 3. Vorbericht. *Ausgrabungen und Funde* 30, 57-67.

Gramsch, B. 1987. Ausgrabungen auf dem mesolithischen Moorfundplatz bei Friesack, Bezirk Potsdam. *Veröffentlichungen des Museums für Ur-und Frühgeschichte Potsdam* 21, 75-100.

Gramsch, B. 1989. Excavations near Friesack: an Early Me-solithic Marshland Site in the Northern Plain of Central Europe. In C.Bonsall (ed.), *The Mesolithic in Europe*, 313-24. Edinburgh: John Donald Publishers.

Gramsch, B. 1990. Die frühmesolithischen Knochenspitzen von Friesack, Kr. Nauen. *Veröffentlichungen des Mu-seums für Ur-und Frühgeschichte Potsdam* 24,7-26.

Gramsch, B. 1991. Ausgrabungen auf einem weiteren frühme-solithischen Fundplatz bei Friesack, Kr.Nauen. *Ausgra-bungen und Funde* 36, 51-56.

Gramsch, B. in press. Ein mesolithischer Birkenrindenbehälter von Friesack. *Veröffentlichungen des Museums für Ur-und Frühgeschichte Potsdam* 26.

Hedges, R.E.M., Housley,R.A., Law,I.A., Perry,C., and Gow-lett, J.A.J. 1987. Radiocarbon dates from the Oxford AMS System: Archaeometry datelist 6. *Archaeometry* 29(2), 289-306.

Kernchen, I., Gramsch, B. 1989. Mesolithische Netz-und Seil-reste von Friesack, Bezirk Potsdam, und ihre Konservie-rung. *Veröffentlichungen des Museums für Ur-und Frühgeschichte Potsdam* 23, 23-28.

Kloss, K. 1987a. Pollenanalysen zur Vegetationsgeschicte, Moorentwicklung und mesolithisch-neolithischen Besied-lung im Unteren Rhinluch bei Friesack, Bezirk Potsdam. *Veröffentlichungen des Museums für Ur-und Frühge-schichte Potsdam* 21, 101-20.

Kloss, K. 1987b. Zur Umwelt mesolithischer Jäger und Samm-ler im Unteren Rhinluch bei Friesack.*Veröffentlichungen des Museums für Ur-und Frühgeschichte Potsdam* 21, 121-30.

Schneider, M. 1932. *Die Urkeramiker*. Leipzig: Curt Ka-bitzsch.

9

RECENT DEVELOPMENTS IN WETLAND ARCHAEOLOGY IN POLAND

Wojciech Brzeziński

SYNOPSIS

Some 300 archaeological sites have been excavated in Poland every year since 1967. Not more than 70 researched during this period can be recognised as wetland sites. The bulk are dated to the Neolithic, Early Iron Age and Medieval Period; however a few occur in other periods too. The wetland sites are situated mainly in western, northern and north-eastern Poland, in the areas abounding with lakes, swamps, bogs etc. Among the most interesting of such sites excavated in recent years are: a Neolithic peatbog settlement at Dudka, Masurian Lakes, an Early Iron Age open settlement at Grzybiany in Silesia, a cult site from the period of Roman Influences at Otalążka, south of Warsaw, and a large Early Medieval Prussian emporium at Janów Pomorski near Elbląg, briefly discussed in this paper.

Study of wetland sites in Poland (Fig. 9.1) carried out by Polish archaeologists goes back to the 1930s, the time of the excavation of the celebrated fortified settlement of the Lusatian Culture at Biskupin in the west of the country. In the public eye, this site remains unmatched until today, even though much has been done quietly over the ensuing decades. Archaeological efforts began to be better reflected in print from the 1960s onwards with the launching of a yearly bulletin, *Informator Archeologiczny*. The present account of wetland archaeology in Poland is based on this source as well as on the small body of publications and courtesy of some Polish archaeologists involved in this research.

According to *Informator*, between 1967 and 1987 some 300 sites were excavated in Poland every year. Out of several thousand sites dug over twenty years only about 70 were wetland in character – just over 1%. Of course, this is only an approximation, since quite often it was difficult to conclude on the basis of a short entry whether the site was a dryland or a wetland one. Moreover, an overwhelming

majority of data obtained through these excavations has yet to be published owing to such well-known obstacles as lack of sufficient financial means to continue fieldwork or to publish, or other, all-too-human failings.

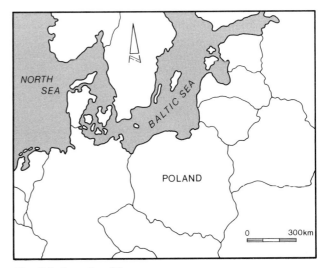

Fig. 9.1 Location Map

Furthermore, the archaeology of wetland areas has yet to become a full-fledged branch of research in Poland. So far, very few comprehensive projects of archaeological survey have been conducted with the single aim of discovering patterns of prehistoric settlement in this type of environment. Wetland sites discussed in the present paper (Fig. 9.2) were studied within the broader framework of such research problems as the study of the spread of and relationship between culture assemblages, micro-and macroregional studies, or conservation requirements. Being well aware that this paper rests on rather frail foundations, the author hopes that his readers will bear with him, even if at times he appears more like a fortune-teller reading the tea leaves than a serious archaeologist.

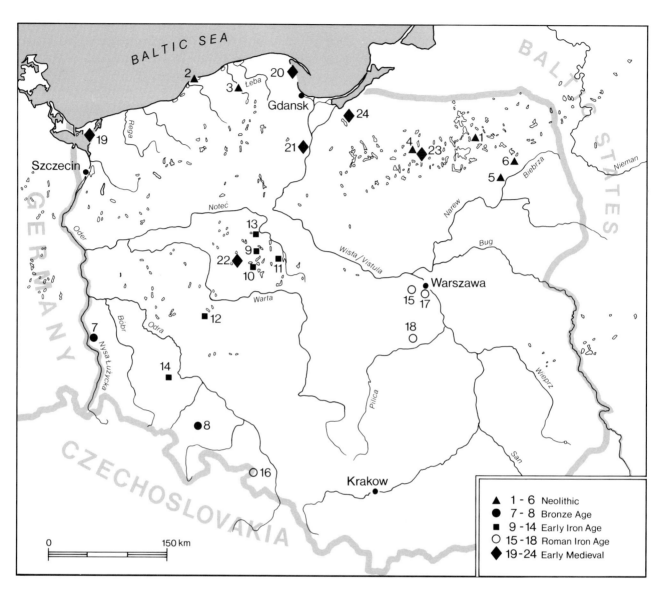

Fig. 9.2 Polish wetland sites mentioned in the paper. 1. Dudka; 2. Dąbki; 3. Poganice; 4. Barkweda; 5. Sośnia; 6. Woźnawieś; 7. Luboszyce; 8. Gołostowice; 9. Biskupin; 10. Izdebno; 11. Jankova; 12. Cichowo; 13. Sobiejuchy; 14. Gryzbiany; 15. Regów; 16. Królowe; 17. Falenty; 18. Otalążka; 19. Wolin; 20. Puck; 21. Gniew; 22. Jezioro Lednickie; 23. Łąkorz; 24. Janów Pomorski

Most of the sites mentioned in this work are situated in northern and western Poland, an area profoundly shaped by glacial activity. It is a region rich in lakes, with a well developed and dense water system and it features extensive tracts of various types of wetland. As elsewhere in Europe (Coles 1984, 26-31),this environment has been undergoing gradual deterioration owing to economic activity, draining in particular, carried out from the second half of the 19th century onwards. It is only to be expected that a large number of archaeological wetland sites in the region, long settled by humans from the time of the withdrawal of the ice sheet, must have been reduced to dryland ones, with accompanying loss of organic remains.

Happily, not all was lost and Poland still features many interesting wetland sites dated to various periods of prehistory. Several Stone Age sites located in wet environments have been studied in the Great Poland Lakeland (Pojezierze

Wielkopolskie), in the Szczecin Lowland (Nizina Szczecińska) and in the Słowińce Coastal Belt (Pobrzeże Slowińskie) but the largest number of sites were discovered and explored in the north-eastern corner of the country in the Mazurian and Suwałki Lakelands (Pojezierza Mazurskie i Suwalskie) and in the northern reaches of the Podlasie Lowland (Nizina Podlaska). This part of Poland is a region long considered as economically backward, which is turning out to be a blessing in disguise for archaeologists and conservationists alike. Many Upper Palaeolithic and Mesolithic campsites situated on its peatlands, marshy lake bays, river valleys or oxbow lakes have survived to our day with their rich trove of organics intact.

Dudka

One such rewarding site is the one at Dudka, in Suwałki province (Fig. 9.3). Traces of human occupation going back

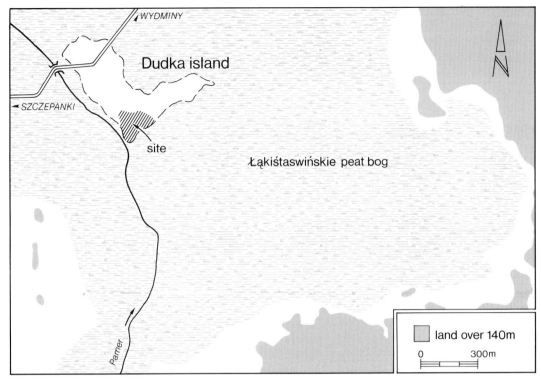

Fig. 9.3 Occupation on Dudka Island (after Gumiński et al 1988, fig.1)

to the Upper Palaeolithic were discovered on a mineral island elevated some 2 to 3 m over an extensive peatbog, some 25 sq. km in area, formerly a shallow, glacial lake. The site covers 3 ha in the southern part of the 15 ha island (Guminski and Fiedorczuk 1988, 113-115; Guminski and Fiedorczuk 1990). The stratigraphical sequence documents repeated episodes of occupation of the site. The earliest finds are flints, antler and bone dated to the Pre-boreal period, which testify to the presence of the Swidry Culture group. Innumerable flints and bone artefacts were later left by Komornica Culture group during the Boreal period. Subsequent occupation is evidenced by pottery finds belonging to cultures of the east European Neolithic woodland zone, dated to the beginning of the Sub-boreal period in the 4th millennium BC. The bulk of finds from Dudka seem to belong to this stage of the occupation of the island. Ceramic material shows closest links to Zedmar types, with some analogies to Narva and Ertebølle Cultures also in evidence – the first such finds in Poland. The final occupation episode documented at Dudka was by a Corded Ware population (Guminski and Fiedorczuk 1988, 117, 140-144).

Three seasons of fieldwork at Dudka stripped an area roughly 48 sq.m producing a vast body of evidence: over 50,000 remains of animal bone, over 2000 flints, 3500 potsherds and several score of antler and bone artefacts. No traces of dwelling structures were discovered, barring the remains of a posthole (Guminski and Fiedorczuk 1988, 118). Bone material was examined but owing to its highly fragmented condition it was possible to identify the animal species in only 500 cases; 91% turned out to be fish bone. Bones of mammals documented the presence of species

typical for forests of wetland environments such as red and roe deer and elk (Guminski and Fiedorczuk 1988, 138).

The vast amount of organics recovered at Dudka testifies to the repeated occupation of the island from the early Holocene to the end of the Stone Age. On the basis of follow-up research done so far, the economy seems to have relied on fishing and hunting and no traces of agriculture or stock-breeding have been discovered. Excavations at Dudka are still in progress as is the study of pollen and macrobotanical evidence.

Other Neolithic sites surviving in wet conditions

These include the following: an interesting settlement at Dąbki, Koszalin province, on the Baltic coast. (*Informator* 1981, 30;1985, 18). This peatbog site featured a rich culture layer containing large quantities of charcoal, plant remains, fish and animal bones as well as antler fragments. Similar data were recovered from a Funnel Beaker Culture settlement at Poganice, Słupsk Province (*Informator* 1974, 24; 1985, 29). Further to the east, a peatbog settlement at Barkweda, Olstztyn Province, produced large quantities of timber, charcoal and other organic materials (*Informator* 1974, 23-24). Two sites at Sósnia (Kempisty and Więckowska 1983) and Woźnawieś (*Informator* 1983, 59) in Łomża Province, situated on dune and bog margins, were also excavated.

Bronze Age (c 19th-7th centuries BC)

Wetland sites dated to the Bronze Age studied in the 1970s and 80s included a Lusatian Culture settlement at Luboszyce, Zielona Góra province, accidentally discovered in a draining ditch section and later followed by a rescue excavation (*Informator* 1975, 63). Another Bronze Age site in Lower Silesia, the Unetice Culture settlement at Goĺostowice, Wrocĺaw Province, established on a flood terrace of a small river, was excavated by sondages (*Informator* 1986, 46).

Early Iron Age (c 7th-2nd centuries BC)

Early Iron Age wetland sites were more numerous and more rewarding. The last twenty years have seen the continuation of research at Biskupin (Niewiarowski *et al* this volume). A similar fortified Lusatian Culture settlement in the region at Izdebno, Bydgoszcz Province, produced well preserved timber remains of a breakwater, pier and trackway (*Informator* 1978, 85; 1979, 84). Excavation at Jankowo, Bydgoszcz Province and Cichowo, Leszno Province, brought comparable results (*Informator* 1972, 96-97). Another Iron Age village at Sobiejuchy, Bydgoszcz province, completes the list of this type of site (*Informator* 1981, 111-113; 1982, 120; 1983, 95-96). All such fortified settlements were found to have been established on lake islands or peninsulas, joined to the mainland by wooden causeways. They had been enclosed by earth-and-timber walls and a timber breakwater usually of oakwood. The dwellings were generally grouped in the centre of the interior and were encircled by a wooden road. All these structures were well-preserved in their lower sections in the waterlogged culture layers.

Grzybiany

Another example of a Lusatian Culture site dated to the period in question is the open lake settlement at Grzybiany, Legnica Province in Lower Silesia (Bukowski 1982). Intensive excavation of the site showed the settlement to have covered some half a hectare in area, occupying several sandy outcrops raised almost 1 m above the water level and separated from the mainland by a broad stretch of shallows. The lake lies at the bottom of a wide and elongated depression, one of the series of lakes connected to the Kaczawa river. Several of them have since prehistoric times become overgrown by peatbog. The settlement at Grzybiany occupied a point commanding the most convenient valley crossing (Bukowski 1982, 14).

It is possible to discriminate between at least 3 occupation layers in the settlement (Bukowski 1982, 15). The natural base of what used to be sandy clumps and today is a peninsula, was formed of clayey-sandy deposits covered by gyttja. Their uppermost layer contained the oldest level of occupation with preserved remains of a wooden trackway, pottery, red deer and elk antler with traces of working, as well as fragments of animal and human bone. This level is dated to Hallstatt B.

Wooden structures from this period followed the shoreline, being seperated from the water by a number of breakwater piles. Presumably, they are the remains of a pier constructed from timbers between 3 and 3.5 m long, some

20 to 40 cm in diameter, set according to a regular pattern of parallel and recurring series. This structure was reinforced by piles and bundled brushwood. A row of posts running parallel to the presumed pier on its inside probably marks the extent of the dwellings. The southern stretch of the "pier" is reminiscent of a breakwater and has a more elaborate construction, framelike in character. These box-like structures were often found to contain several entire or broken vessels - possibly some sort of offering. The pier-cum-trackway probably gave onto a landing jutting out into the lake. A grid construction just off the waterline seems to suggest such an interpretation. Another interesting find from Grzybiany was a large steering paddle, some 1.35 m long, found within the settlement (Bukowski 1982, 20, fig. 7).

The next occupation level contained remnants of dwellings: hearths and burnt beams, as well as a wealth of artefacts such as pottery, spindle whorls, bone and antler objects, notably pins, mallets, mattocks and digging sticks. Some bronzes were also discovered. The most remarkable find in this layer was a large bronze-working area featuring an abundance of artefacts which dated the feature to 6th century BC.

Occupation level III contained more hearths along with large concentrations of burnt daub, charcoal and ashes suggestive of repeated fires. A number of dwellings may be identified from the presence of hearths, but their shape and dimensions remain to be defined. Level III is reliably dated by pottery and metal finds to Hallstatt D (Bukowski 1982, 26).

In the light of the recovered evidence, the settlement at Grzybiany seems to be unparalleled in this part of Poland. No other open lake settlements are known from Silesia. In terms of preservation of timber constructions the site may be likened to Biskupin in Great Poland. A wealth of pollen, paleobotanical and paleozoological as well as mollusc and tree ring samples are still in the process of study and have yet to be published.

Period of Roman Influences (c 1st-5th centuries AD)

From this period, the wetland sites studied so far were usually open settlements established on wet meadowland margins on the banks of small watercourses. One interesting site, at Regów in Warsaw Province, featured an antler comb manufacturing workshop with a remarkably well preserved inventory of artefacts (Brzezinski 1980). Other settlements dated to the period included one at Królowe, Opole Province in Lower Silesia and an iron-smelting centre at Falenty, Warsaw Province, both discovered during draining activities (*Informator* 1968, 141-142; 1985, 99).

Otalążka

By far the most impressive and unusual finds were produced by excavation of a peatbog site at Otalążka,

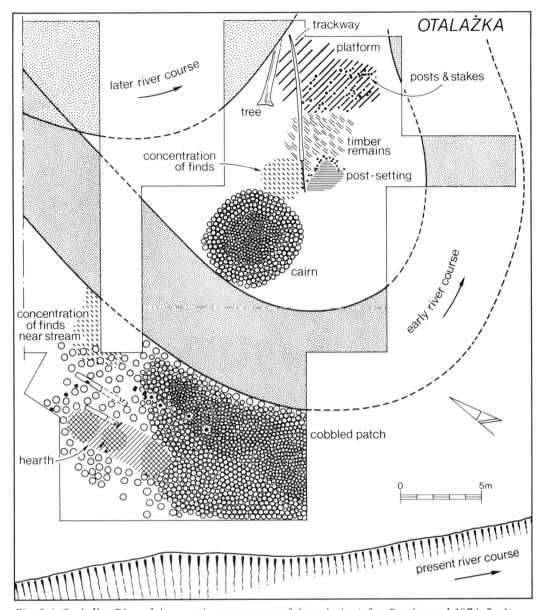

Fig. 9.4 Otalążka. Plan of the most important part of the cult site (after Bender et al 1974, fig.1)

Radom Province, in central Poland (Fig. 9.4). A settlement discovered there, thought to have been a ritual site, was established at the narrowing of a small river valley on either bank of the stream, in an area empty of other archaeological sites for the period when the presumed sanctuary was in function (Bender 1969).

Geological studies conducted at Otalążka revealed a stratigraphy consisting from top to bottom of a humic layer, overlying modern sands, gytta and river-mud deposits resting on peaty deposit I. The culture layer was found at a depth of some 2 m, sandwiched between peaty deposit I and II and it consisted of peat with a sandy admixture (Bender and Stupnicka 1974, 308).

It was also established that until the turn of the 5th century AD the level of the water table and of the stream had been much lower than at present and the original ground surface was between 1.5 to 2.5 m below the modern level of the flood terrace. Owing to climatic changes, notably increased

humidity in the second phase of the Sub-atlantic period, the groundwater table rose(Bender and Stupnicka 1974, 325).

Extensive fieldwork at Otalążka revealed a number of stone and timber structures of a strikingly non-dwelling or production function. On the right bank were found 3 hearths banked in with stone-settings and fenced in on north and east sides by a bundle brushwood and peg fence. Between the fence and the bank of the stream a cobbled patch was uncovered resting on peaty deposit II. To the north of the fence was a concentration of potsherds and animal bones. Interestingly enough, the pots were evidently intentionally broken before deposition, while the bones came from the heads and limbs of the animals.

On the left bank, the inner bend of the river was occupied by a cairn, some 0.6 m high, 6 m in diameter, also resting on peaty deposit II. Two of its sides were washed by the stream. The cairn contained a dozen-odd potsherds and animal bone. Several entire earthenware vessels, fragments of bone, potsherds and a part of a wheel rested at its base. A depression to the southeast of the cairn was spanned by a trackway, some 10m long, made of roundwood. On both sides of the trackway, notably to the south of it, were uncovered fragments of raw and worked timber deposited in layers with 8 crushed vessels between individual layers. Another puzzling find was a structure consisting of a dozen-odd pegs driven into the ground forming something like a corner, uncovered some 2 m distant from the cairn. Inside it was a large stone, possibly an altar, and small wooden vessels next to it, resting on a plank along with 2 small earthenware bowls.

Yet another structure was revealed on the left bank at the extremity of the trackway. It covered some 10 m and consisted of several-score pegs of varying dimensions driven vertically and at an angle into the ground. Presumably, they were the remains of a grid-construction platform raised over a periodically inundated area. Around this structure was found the largest concentration of cattle bone on the site (40% of all bones), a dozen-odd almost complete vessels and a three-layered comb together with a zoomorphic brooch.

The body of evidence from Otalążka testifies to the ritual character of the site. Imaginably, here was an open air sanctuary situated in a desolate marshy area, a stark, eerie environment. Perhaps some sort of ritual feast used to be held around the hearths on the right bank while three structures on the left connected by a trackway witnessed other awesome rites (Bender and Stupnicka 1974, 354).

Few sites comparable to Otalążka are known from the territory of non-Celtic and non-Roman Europe. In Poland it is the only one of its kind, but finds from Scandinavia and central Germany suggest that more may be still hidden in Polish peatbogs and marshes.

Medieval sites (c 6th-14th centuries AD)

As a rule, one third of all sites excavated in the last two decades were medieval ones. Hillforts raised during this period were frequently situated in inaccessible surroundings, which in Poland's conditions usually signify heights surrounded by marshland, crossings through bogs, peninsulas extending far into lakes, lake islands and so on. It would seem far from wrong to anticipate a plethora of wetland sites. Unfortunately, this is not so, since many of these medieval sites have survived to this day only as dryland ones, as a result of climatic change, fluctuations in water tables and draining.

The most interesting discoveries were made on the coast of the Baltic. Some of them are quite spectacular, such as the Early Medieval settlement complex on the island of Wolin – dated to 9th-10th centuries AD. More than ten years of excavation there revealed large fragments of a rough-plank waterfront. The timbers were triangular in section, reaching in length up to 2.5 m. They formed a palisade anchored with horizontal stays, resting in a 60-80

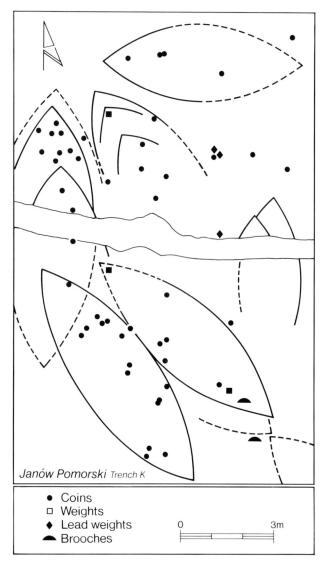

Fig. 9.5 Janów Pomorski. Outlines of boats and distribution of finds (after Jagodziński 1991, fig. 15)

cm thick peaty mud deposit. Wooden platforms led off from the waterfront, becoming timber-lined tracks inside the settlement (*Informator* 1979, 198-199; 1980, 179; 1981, 208-209; 1985, 152). The late 1970s saw the excavation of a port in Puck, in the bay to the north of Gdańsk. Underwater exploration dominated, producing traces of a wooden waterfront and a 50 m long pier. The waterfront had been built in a trestle construction. Other interesting finds from Puck included fragments of boats, such as rowlocks and oakwood ribs. The port is thought to have functioned from the 8th to 13th centuries AD. A later waterfront. dated to the 14th century AD, was discovered during excavation at the medieval town of Gniew (*Informator* 1982, 253). Coming back to the depleted hinterland, it is not totally devoid of wetland discoveries. Excavation of a number of Early Medieval earthworks on lakeshores or river banks revealed the presence of wooden bridges and platforms. Underwater exploration has been on the agenda frequently (Kola and Wilke 1989). An interesting discovery was made at Łąkorz, Olsztyn Province, in the Masurian Lakeland. Here, systematic underwater exploration uncovered a pile construction thought by some to have formed a part of a hunting lodge used by the elders of the Order of Teutonic Knights in the 14th century AD, presumably a type of platform with a landing (Grażewski 1989).

Janów Pomorski

Finally, the remarkable results of systematic excavation started in 1984 of a trading-and-craft centre at Janów Pomorski should be discussed (Fig. 9.5). This settlement with area of *c* 10 ha was situated in a waterlogged area, partially peatland, stretching along the shore of Lake Drużno. In the Early Medieval period this lake was connected with the Gulf of Gdansk and the open sea (Jagodziński and Kasprycka 1990, 12; Jagodzinski and Kasprycka 1991). Traces of three-part dwelling structures with hearths were discovered. The trading part of the settlement was located close to the shore of the lake. In this area a lot of amber products, fragments of glass vessels, Arabic coins and the remains of an antler-workshop were excavated. Most striking was the discovery of partially overlapping traces of 9 boats of stave construction (Jagodziński and Kasprzycka 1990, fig. 23)

Thanks to favourable wet conditions a great amount of animal bone was preserved. They show domination of such species as pig(48%) and cow(42%). Fish bones mostly belong to pike-perch (Jagodzinski 1991,150). The site can be dated to the 9th-10th centuries AD. In the light of obtained results the settlement can probably be identified

with the famous Truso trading centre, mentioned in a description by the Anglo Saxon traveller Wulfstan(Jagodzinski 1991, 154-155).

CONCLUSION

It must be stressed once again that this brief review of wetland sites presented is far from complete. This account is focussed on what the author considers major wetland excavations conducted in recent years. As it can be seen, the bulk of data still awaits publication to reach a wider audience. Obviously, many conclusions may lose weight once more information is in circulation.

Much work is to be done in wetland archaeology in Poland. The foremost task would be to conduct a nation-wide survey of vanishing wetlands. More emphasis should be placed on this branch of study in the education of future archaeologists. Finally, closer cooperation with naturalists and conservationists is needed if Poland is to retain its invaluable wetland heritage.

Acknowledgements

W. Bender MA, Państwowe Muzeum Archeologiczne, Warsaw, Poland. Prof. Z. Bukowski, Instytut Historii Kultury Materialnej PAN, Warsaw, Poland. Dr W. Gumiński, Instytut Historii Kultury Materialnej PAN, Warsaw, Poland. M. Jagodziński MA, Państwowa Służba Ochrony Zabytków, Elbląg, Poland.

BIBLIOGRAPHY

Bender, W.1969. Prace terenowe w miejscowości Otalążka, pow. Grójec, w latach 1966-1967. Fieldworks at Otalaz-ka,Grójec district, in years 1966-1967. *Sprawozdania Archeologiczne* 21, 91-96.

Bender, W. and Stupnicka, E. 1974. Z badań archeologiczno-geologicznych stanowiska torfowego w miejscowości Otalążka, pow. Grójec.
Archaeological-geological investigation of a peatbog site at Otalążka, near Grójec. *Archeologia Polski* 19, 307-366.

Brzeziński, W. 1980. Przyczynek do znajomosci rogownictwa na ziemiach polskich u schyłku starożytności (IV w.-V wn.e). Contribution to research concerning antler handicraft in Poland in Late Roman Influences period. *Kwartalnik Historii Kultury Materialnej* 1, 27-39.

Bukowski, Z. 1982. Osiedle otwarte kultury łużyckiej w Grzybianych,woj. legnickie w świetle dotychczasowych badań. Open settlement of the Lusatian Culture in the light of recent excavation. *Pamiętnik Muzeum Miedzi* 1, 13-29.

Coles, J. 1984. *The Archaeology of Wetlands.* Edinburgh: University Press.

Grażewski, K. 1989. Parthaczyn-przyczynek do badań nawodnych dworów myśliwskich w Prusach krzyżackich. Parthaczyn – a contribution to research of lacustrine hunting-lodges in Prussia. *Kwartalnik Historii Kultury Materialnej* 3-4, 577-587.

Gumiński, W. and Fiedorczuk, J. 1988. Badania w Dudce, woj. suwalskie a niektóre problemy epoki kamienia w Polsce północno-wschodnie. Some problems of Stone Age in north eastern Poland in the light of excavation at Dudka, Suwałki district. *Archeologia Polski* 33, 113-148.

Guminski, W. and Fiedorczuk, J. 1990. Dudka 1. A Stone Age peat-bog site in north-eastern Poland. *Acta Archaeologica* 60, 51-69.

Informator Archeologiczny, 1968-1987. Warszawa: Ośrodek Dokumentacji Zabytków.

Jagodziński, M. 1991. Truso w swietle nowych odkryc. Uwagi na marginesie badan sredniowiecznej osady rzemieslniczo-handlowej w Janowie Pomorskim (gmina Elbląg). Truso in the light of new discoveries. In *Archeologia Bałtyjska*, 136-155. Olsztyn.

Jagodziński, M. and Kasprzycka, M. 1990. Zarys problematyki badawczej wczesnośredniowiecznej osady rzemieslniczo-handlowej w Janowie Pomorskim,(gmina Elbląg). An Outline of the research problems concerning the early medieval artisan trade settlement at Janów Pomorski(Elbląg Parish). *Pomorania Antiqua* 14, 9-48.

Jagodziński, M. and Kasprzycka, M. 1991. The early medieval craft and commercial centre at Janów Pomorski near Elblag on the South Baltic coast. *Antiquity* 248, 696-715.

Kempisty, E. and Więckowska, H. 1983. *Osadnictwo z epoki kamienia i wczenej epoki brązu na stanowisku 1 w Sośni,woj. łomżyńskie.* Settlement of the Stone and Early Bronze Ages on site 1 in Sośni Łomża, Voivodeship. Wrocław, Warsawa, Kraków, Gdańsk,Łodz: Ossolineum.

Kola, W. and Wilke, G. 1989. Sprawozdanie z archeologicznych badań podwodnych reliktów wczesnośredniowicznego mostu "poznańskiego"(Rybitwy,stan.3a) w jeziorze Lednickim w latach 1986-1987. Report on underwater excavation of remains of early medieval "Poznań bridge" (Rybitwy, site 3a) in Lednica lake. *Studia Lednickie* 1, 77-95.

10

BISKUPIN FORTIFIED SETTLEMENT AND ITS ENVIRONMENT IN THE LIGHT OF NEW ENVIRONMENTAL AND ARCHAEOLOGICAL STUDIES

Władysław Niewiarowski, Bożena Noryśkiewicz, Wojciech Piotrowski and Wiesław Zajączkowski

Biskupin is situated at a distance of 75 km north-east of Poznań and 50 km south-west of Bydgoszcz, in the so-called Pałuki region, geographically lying between Great Poland and Pomerania (Fig. 10.1). The name Pałuki – *Terra Palucensis* in early medieval manuscripts – indicates rolling countryside amidst lakes and meadows. In 1933 on a peninsula of Lake Biskupin a fortified settlement of Early Iron Age date was discovered. This was possible because the lake level had been lowered by 1 m – a result of irrigation works in the Biskupin surroundings. Archaeological investigations were carried out from 1934 until 1974, but with a break during World War II, although the Germans undertook some excavations in 1941 and 1942. The fortified settlement, erected most probably in the 7th century BC, was built on land which was boggy, oval in shape, about 2 ha in area and rising 1-1.5 m above the lake, with considerable defensive advantages. The settlement was 190 m long and 120 m wide, surrounded by a breakwater, with a rampart 463 m long and *c* 6 m high. Inside the settlement there was a street system consisting of a wide ring road and 11 transverse streets, and dwelling and storage buildings set as 13 rows of houses containing 102-105 flats of the same space and layout. Prehistorians think Biskupin had 800-1000 inhabitants. Ethnically they belonged to the so-called Lusatian Culture, which extended over large areas of Central Europe between *c* 1200-400 BC (Kostrzewski 1936,1938; Rajewski 1950, 1957, 1958, 1959, 1963, 1974).

Biskupin is the only Lusatian Culture fortified settlement examined on such a great scale (Fig. 10.2) – about 75% of

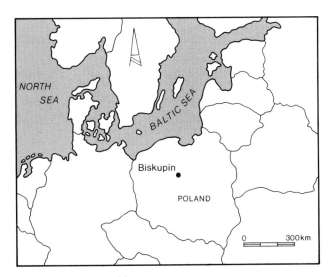

Fig. 10.1 Location Map

the whole site area – and one of the biggest reservoirs of archaeological waterlogged wood in Europe,and it has been a training and experimental centre for archaeologists, naturalists and conservators since the pre-war period. We have a long tradition of interdisciplinary cooperation, but still a lot of the problems connected with Biskupin remain to be solved. The evidence so far recovered was obtained mainly from within the settlement area, while the immediate surroundings were searched only on a small scale. New environmental investigations carried out in recent years by specialists from the Institute of Geography, Nicholas

Fig. 10.2 Aerial view of the Biskupin excavations 1934-38, taken in 1938. Photo Biskupin Archive

Copernicus University in Toruń – W. Niewiarowski, B. Noryśkiewicz and M. Sinkiewicz – have significantly enlarged our knowledge about the environment of Biskupin and its hinterland. Recent archaeological studies and activity in the field of experimental archaeology have provided new evidence for the reconstruction of Biskupin's economy as well. Some of these environmental and archaeological aspects will be presented in this article.

ENVIRONMENT

The Early Iron Age fortified settlement at Biskupin is situated in a young glacial landscape, its main deposits and landforms shaped during the last Scandinavian Glaciation, about 18,000 uncal BP.

The main elements of land relief (Fig. 10.3)

1. a flat and undulated moraine plateau exposed at an altitude 95-105 m above sea level, consisting of more or less loamy till.

2. subglacial channel of a complex origin (Niewiarowski in press) and variable width (0.4-3.0 km), cut into the moraine plateau to a depth of 10-35 m bordered by escarpments of 7-26 m elevation and inclined 8-20°. The following landforms occur there:

   a) relatively flat glacial levels built of till,

   b) kame hillocks, hills and ridges built of sands and silts, created in crevasses of stagnant ice,

c) undulations with fluvioglacial sand and gravel cover, placed above glacial forms built of till,

d) plains built of ice-dammed lake sediments (sands and silts, locally clay), in some places with an admixture of organic matter,

e) numerous lakes developed during the Allerød period (11,800-10,700 uncal BP) after melting away of buried ice. These lakes vary in shape and depth; Lake Ocwieckie is the deepest one (42.5 m). Lake Biskupin covers 116.6 ha, its maximum depth is 13.7 m, and the mean water level in the years 1955-1980 was 78.77 m above sea level. The lakes are joined and drained by the Gąsawka rivulet, tributary to the river Noteć.

f) biogenic plains built mostly of gyttja and peat, formed in the Holocene due to overgrowing of the lakes by vegetation,

g) lake terraces built of sands and silts as well as organic deposits, and locally of lacustrine chalk, clear indicators of oscillations in the water level of the lakes.

On such differential land relief and lithology of surface deposits, a mosaic soil cover was formed. In general, relatively fertile soils, mainly brown and lessivés ones, were formed on the moraine plateau and on glacial landforms in the subglacial channel; podsolic and rusty soils formed on glacial-aquaeous sediments; black earths, peat-muck and mineral muck-soils were created in flat areas with a high level of underground water.

Biskupin's surroundings are now mostly used as arable land. Small patches of forest appear on the least fertile soils, for example on some kames. Meadows and pastures occur on wetlands, mainly on biogenic plains. Thick beds of peat were exploited by men, for example the peat bog between Lake Godawskie and Lake Biskupin, where secondary water reservoirs were created after extraction of peat.

Changes in the natural environment

In this paper we examine changes of Biskupin's natural environment only from the appearance of the first neolithic farmers there, in the second half of the 7th millennium uncal BP. From this time, parallel to climatic changes especially in humidity, the influence of human activity has been growing gradually. This activity caused changes in all components of the natural environment, but in this paper we will examine only changes in vegetation cover and in hydrology.

On the basis of palynological analysis from the upper 5 m of the 10.8 m of Lake Biskupin sediments, we are able to state the following: in Biskupin's surroundings at the end of the Atlantic period (c 6000-5000 BP) deciduous forest with oak, lime, elm and hazel dominated on the areas of till, mixed forest with pine prevailed on the sandy areas, alder, ash and peat bog vegetation dominated on the wetlands.

The simplified palynological diagram (Fig. 10.4) shows the percentage values of pollen grains of trees and shrubs, pollen sums of herbaceous plants and more important indicators of human activity. Because of the lack of radiocarbon

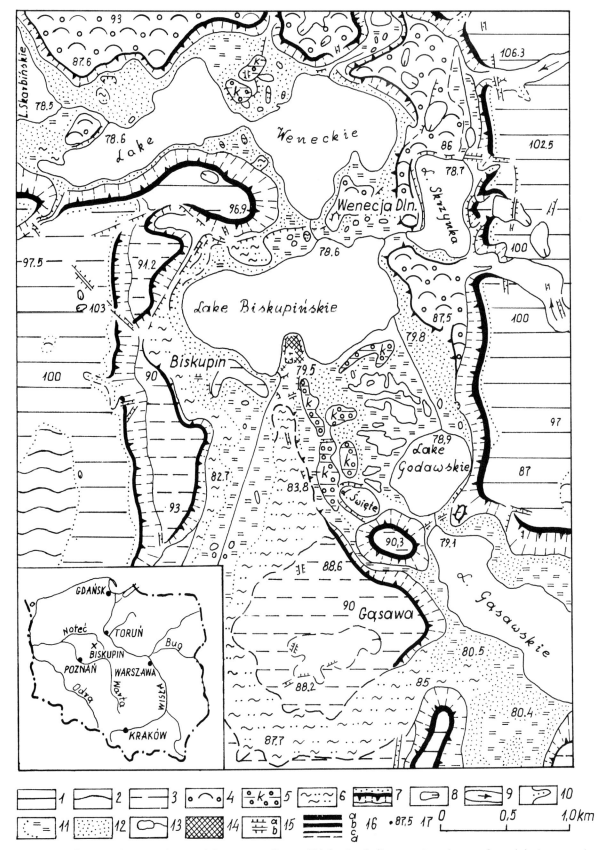

Fig. 10.3 Geomorphological map of the surroundings of Biskupin: 1. flat moraine plateau; 2. undulating moraine plateau; 3. plains and morainic undulations in the bottom of sub-glacial channel; 4. morainic undulations with sandy and gravelly fluvioglacial cover; 5. kame hillocks, hills and ridges; 6. plains built of ice dammed lake sediments; 7. slopes and degradation zone; 8. kettles; 9. melt-water valleys; 10. periglacial denudation valleys; 11. biogenic plains, mainly peat plains; 12. minerogenic lake terrace deposits; 13. lakes, ponds, and streams; 14. Early Iron Age fortified settlement at Biskupin; 15. anthropogenic forms (ditches, embankments etc.); 16. height of escarpments: a. 10-20 m; b. 5-10 m; c. up to 5 m; d. undistinct; 17. altitude points

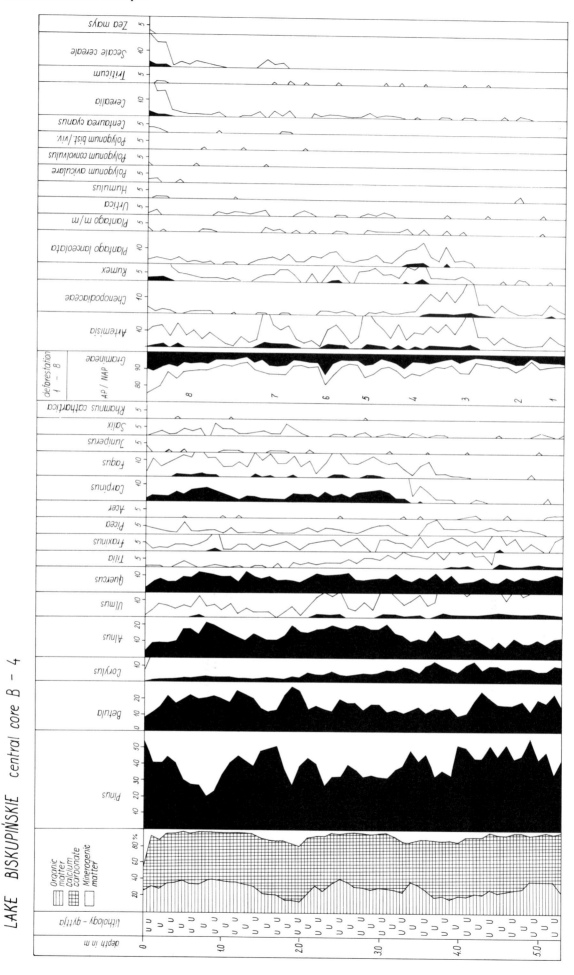

Fig. 10.4 Simplified pollen diagram from upper part of Lake Biskupin sediments

datings from the profile the chronology of changes in vegetation cover is based upon correlation of these changes noticed in other profiles with radiocarbon dates in the adjacent Great Poland region (Stach 1985; Filbrandt – in manuscript) and in Tuchola Forest (Miotk-Szpiganowicz 1989).

Eight local settlement phases were distinguished according to changes of pollen values of synanthropic plants and some trees. Traces of deforestation in the first settlement phase(late Atlantic) are characterised by a slight growth of pollen of *Artemisia, Rumex* (sorrel), *Urtica* (nettle) and spores of *Pteridium aquilinum* (bracken), a fall of pollen value of *Ulmus* (elm), *Fraxinus* (ash) and *Tilia* (lime). This phase probably correlates with the activity of an early neolithic population.

During the second settlement phase some *Cerealia* (cereal) pollen appeared in the lacustrine sediments. The appearance of *Carpinus* (hornbeam) and *Fagus* (beech) *c* 3900 uncal BP in the deciduous forest was a natural change due to the succession of vegetation and to climatic changes of the Sub-boreal. The third settlement phase probably correlates with the late Neolithic; pollen of synanthropic plants, including cereals, takes a bigger part than in the previous phases, but generally agriculture was in an initial state.

The 4th and 5th phases are probably to be dated to the Bronze Age. The biggest Holocene pollen value for *Plantago lanceolata* and rise of *Rumex* pollen with parallel decline of oak, hazel, elm and ash pollen but with a rise of pine pollen, appeared in the 4th phase. Such a situation suggests a predominantly pastoral economy and newly deforested areas. A rise in cereal pollen was manifest at the beginning of the 5th phase, but later a regression of human activity was indicated by a decline of synanthropic plants as well as by a growth of oak and elm pollen.

Changeable climatic conditions,especially temperature and humidity, caused significant lake level oscillations during the Late Glacial and Holocene periods. Shallow lakes and littoral parts of existing lakes were disappearing under minerogenic and organic sediments, as well as being overgrown by vegetation during the Holocene period. Some lakes were overgrown in periods of low water level, but they returned to their previous state when the water level was higher. The detailed sequence of lake water oscillation has not been fully established yet because the whole microregional project is still under realization. Certainly we may state that from the Allerød until the end of the fortified settlement at Biskupin the water level of the lakes oscillated but even at its highest position it did not transgress the recent water level of Lake Biskupin.

The formation of the Biskupin peninsula on which the fortified settlement was erected was possible to recognize more clearly on the basis of the new geomorphological and geological investigations. The peninsula was formed by the continuation of a kame ridge, and kame deposits caused by

a creation of shallows in the lake which was posterior to them. Ice-dammed lake deposits found in the southern part of the peninsula had been precipitated, as it is shown in profile 3 (Fig. 10.5), on the kame deposits. In the lower part of the profile there are intercalations of organic matter (17,000 ± 200 uncal BP; Gd-5769) within the ice-dammed lake sediments. However, a larger part of the peninsula is built of Late Glacial and Holocene lacustrine sediments like sands, slime, warp, gyttja and peat. Looking at profile 1 (Fig. 10.5) taken in the settlement area, we find minerogenic lacustrine sediments with the Pre-boreal peat over them, which occurs at the depth of 1.85-2.03 m below surface. The radiocarbon dates obtained from this peat are clearly too young and they do not correspond to the results of palynological analysis. Later oscillations of a high water level of the lake resulted next in a reduced thickness of lacustrine sediments (from Boreal and Atlantic periods), which contained sedimentation hiatuses.

An important matter is the determination of the age of the peat beneath the houses of the settlement. Radiocarbon dates suggest a peat began to form there *c* 4000 BP and that the growing process continued probably until the erection of the settlement, although it is clear from the traces of peat-muck soil (Jaron 1936) that at least in higher parts of the peninsula it dried out and mineralised. It is a *Carex* and *Phragmites* lowland peat, its surface at 78-79 m above sea level.

The sixth settlement phase in the palynological diagram (Fig. 10.4) is probably connected with the Late Bronze Age and Hallstatt period, and it is characterised by a significant growth of herbaceous plants, including *Graminae* (grasses) and cereals, and this indicates intensive economic activity by man. Although a great amount of oak timber had been used for constructional purposes, after examination of the palynological diagram we did not find a reduction of oak pollen, but on the contrary an increase was noticed. It is possible to explain such a situation by suggesting that after cutting of younger and thin trees, single, thick and older free-standing oak specimens flowered much more abundantly than in a dense forest canopy.

After the above-mentioned settlement phase, we note in the diagram a significant reduction of pollen from synanthropic plants which indicates a regression in the settlement economy. Later in the 7th phase we find much more cereal pollen than in the 6th phase, rye pollen appeared, and there was a clear reduction of hornbeam and oak pollen. This phase is linked to the period of Roman Influences. After a reforestation phase, very intensive growth of cereals and an increase of deforestation began in the Middle Ages.

One of the most important palaeohydrological problems is the level of Lake Biskupin's water table at the time of building the settlement. There is a lack of direct evidence but we may infer the following. That, firstly, the water level had to be lower than the peat surface and foundations of the houses; secondly, it had also to be lower than seasonal high water levels, which occur 0.8 m above mean lake level. This

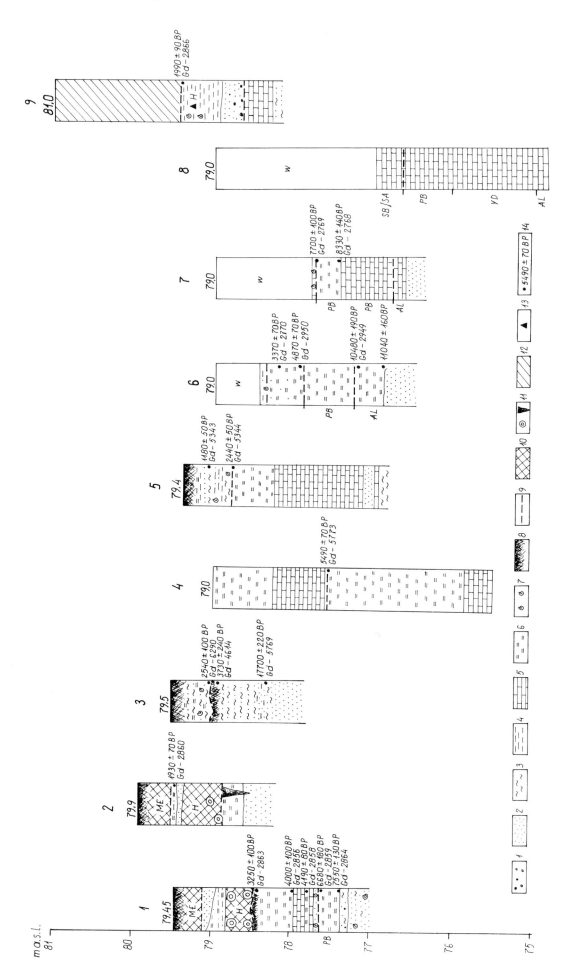

Fig. 10.5 Selected geological profiles from Biskupin Lake and its surroundings; 1. gravels; 2. sands; 3. silts; 4. slime and mud with organic matter; 5. calcareous sediments (gyttja,marl,chalk); 6. peat; 7. mollusc shells; 8. fossil and recent soils; 9. hiatus; 10. culture layers; 11. fossil wood constructions; 12. anthropogenic denudation deposit; 13. artefacts; 14. location of samples taken for ^{14}C datings. Designation of letters: AL – Allerød, YD – Younger Dryas, PR – Pre-boreal, SB – Sub-boreal, SA – Sub-atlantic, H – Hallstatt, ME – Middle Ages, w – water

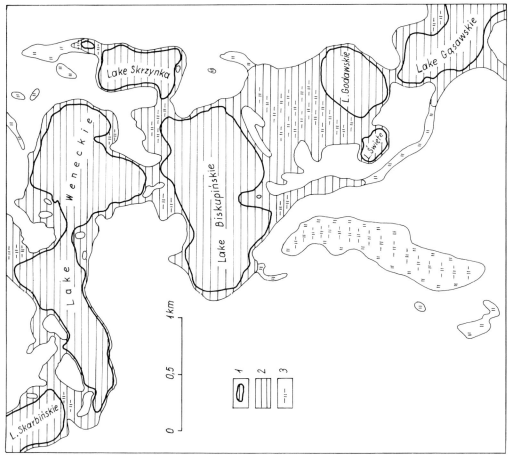

Right: Palaeohydrography during the maximum extent of lakes:
1. present lakes;
2. former extent of lakes;
3. bogs and mires.

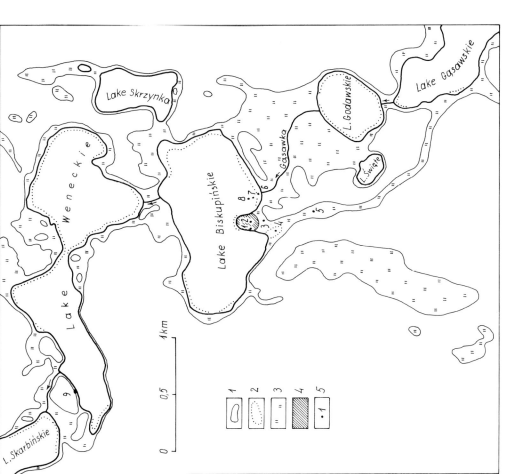

Fig. 10.6   Left: Palaeohydrography at the end of Bronze Age:
1. present lakes;
2. extension of lakes at the end of Bronze Age;
3. peat bogs;
4. Early Iron Age fortified settlement at Biskupin;
5. location of geological profiles presented in Fig. 10.5

means that the water level could not be higher than 77-77.5 m above sea level, so at least 1 m and even a little bit more below the recent level. Accepting such a figure for the water level - and this opinion is strengthened by the analysis of a bog sediment structure in profiles 1,4 and 5 (Fig. 10.5) – we may state the palaeohydrographical situation within Biskupin's surroundings was similar to that shown in Fig. 10.6.

New geological investigations realized within the exposed part of Biskupin peninsula resulted in new data relevant to the problem of whether the settlement had been built on a peninsula or on an island. Following the profile, sediments of the glacial ice-dammed lake with a fossil soil of degraded black earth type on them (3730 ± 240 uncal BP; Gd-4614) are clearly manifested in the southern part of the peninsula. The fossil soil occurs at an altitude of 79 m above sea level. On the partly destroyed surface of the fossil soil lie sandy-silty lacustrine sediments with organic matter (2540 ± 100 uncal BP; Gd-6290). This profile records clearly that before 2500 uncal BP the Biskupin lake never reached as high as 79 m above sea level, and that whilst the settlement was being built the peninsula was joined to the mainland, and rose at least 1.6 m above the contemporary water level. Therefore, our conclusion is that there is no geological evidence to support the hypothesis that the settlement location was an island at the time of building. It was a peninsula.

It is known from the archaeological evidence that the water level in Biskupin Lake was rising during the settlement's existence, and this is clearly testified by the floors of the houses being raised 0.2-0.5 m and placed on an artificial embankment during the settlement's younger phase (Kostrzewski 1936). The rise in lake level seems to have been quite rapid, because after the disappearance of the settlement *c* 2400 uncal BP it exceeded 79 m above sea level and almost the whole peninsula must have been deluged. This was not only a local phenomenon, as Piasecki (1957) has argued, but a wide event which has been noticed in Middle, Western and Northern Europe at that time (see among others, Godwin and Willis 1959; Ragnon 1983; Gaillard 1985). In the neighbourhood of Biskupin it is evident in Lake Pakoskie (Niewiarowski 1976) and in Lake Wolskie (Nowaczyk *et al* 1981). This process has been linked with progressive cooling and a significant increase in humidity. The higher water level was probably one of the main reasons for the settlement's decline.

Raising of water levels in the lakes caused them to enlarge, with flooding of some peat-bogs (profiles 1,2,4,5 in Fig. 10.5). Because of the existence of lake terraces and due to the dating of lacustrine sediments in a high position in the profiles 2,5 and 9, we are able to state that the maximum level of Lake Biskupin and other neighbouring lakes was *c* 80-80.5 m above sea level, which means 1.2-1.7 m higher than the recent level. This maximum lake level probably occurred at the break of La Tène and Roman Influences periods, and the palaeohydrological situation of Biskupin's surrounding at this time is shown in Fig. 10.6.

The flooding of the Biskupin fortified settlement is proved by shallow lacustrine sediments, which cover the cultural layer of the settlement, among them lacustrine sands with washed traces of the burnt ruins (Paulo 1936; Gadomska-Czekalska 1950). The lack of a settlement phase between the abandonment of the Early Iron Age and the 3rd century AD is also proof of flooding (Kostrzewski 1950).

A detailed study of the post-Hallstatt stratigraphy of the peninsula is made more difficult by a significant disturbance of the upper layers by Early Medieval settlement, which existed from the 7th to 11th centuries AD. Analysis of the molluscan fauna found within these upper layers, with species from shallow water and also from wet meadows, suggests however that even the maximum water level oscillated, and lakes floods did not last too long.

Later lowering of the lakes was caused by natural (climatic) reasons and by anthropogenic activity, especially by regulation of the channel of the rivulet Gasawka in the last century.

The fortified settlement

Every square metre of the peninsula was used by the prehistoric fort builders for some type of architectural construction (Fig. 10.2). It was surrounded by a *breakwater* made of 3 to 9 serried rows of oak and pine stakes, at an angle ot $45°$ (18,000-20,000 stakes = *c* 4000 trunks). Ice-floes, which built up in the wintertime, pushed by the strong north-west winds, were kept at bay by additional stakes rammed into the lake bed itself on that side of the peninsula.

The *defence ramparts* were built behind and parallel to the breakwater, on a foundation of oak logs placed in rectangles measuring 3-3.5 m. The rampart logs were interlocked at the corners, and the rampart boxes were filled with earth and sand and plastered from both sides with clay. The gateway was cut in the south-west region, the gates turned on pegs fixed in the threshold and lintel of the gateway. Over the gateway a defence and watch tower was built (Fig. 10.7) which probably dominated the whole settlement (Rajewski 1950). An oak *causeway*, *c* 250 m long, was built above water level leading from the gateway and entrance to the south-western shore of the lake, not far from a freshwater spring.

The positioning of the settlement's *streets* and their slight bend indicate that the aim was to achieve optimum utilization of light and solar heat. The streets were corduroys built from oak or pine logs and covered with clay. A uniform building technique was used for all the *houses*. This technique consisted in erecting walls of horizontal logs, tongued and keyed into grooved uprights. These uprights were reinforced at the sides with pegs, and at the bottom evenly cut and rammed into the soft foundation. Such a technique made it possible to build long wall sections using lengths of timber packed with moss and clay. A house measured 9 x 8 m, giving 70-80 sq. m floor space and was probably occupied by one extended family. In all, houses covered

8300 sq.m or about 42% of the total built up area of the settlement (Rajewski 1959; 1963).

Generally the defended settlement had 2 phases (Rajewski 1950). The older one covered the bigger area, and was built mostly of oak trunks and was damaged maybe during intertribal wars. The younger phase had a reduced internal surface, and used mostly pine wood. In addition to oak and pine, Biskupin's inhabitants also used alder, poplar, birch, ash, willow, hornbeam and hazel wood.

We have to mention, as well, a 3rd phase – quite enigmatic, small and poorer but existing in the form of an open settlement dated towards the end of the Iron Age occupation on the peninsula.

Stratigraphy

The stratigraphy of the fortified settlement is complicated and not clear; the general division consists of six levels (Kostrzewski 1936; fig. 6):

I   top soil, mostly without artefacts
II peat with Lusatian Culture artefacts in the southern part of the site, and with Early Medieval artefacts in the middle and in the eastern part
III silt and peat with artefacts from Neolithic until the Early Medieval period

Fig. 10.7 The reconstruction of the watch tower and the entrance to the settlement, 1988. Photo: A.Ring

IV loam covering floors of the younger phase of the settlement
V   remains of the younger phase of the settlement
VI remains of the older phase of the settlement.

This indicates the kind of disorder and dislocation which is evident especially in the 3 upper levels. For a slightly clearer situation let us corellate these levels with the geological profile (Pazdur *et al* 1992) of thickness *c* 1 m:

1) levels I-IV - humus deposits
2) level V - upper beams of the street of the younger phase
3) level V - lower beams of the street of the younger phase
4) level VI - upper beams of the street of the older phase
5) level VI - lower beams of the street of the older phase
6) peat with thin layers of sand
7) deposits with malacofauna shells
8) lacustrine sediments.

ECONOMY

The main source of livelihood of the Biskupinians was cultivation of the land and breeding of domestic animals (Rajewski 1957; 1958; 1959; 1963; 1974).

Plants

The Biskupinians were burning forest, to prepare soil for cultivation, as well as using crop rotation and fallowing techniques. Wooden ploughs and antler hoes and picks were in use. From the plant macrofossil analyses (Jaroń 1938) we know 4 species of wheat and 2 species of barley were sown, also millet, peas, beans, lentils, poppy, turnip, false flax and flax, harvested using bronze sickles. They were also gathering hazel nuts, sorrel, goosefoot, orache, as well as oregano, hogweed and plants used for magical or medical purposes like knot-grass. Biskupinians gathered plants used for dyes, too, such as lilac and Lady's Bedstraw.

Rye grains were not found, and rye is not known as a cereal crop in this part of Europe in the Hallstatt period. It was a surprise for us to learn the results of the newest palynological analyses (Fig. 10.4) which showed a growth of cereal pollen in the 7th settlement phase (Roman Influences period) especially wheat and rye, which is characteristic for this period in Poland, more extensive even than during the phase connected with the fortified settlement. These results are in opposition to our recent archaeological knowledge that Roman Influences period settlement at Biskupin and in its surroundings was quite poor. We have only some small "Roman" settlements in our archaeological inventory. All these palynological data induce us to start thinking about some of Biskupin's economic and settlement aspects in new ways, not only during the Hallstatt period but during Roman Influences and post Roman Influences periods as well.

Animals

The latest results of archaeozoological analyses (Lasota-Moskalewska 1992) are based on material from Biskupin and other settlements of Biskupin type. The Biskupin material analysed included 2885 fragments of mammal bones, 3 bird bones and numerous fish bones. Of the mammal bones, 9.6% came from game. For consumption however, and probably in breeding, cattle was of prime importance, followed by sheep and goat and, in 3rd place, pig. Most of the cattle from Biskupin were small (*c* 100 cm in height). The sheep were of medium size, of peat-sheep and heath-sheep type and similar to early medieval sheep in Poland. Pigs were large, varying little from wild boars. This suggests that pigs were allowed to graze freely in the woods where cross-breeding could occur. The Biskupinians also kept big dogs. The horses were the size of the tarpan and were used for riding and as pack animals.

On the basis of archaeological data, the osteological material from Biskupin was divided into 3 groups corresponding with the three settlement phases. In the first place there is a statistically significant excess of pig bone, a result of ecologic conditions which favoured pig breeding. The devastation of oak forests for building material could then have increased interest in the breeding of ruminants. A comparison of bone material according to species from Biskupin and 5 other neighbouring fortified settlements – Jankowo, Izdebno, Sobiejuchy, Smuszewo and Slupca – showed that there were differences in animal breeding. For example, at Smuszewo pigs prevailed, and maybe the place was surrounded by large deciduous forests suitable for pig feeding. The greater number of horse bones in the material from Slupca and Jankowo may be evidence that the inhabitants of these settlements were more often engaged in armed expeditions and, therefore, horses were very important. The different breeding patterns in the settlements studied suggests that local differences of sites and natural conditions modified the type of economy (Lasota-Moskalewska 1992).

But even these conclusions are not firm. We should mention that the Biskupin environment was very similar to that of the Smuszewo fortified settlement – so why such a difference in animal breeding structure? The problem ought to be solved through close interdisciplinary cooperation, but now we know that maybe it would not be so unreasonable to put another question - are we not too strongly attached to the idea that every kind of human activity should be reflected in the natural environment? Maybe sometimes people left no noticeable traces in the environmental record. And this means we have to learn about environmental rules more than before.

Game animals of the Biskupin area included wild boar, red deer, roe deer, wolf, hare, bear, beaver, lynx, otter and duck. The only aurochs bone found is a part of a skull discovered near the gateway. Wild animals, apart from meat and skins, also provided the inhabitants of Biskupin with horn and bone for the manufacture of various articles - for example most hoes and picks were made from antler. The Biskupinians fished from dug-out boats with nets, and also with rods and lines fixed with small bronze hooks - and caught tench, pike, perch, sheatfish (*Silurus Glanis L.*), bream and roach.

Territory and population density

Since 1934, Biskupin's microregion has been quite well examined from an archaeological point of view, but we are still far from a total picture. The latest surface investigations organized in the last decade on a big scale, an enterprise realized within the general project known as the Archaeological Map of Poland, mapped 115 sites of varied type and date in an area of *c* 30 sq. km (Piotrowski and Zajączkowski, in manuscript).

In our opinion the Biskupin territory occupied an area of *c* 25 sq. km; on the west, south and east it was bordered by forest complexes, on the north it had probably an open border with another fortified settlement at Sobiejuchy. The shape of the territory was influenced by the hydrology, especially by a chain of lakes going from south to north, which served in prehistoric times as a major transport and communication route. The area of intensive economic exploitation is marked by permanent and seasonal settlements, camp sites and stray finds.

Here we will try to construct an ecological model of economy for the prehistoric population living in this area around 500 BC. We should like to mention that our model differs from one created in the 1970s and still being developed by M.Henneberg and J.Ostoja-Zagórski (Henneberg and J.Ostoja-Zagórski 1977; 1984). We hope that our proposals will awaken a discussion about possibilities of reconstructing prehistoric economies in this region.

We suppose that the population of the fortified settlement at Biskupin plus that from satellite settlements was *c* 800 persons. On the basis of results obtained from Biskupin's experimental archaeology projects, we suggest (with full awareness of the problems of such a hypothesis) that the approximate amount of crop yield for species of wheat (*Triticum dicoccum* Schrank.;*Triticum Spelta; Triticum vulgare* Vill.;*Triticum compactum* Host.) was 6-8 grains from one. One person could consume *c* 0.5 kg of cereal per day. Eight hundred persons x 365 days x 0.5 kg = *c* 150 tonnes. The yield from 1 ha could be 800-1000 kg, so fields of 150-200 ha would produce *c* 150 tonnes of grain. Of course Biskupinians had to collect seed grain first of all, and needed *c* 170 tonnes in order to have *c* 150 tonnes for consumption. If we hypothetically enlarge the area of 200 ha to 250 ha, this would be the maximum arable territory which the Biskupinians cultivated, including patches occupied by oleaginous and leguminous plants like beans and lentils, which played quite an important role in the Biskupinian's menu.

Another aspect connected with food consumption is the share of animal protein in total consumption. Probably 1

Fig. 10.8 Biskupin archaeological reserve park – a view from the west, 1990. Photo: A.Ring

cow (short horn species – *c* 100 cm tall) produced per year *c* 700 litres of milk, and males were slaughtered as well as used for ploughing and as draught power. One sheep produced *c* 50-60 litres of milk per year and delivered 1.5-2kg of rough wool (Lasota-Moskalewska 1992). But although we know quite a lot as the result of the latest osteological analyses, the yield from animals still needs more scientific examination and attention, closely linked with experimental archaeology.

The Future

Biskupin and its surroundings (Fig. 10.8) need very active protection and care because of the significant danger coming from industrial activity as well as from modern agriculture. Happily we have got good contacts with local politicians and administration, and we really hope that cooperation with Polish and foreign scientists will be reflected by satisfactory results. In the summer of 1991 we have started (together with John and Bryony Coles as consultants) a project monitoring the water-levels on the Biskupin peninsula, and we should like to initiate – not in the far future – a new undertaking which can be called the Biskupin International Project. Nowadays we feel deeply the lack of a dendrochronological laboratory, and we suffer because of financial cuts to our programme for the conservation of the settlement's waterlogged construction, but all things considered we are optimistic about our recent activity as well as our plans for the coming years.

BIBLIOGRAPHY

Gadomska-Czekalska A. 1950. Podłoże geologiczne grodu prasłowiańskiego w Biskupinie (*Rés.* Le substratum géologique de l'enceinte fortifié de Biskupin). In J. Kostrzewski (ed.), *III Sprawozdanie z prac wykopaliskowych w grodzie kultury łużyckiej w Biskupinie w powiecie żnińskim za lata 1938-1939 i 1946-1948*, 28-38. Poznań.

Gaillard, M.J. 1985. Postglacial palaeoclimatic changes in Scandinavia and Central Europe. A tentative correlation based on studies of lake level fluctuations. *Ecologia Mediterranea* 11, 159-75.

Godwin, H. and Willis, E.H. 1959. Radiocarbon dating of prehistoric wooden trackways. *Nature* 184, 490-491.

Henneberg, M. and Ostoja-Zagórski, J. 1977. Próba modelowej rekonstrukcji gospodarki mieszkanców halsztackich grodów typu biskupińskiego (*Sum.* An attempt to the model description of economy in a population related to a fortified settlement of the Biskupin type). *Kwartalnik Historii Kultury Materialnej* 25.3, 319-40.

Henneberg, M. and Ostoja-Zagórski, J. 1984. Use of a General Ecological Model for the Reconstruction of Prehistoric

Economy. The Hallstatt Period of Northwestern Poland. *Journal of Anthropological Archaeology* 3. 1, 41-78.

Jaroń, B. 1936. Torfowisko z kulturą łużycką w Biskupinie (*Rés.* Tourbière avec les restes d'un village fortifié de la civilisation lusacienne à Biskupin).*Osada bagienna w Biskupinie w pow.żnińskim*, 21-7. Poznań.

Jaroń, B. 1938. Szczątki róślinne z wczesnego okresu żelaznego w Biskupinie (Plant remnants from the Early Iron Age at Biskupin, Great Poland). In Polish only. In J. Kostrzewski (ed.) *Gród prasłowiański w Biskupinie w powiecie żnińskim. Sprawozdanie z prac wykopaliskowych w latach 1936 i 1937, z uwzględnieniem wyników z lat 1934-1935*, 104-32. Poznań.

Kostrzewski, J. 1936. *Osada bagienna w Biskupinie w pow. żnińskim* (*Rés.* Un village fortifié sur le marais du premier âge du fer découvert à Biskupin, Grande Pologne), 1-20. Poznań.

Kostrzewski, J. (ed.) 1938. *Gród praslowianski w Biskupinie w powiecie zninskim. Sprawozdanie z prac wykopaliskowych w latach 1936 i 1937,z uwzględnieniem wyników z lat 1934-1935* (The preslavonic settlement at Biskupin. The excavational report of 1936 and 1937, with additional results of 1934-1935). In Polish only. Poznań.

Kostrzewski, J. 1950. Zabytki z okresu rzymskiego w Biskupinie (*Rés.* Trouvailles de la période romaine à Biskupin). In J.Kostrzewski (ed.) *III Sprawozdanie z prac wykopaliskowych w grodzie kultury łużyckiej w Biskupinie w powiecie żnińskim za lata 1938-1939 i 1946-1948*, 370-73, Poznań.

Lasota-Moskalewska, A. (1992). Hodowla i łowiectwo w Biskupinie na tle innych osiedli obronnych kultury łużyckiej (*Sum.* Animal breeding and hunting at Biskupin compared with other Lusatian Culture fortified settlements). In J.Jaskanis (ed.), *Prahistoryczny Gród w Biskupinie* 185-195. Warszawa.

Miotk-Szpiganowicz, G. 1989. Type Region P-s: Bory Tucholskie. *Acta Palaeobotanica* 29, 81-4.

Niesiołowska-Wędzka, A. 1970. Ze Studiów nad procesem kształtowania się grodów kultury łużyckiej (*Sum.* From the studies on the process of formation of fortified settlements of the Lusatian Culture).*Archeologia Polski* 15.1, 35-81.

Niesiołowska-Wędzka, A. 1976. Problem genezy i funkcji frodów "typu biskupińskiego" w świetle oddziaływań kultur poludniowych (*Rés.* Recherches sur la genèse et la fonction des castra du "Type Biskupin" à la lumière de l'influence des civilisations méridionales). *Slavia Antiqua* 23, 17-38.

Niesiołowska-Wędzka, A. 1989 *Procesy urbanizacyjne w kulturze łużyckiej w świetle oddziaływan kultur południowych* (*Zsf.* Urbanisierungsprozesse in der Lausitzer kultur angesichts der Einwirkungen der südlichen Kulturen). Wroclaw: Polskie Badania Archeologiczne 29.

Niewiarowski, W. 1976. Wahania poziomu wód w Jeziorze Pakoskim w świetle badań geomorfologicznych i archeologicznych (*Sum.* Oscillations of the water level in Lake Pakość in the light of geomorphological and archaeological investigations). In W. Niewiarowski (ed.), *Problemy geografii fizycznej. Studia Scientiarum Torunensis*, sec.C.8, 193-211.

Niewiarowski, W. (in press). Morphogenesis of the Żnin channel as an example of a subglacial channel of complex origin in the Polish Lowland. *Quaestiones Geographicae*.

Nowaczyk, B., Ostoja-Zagórski,J., Pazdur, A. and Romanowska-Grabowska, O. 1982. Zmiany poziomu wód w Jeziorze Wolskim w świetle badań archeologicznych i datowań [14]C (*Sum.* Water-level changes in Lake Wolskie reflected in archaeological research and radiocarbon datings). *Badania Fizjograficzne nad Polską Zachodnią, ser A., Geografia fizyczna* 34, 141-6.

Paulo, K. 1938. Cztery profile geologiczne z półwyspu Jeziora Biskupińskiego (Four geological profiles from the peninsula of Lake Biskupin). In Polish only. In J.Kostrzewski (ed.) *Gród prasłowiański w Biskupinie w powiecie żnińskim. Sprawozdanie z prac wykopaliskowych w latach 1936 i 1937, z uwzględnieniem wyników z lat 1934-1935*, 132-9. Poznań.

Pazdur, M.F., Mikłaszewska-Balcer, R., Węgrzynowicz, T. and Piotrowski, W. 1992. Chronologia bezwzględna osady w Biskupinie w świetle datowań radiowęglowych (*Sum.* The absolute chronology of the Biskupin settlement in the light of Radiocarbon Dating). In J.Jaskanis (ed.), *Prahistoryczny Gród w Biskupinie, 115-25. Warszawa.*

Piasecki, D. 1957. Zagadnienie zalewu prehistorycznego grodu biskupińsikiego (*Zfg.* Das Problem der "Überflutung der praehistorischen Siedlung in Biskupin bei Gniezno"). *Zeszty Naukowe UAM Geografia 1*, 87-118.

Ragnon, P. 1983. Quelques crises climatiques des douze dèrniere millénaires. *Bulletin de l'Association de Géographes Français* 60, 144-55.

Rajewski, Z.A. 1938 Sprawozdanie z organizacji badań w latach 1936 i 1937 (Organizational report of the excavations done in 1936 and in 1937). In Polish only. In J.Kostrzewski (ed.) *Gród prasłowiański w Biskupinie w powiecie zninskim. Sprawozdanie z prac wykopaliskowych w latach 1936 i 1937, z uwzglednieniem wynikow z lat 1934-1935* 1-14. Poznań.

Rajewski, Z.A. 1950. Budowle grodów kultury łużyckiej na półwyspie jeziora biskupińskiego w powiecie żnińskim. (*Rés.* Le construction des deux encientes fortifiées de civilization lusacienne). In J. Kostrzewski (ed.), *III Sprawozdanie z prac wykopaliskowych w grodzie kultury łużyckiej w Biskupinie w powiecie żnińskim za lata 1938-1939 i 1946-1948*, 239-85. Poznań.

Rajewski, Z.A. 1957. Osadnictwo w czasach pierwotnych w Biskupinie i okolicy (*Sum.* The primary settlement of Biskupin and its environs). *Wiadomości Archeologiczne* 24.3, 165-88.

Rajewski, Z.A. 1958. New discoveries in Western Poland. *Archaeology* 11.1, 40-47. New York.

Rajewski, Z.A. 1959. Settlements of a Primitive and Early Feudal Epoch in Biskupin and its surroundings. *Archaeologia Polona* 2.1, 85-124.

Rajewski, Z.A. 1963. Über befestigte Siedlungen der Lausitzer Kultur aus der Hallstatt Periode im Gebiet Polens. *Arbeits und Forschungsberichte zur Sächsischen Bodenkmalpflege* 11/12, 483-510.

Rajewski, Z.A. 1969. Wehrsiedlungen und offene Siedlungen. *Beiträge zur Lausitzer Kultur*, 221-8. Berlin.

Rajewski, Z.A. 1974. Was Wehrsiedlungen-Burgen sowie deren Überbauung an wirtschaftlich-gesellschaftlichem Wert bergen. In B. Chropovsky (ed.), *Symposium zu Problemen der jüngeren Hallstattzeit in Mitteleuropa*, 427-33. Bratislava.

Stach, A. 1985. Analiza pyłkowa osadów torfowiska przy jeziorze Bakorce (Pojezierze Gnieźnieńskie). (*Sum.* Pollen Analysis of peatbog sediments in the vicinity of Lake Bakorce, the Gniezno Lakeland). *Sprawozdania Poznańskiego Towarzystwa Przyjaciół Nauk* 104, 223-4.

11

EVOLUTION OF LAKES AND PREHISTORIC SETTLEMENT IN NORTHWESTERN RUSSIA

P.M.Dolukhanov

SYNOPSIS

The evolution of prehistoric settlements in northwestern Russia proceeded against the background of major changes in the lacustrine environment. The initial settlement occurred in the Late Glacial. Stable lake settlements with an efficient forager-type economy emerged during the Climatic Optimum (6200-5000 uncal BP) and the Post-optimum (5000-3600 uncal BP). The spread of Corded Ware pottery (4000-3600 uncal BP) failed to modify the stable settlement and subsistence pattern there.

The wetland landscape played an extremely important role in the evolution of prehistoric mankind. It can be shown (Dolukhanov 1979,38) that the earliest stages in the development of tool-producing hominids were restricted to lacustrine and riverine environments. These types of biome provided early humans with the necessary resources of life, while protecting them from their numerous enemies.

Wetland landscapes became particularly important for social groups in northeastern Europe in the course of Late Pleistocene and early/middle Holocene. The entire pattern of socio-economic evolution of prehistoric communities in this part of Europe may be interpreted in terms of increasingly successful adaptation to the riverine-lacustrine environment by means of intensified foraging strategies. The success of these foraging strategies was largely dependent on the evolution of particular types of wetland landscapes, which eventually became the main arena for human economic and social behaviour.

A detailed picture of the development of wetland-type settlements against the background of environmental

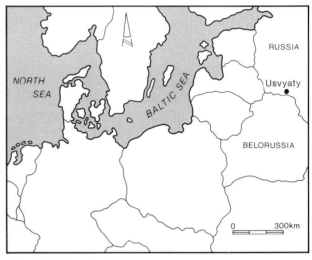

Fig. 11.1 Location Map

change has emerged from the multidisciplinary research into prehistoric lake dwellings in the northwestern provinces of Russia, notably in the south of Pskov and in the north of Smolensk oblast'. In the area which belongs to the catchment of the upper West Dvina (Duna, Daugava) River, a number of prehistoric sites were discovered and studied by A.M. Miklyayev and his associates. In these studies, which are reflected in a number of publications, the present writer took part in 1965-1986 (Miklyayev and Semyonov 1979; Miklyayev *et al* 1984; Miklyayev *et al* 1990; Dolukhanov and Miklyayev 1969, 1986; Dolukhanov *et al* 1989).

The studied area (Fig. 11.1) lies in the extreme southeast of the Pskov and the northwest of the Smolensk oblast'

93

close to the limits of Byelorussia. The main features of the relief were formed during the maximum stages of the last glaciation, when a system of end-morainic belts was formed. Closely spaced end-moraines took the form of alternating ridges and hollows. In the upper West Dvina area the morainic highland directly abutted the terraced sandy plain, which resulted from the activity of the ice-dammed lakes. Kvasov (1979) convincingly proved the existence of a large ice-dammed 'Kasplya' lake in the upper stretches of the West Dvina basin, and the subsequent drainage of this lake led to the emergence of the new 'Plotsk' basin in the middle stretches of the West Duna valley, at an altitude of *c* 160-130 m. The terraces of the ice-dammed lakes are clearly visible in the present-day relief. In some cases sand-dunes were developed on their surface.

One may distinguish four main stages in the evolution of the environment, each of which corresponds to particular features in the interplay between population and the resources:

1. Late Glacial: 15,000-10,000 uncal BP
2. Early Holocene: 10,000-8000 uncal BP
3. Climatic Optimum: 8000-5000 uncal BP
4. Post-optimum: 5000-2000 uncal BP

Initial Settlement

The initial penetration of human groups into northwestern Russia occurred during the Late Glacial. The earliest sites in the West Dvina area of the Pskov oblast' (sites of Ivantsov Bor, Lukashenki and others) were found on the sand dunes developed on the surface of the terraces of the residual ice-dammed lakes. The tool-kits of the surface sites include tanged points of the Swiderian type, an Epi-Palaeolithic tradition spread predominantly in central-eastern Poland, Bielorussia, and in northern Ukraine. Existing geochronological evidence suggests that these sites corresponded to the Younger Dryas, a cold spell which occurred between 11,000 and 10,000 uncal BP, when full glacial conditions were re-installed in Europe (Berger, 1990).

There exist several hypotheses concerning the origin of the Swiderian tradition. Several scholars, focussing on the typological similarity of Swidry points with leaf-shaped Upper Palaeolithic implements, link the Swiderian with the Central European Upper Palaeolithic (Schild 1975). Gurina (1965) saw the origin of the Swiderian in the assemblage of Borshevo II on the river Don. The stratified site of Grensk on the river Sozh (Bud'ko 1970) seems to prove the local development of the Swiderian in that area. The lower level of the site contains implements similar to those of the Upper Palaeolithic sites situated in the same basin (Yudinovo, Gontsy etc.).

Hence one may conclude, that the Swiderian assemblages in the Northern and Northeast European plain resulted mostly from the gradual migration of population groups from the areas of Upper Palaeolithic sites in the periglacial zone: from sites in Central Europe, and from the basins of Dnieper and Don. The subsistence of these groups was mostly based on nomadic hunting of reindeer. Their seasonal camps were restricted to the areas richest in biomass: the shores of residual ice-dammed basins and the related hydraulic network.

While retaining their cultural identity, Swiderian groups were in constant contact with economically and socially similar groups of different origin within the wider area of Northern Europe. These contacts were responsible for the culturally related types of tools, such as Ahrensburg and Lyngby points, which have been occasionally discovered in the studied area.

Mesolithic

The transition to the Holocene saw a marked increase in temperature throughout Europe. Considerable thermal maxima were recorded in the Boreal (9000 ±200 uncal BP), and Early Atlantic (7500 ±200 uncal BP). At the same time, due to the drainage of the Baltic Ice Lake, and the subsequent lowering of the base of erosion, the level in the residual ice-dammed lakes dropped in the Early Holocene.

Throughout Northern Europe, the Early Holocene featured the development of mesolithic groups. In the eastern Baltic area and in the neighbouring regions of Russia, sites belong to the Kunda culture. These sites were normally located in wetland landscapes: either within inshore lagoons in the coastal area, or on the banks of shallow lakes. The subsistence pattern was based on hunting of forest game (elk, wild pig, red deer), sea mammals (seal) and waterfowl, and on fishing (Paaver, 1965). Culturally, the Early Holocene mesolithic in the area may be seen as a direct continuation of the preceding Late Glacial tradition. One notes no significant changes in the settlement and subsistence patterns.

No major mesolithic sites have so far been found in the upper West Dvina area. Scattered finds of flint, bone and antler tools of mesolithic type, found predominantly on the low-lying terraces of lakes and rivers, suggest the existence of a mesolithic tradition basically similar to Kunda. One may argue that the early mesolithic sites in the area were located on the contemporary lake shore-lines during a considerable drop in the level of the lakes. In that case these sites could have been buried under lake sediments of a later age.

Early Neolithic

According to the modern evidence of Soviet scientists (Khotinsky *et al* 1991) based on palynological records and radiocarbon measurements from various parts of the Russian Plain, the Climatic Optimum (Atlantic) manifested itself in at least two warm culminations: 7500 ± 200 uncal BP (AT-1) and 5000 ± 500 uncal BP (AT-3). Based mostly on the palynological records, Zubakov (1986) argues that the Climatic Optimum in the northern hemisphere took effect from a 7% increase of the mean summer temperature combined with a pronounced increase in the concentration of carbon dioxide in the atmosphere . Investigations carried out in the Upper Dvina basin (Dolukhanov *et al* 1989) have indicated a pronounced cool interval (AT-2) which separated two culminations of the warm-loving species. The cool interval was dated to *c* 6200 uncal BP.

Another important feature of the Climatic Optimum in northwestern Russia was repeated fluctuation in the lake-levels. Systematic investigations carried out in a number of lacustrine basins in Latvia and in the southern part of the Pskov oblast' (Dolukhanov 1978) have identified a number of fluctuations in lake-levels, which were more or less synchronous with that of the level of the Littorina sea. The following pattern emerges based on the evidence obtained for three lake basins: Lubana in eastern Latvia, and Usvyaty and Zhizhitsa in the Pskov oblast' :

Table 1

Age uncal BP	Lake	Phenomenon
7500-6000	Lubana	Transgression
6000-5000	Lubana, Usvyaty, Zhizhitsa	Regression
5000-4500	Lubana, Usvyaty, Zhizhitsa	Transgression
c 4500	Lubana, Usvyaty	Regression
4500-4000	Lubana, Usvyaty, Zhizhitsa	Transgression
4000-3800	Lubana, Usvyaty	Regression

Rudnya Serteya (Fig. 11.2)

The next important innovation in the cultural development of the local population in the eastern Baltic area was the beginning of the production of pottery. One of earliest sites with evidence of pottery is Rudnya Serteya in the Upper West Dvina (Dolukhanov *et al* 1989). Judging from the geomorphology of the river valley and from the stratigraphy of deposits, one may suggest that during Late Glacial times there occurred a chain of small residual ice-dammed lakes. The Rudnya Serteya site was located in the off-shore area of the northern lake, 2.5 km south of the discharge channel.

The finds belonging to the earlier layer (A) were made in a layer of calcareous gyttja overlying silt of Late Glacial age. The stone inventory included an axe-like tool, retouched blades and fragments, and unretouched flakes. The same layer contained fragments of 10-12 pottery vessels. This pottery was of a poor quality; it was made of clay tempered with sand, which included quartz, muscovite, feldspar and organic matter. The walls of vessels were either 5-8 or 10 mm thick. The diameter of neck was 16-22 cm. Rims were straight, bottoms conical. Judging from the pot-sherds one may suggest mitre-shaped vessels, 30-40 cm high. Simple ornamental patterns consisted of horizontal, vertical or diagonal rows of triangular impressions. On the bottom one notes rows of impressions radiating from the centre. The pottery assemblage has no direct analogies in

the neighbouring territory. Miklyayev *et al* (1990) suggest relationship with the Russian southeast.

The site was abandoned due to an abrupt rise in the level of the lake. In the course of the following transgression of the lake, the earlier cultural deposits were partially washed away, partly redeposited in the calcareous gyttya. Several radiocarbon measurements of the sample from this layer show an age of 6200 uncal BP. Pollen analysis shows a considerable reduction in the percentage of species of mixed oak forest (oak, elm, lime). Alder was the most common tree pollen.

The geochronological data recently obtained at various sites seem to indicate that large-scale production of pottery started more or less synchronously in the entire area of the northeastern Baltic. The following dates were obtained for the earliest pottery-bearing levels at Zvidze in Lubana: 6315 ± 60 uncal BP and 6260 ± 60 uncal BP (Loze 1988). Practically the same age (*c* 6200 uncal BP) is attested by Siiriainen (1974) on the basis of the gradient/time curve, for the earliest comb ceramic style in Finland. In the southwestern Baltic, in the off-shore area of Denmark, only slightly younger dates (6010 ± 95 uncal BP and 5970 ± 95 uncal BP) were obtained for the earliest Ertebølle sites (Andersen and Johansen 1986).

It is noteworthy that these dates for the beginning of pottery production in the Baltic area coincide with the cool interval (AT-2) which interrupted the Climatic Optimum and with a marked regression of both the lakes and the

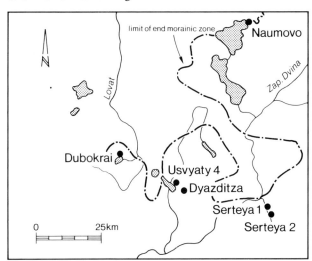

Fig. 11.2 Prehistoric lake settlements in Northwestern Russia

Littorina Sea. The mechanism of interaction of cultural process and ecological change is far from being clear, but it hardly could be unrelated.

The overlying stratum (layer B) at Rudnya-Serteya contained remains of some 30 vessels, 20 to 30 cm in diameter. The vessels were made of clay tempered with sand, organic matter and crushed shells. A series of smaller vessels (diameter: 10-20 cm) were made of clay tempered predominantly by crushed shells and organic matter. The walls were

4-5 mm thick. Both the outer and inner surface of the vessels were smoothed by denticulated stamps. Rims were either straight or S-shaped with either rounded or sharpened rims. In one case a fragment of rounded bottom was found. The vessels were ornamented by comb and triangular impressions, dots and strokes which formed horizontal and (rarely) diagonal rows. One notes zonal patterns: the ornaments were clustered either beneath the rim or in the upper part of the body. In one case a conical asymmetric beaker was found: 11 cm high, 12 cm in diameter, decorated by concentric circles of comb impressions.

The stone industry included bipolar and unipolar cores, end-scrapers, angular burins, ovoid axes with partially retouched cutting edge, an elliptic adze, rhomboid arrowheads, blades and flakes. The bone and antler industry consisted of 12 implements, which included a unilateral tanged harpoon, biconical needle-like points, a tanged point, a knife and several points and axes made of tubular bones.

Thirty radiocarbon measurements obtained so far fall into a limited time-span: 6200-6000 uncal BP. The pollen spectra obtained for layer B show the maximum in content of broad-leaved species, reaching 34%, and a reduction in the percentage of alder. Numerous seeds and macrofossils of aquatic plants include *Nymphaea* sp. and *Ceratophyllum* sp.

The overall appearance of the cultural assemblage is compatible with the Narva culture which was widely spread at that time in the surrounding areas and which lasted till *c* 5000 uncal BP. The economy of the Narva sites in the eastern Baltic area was largely dependent on the hunting of forest game: elk, wild pig were the most common. Red deer, brown bear, marten, beaver, badger are identified among the prey. Seal was common in the coastal sites (Paaver

1965). *Anatidae* and, particularly, mallard were dominant among waterfowl. Pike was the most common among the fish remains. Other species include: catfish, pike-perch, carp, perch, carp-bream. Gathering is evident from the occurrence of water chestnut in large numbers.

The artefactual assemblages of the early pottery-bearing sites in the entire Baltic area bear witness to cultural continuity from the preceding stage. This continuity is particularly well attested in the typology of lithics and bone and antler implements. If one adds to that the basic similarity in settlement and subsistence pattern, the implication that the transition to pottery production was not accompanied by any kind of population change seems obvious. On the other hand, one notes similarity in the ornamental patterns found on Narva pottery on the one hand, and that of the Early Neolithic 'monochrome' pottery of Southeast Europe on the other. One of the possible explanations lies in the existence of large-scale contacts between agricultural and non-agricultural groups in eastern and northeastern Europe (Dolukhanov 1978).

Developed Neolithic

The overlying deposits found at Rudnya and other sequences in the West Dvina basin and elsewhere in the northwest and in the centre of the Russian Plain palynologically correspond to the Early Sub-boreal stage (SB-1), 5000-4000 uncal BP. The corresponding pollen spectra featured the maximum values of spruce pollen (38-42%), with elm, oak and lime diminishing down to 7-9%, and alder constituting 7-9%. One should note that various palaeoclimatic records (Zubakov 1986,250) indicate the global cooling of climate about 5200-5000 uncal BP, which corresponded to a decrease in the concentration of carbon dioxide in the atmosphere, reaching the present-day level.

The Early Sub-boreal stage in the investigated area coincided with an extremely important phase in the development of wetland settlement. In a number of residual lakes (Usvyaty, Zhizhitsa, Rudnya and others), one can see the emergence of large pile-dwelling types of settlement. Such neolithic lacustrine dwellings are known also from other regions of European Russia. Among the best investigated sites, Modlona in the Vologda oblast' (Bryusov 1951) should be mentioned. Occurrence of pile constructions was attested at the Šventoji sites in northwestern Lithuania (Rimantiene 1980), in the Sarnate lagoon in western Latvia (Vankina 1970) and at the sites in the Lubana lowland in eastern Latvia (Loze 1979).

The spatial analysis of pile-dwelling sites in the area studied revealed a clear settlement pattern. In all cases the catchment area of the sites included three distinct landscape features: 1) lake including low-lying terraces and inshore mires; 2) end-morainic highland with predominantly clayey soils; 3) glaciofluvial plain with podzolic sandy soils (Fig. 11.3). The economy of the sites was based on the effective exploitation of wild resources of all the three landscape features. At least 40 species of mammals and

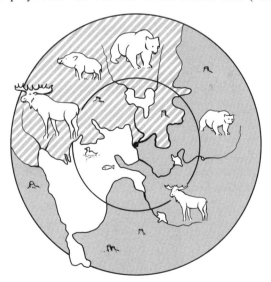

▨ End-morainic upland
▦ Glaciofluvial plain

Fig. 11.3 Neolithic site catchment pattern, based on Naumovo

birds were identified in the layers of the studied sites. They included large mammals: elk, brown bear and wild pig. The hunting of these animals provided the bulk of the meat diet. Among the fur animals, one notes marten, otter and squirrel. Judging from the age groups, elk was hunted the year round. Large amounts of fish-bone suggest the considerable economic importance of fishing. Pike, perch and pike-perch were the most common. Food-gathering was extremely important. Gathering of hazel-nut and water chestnut provided the main sources of protein intake.

The archaeological assemblages corresponding to the initial stages in the development of pile-dwellings are considered by Miklyayev as belonging to the 'Usvyaty culture'. They include rich lithic and bone and antler industries. Pottery includes conical vessels made of clay tempered with sand, crushed shells and crushed pottery (chamotte). The pottery was decorated by extremely rich and varied ornamental patterns, some of which show similarity with ornamentation of Funnel beakers in the western Baltic area.

Detailed multidisciplinary research which included minute stratigraphic control, enabled one to follow the development of the pile settlement in relation to fluctuations in the lake level. The initial settlement at Usvyaty emerged during the transgression of the lake, and radiocarbon dating of the corresponding deposits gave results of 4830 ± 80 uncal BP(TA-242) and 4579 ± 70 uncal BP(TA-105).

The succeeding structures were found in the overlying layers of gyttja. They were located closer to the shore, probably due to a rise in the lake level. Two radiocarbon measurements obtained for this stage were: 4310 ± 80 uncal BP(TA-243) and 4210 ± 70 uncal BP(TA-202). The constructions of this stage were completely destroyed by fire. New structures arose in their place, and their remains were found in the overlying strata. The new dwellings occurred during the subsequent regression of the lake, and one radiocarbon measurement was obtained for this stage: 4100 ± 70 uncal BP(TA-203).

At about the same time, a pile settlement emerged at Naumovo, situated in the inshore area of the lake of Zhizhitsa. A series of radiocarbon measurements obtained for this site has a mean value of 4000± 100 uncal BP. Thereafter a major rise in the lake level was recorded in both lakes, during which course the pile dwellings were buried under thick layers of sand.

Late Neolithic

The subsequent stage in the local pollen sequence is referred to as Middle Sub-boreal (SB-2). This stage, identified elsewhere in the Russian Plain (Khotinsky *et al* 1991) featured a general increase in mixed oak forest and alder accompanied by a corresponding drop in the percentage of spruce. The radiocarbon dates obtained for this stage in the Upper West Dvina area fall within 4000-3600 uncal BP.

In the investigated lakes, a new drop in level is recorded. At this stage, new pile-dwellings arose at the top of the sand deposits which were formed during the preceding transgression. The radiocarbon dates obtained so far for dwellings of this phase at various sites in the area nearly exactly match the age of the SB-2 vegetational phase: 4000-3600 uncal BP.

The archaeological assemblages from the layers of this stage are referred to by Miklyayev as belonging to the 'North-Byelorussian culture'. One notes a rich lithic industry. By contrast, the bone and antler industry is notably poor, as compared to the preceding stage. The most significant change is recorded in the pottery, which contained elements similar to Corded Ware, both in the vessel shapes and in ornamental patterns.

Starting around 4500-4400 uncal BP, groups of the Corded Ware Culture spread through the greater part of central and eastern Europe. The homogenous Corded Ware assemblages (exemplified by the Single Graves in southern Scandinavia) spread in the southwestern Baltic at around 4250-4150 uncal BP. Elsewhere, in Poland and along the southern Baltic coast, one notes heterogeneous cultures: Zlota, Rzuczewo and others. A number of Corded-related assemblages are noted in the eastern Baltic and in the Russian Plain (East Baltic Corded Ware, Fatyanovo, North-Byelorussian etc.).

It is generally accepted that the economy of the Corded Ware groups in central and northern Europe was based on stock-breeding with a dominance of ovicaprids. Malmer (1962, 280) notes that several Corded Ware groups in southern Scandinavia were engaged in agriculture. The economy of the heterogeneous Rzuczewo group, which was located along the southern Baltic coast, was based on hunting and fishing (Machnik 1970).

The spread of the Corded Ware pottery style in the northeastern Baltic area failed to modify the stable settlement and subsistence pattern which had been established there since the Late Glacial. As shown in the faunal analysis of the stratified lake dwellings in the Upper West Dvina (Dolukhanov and Miklyayev 1986), the introduction of Corded pottery there coincided with the appearance of a limited number of the bones of domesticated animals (sheep, goat, pig, cattle),the total number never exceeding 14%. This rate was even lower at the sites in the Lubana depression (*c* 6%). Few cattle bones were recorded at the Corded Ware sites in Estonia (Tamula) and in Lithuania (Šventoji).

Based on the stratigraphical and geochronological evidence, five stages in the development of the lacustrine pile dwellings in the Upper Dvina have been identified (Dolukhanov and Miklyayev 1986). Calculation of the similarity indices for the various groups of archaeological material (Dolukhanov and Miklyayev 1977) shows a change in material culture corresponding with the transition from stage III to stage IV, i.e. from the Usvyaty to the

North-Byelorussian (Corded Ware) Culture. The most abrupt change was observed in the composition of the bone and antler industry; the smoothest in the lithic implements. As for the pottery, the transition was fairly gradual: at least three types of vessels and 12 ornamental patterns remained unchanged throughout the existence of the lakeside settlements. The ornamental patterns of the entire pottery corpus were processed by means of multivariate analysis (Dolukhanov and Fonyakov 1984), which identified two clearly distinguishable clusters, of which the new one (Corded Ware) was gradually absorbed by the old one.

Based on the aforesaid analysis, the conclusion is made that the transition from the 'sub-neolithic' to the Corded Ware cultures in the northeastern Baltic area was a gradual one. No major change in the population was involved. One may assume that in the Post-Optimum climatic conditions, economic and cross-cultural exchange intensified in the entire Baltic area. This included the transaction of matter, energy and information. In symbolic terms it meant the spread of pottery designs, which are seen as indicative of an interaction in the ideational realm. In the sphere of production, one can witness the inclusion of elements of stock-breeding in the pattern of a predominantly foraging economy. Both the ideational and economic novelties failed to disrupt the stable local system based on the dominance of foraging strategies. It took at least one more millennium until the agricultural revolution finally gained ground in the northeastern Baltic area.

BIBLIOGRAPHY

Andersen, S.H. and Johansen,E. 1986. Ertebølle revisited. *Journal of Danish Archaeology* 5, 31-61.

Berger, W.H. 1990. The Younger Dryas cold spell: a quest for causes. *Palaeogeography, Palaeoclimatology, Palaeoecology* 89, 219-237.

Brjusov, A. Ja. 1951. Svajnoe poselenie na reke Modlone i drugie stojanki v Charozjorskom raione Vologodskoi oblasti. *Materialy i issledovanija po archeologii SSSR, Moscow,* 20,7-76.

Bud'ko, V.D. 1980. Paleolit. In V.F. Isaenko(ed.), *Ocerki po arkheologii Belorussii,* 9-48. Minsk: Nauka i Tekhnika.

Dolukhanov,P.M. 1978. *Ecology and Economy in the Neolithic Eastern Europe.* London: Duckworth.

Dolukhanov, P.M. 1979. *Geografija kamennogo veka.* Moscow: Nauka.

Dolukhanov, P.N. and Fonyakov, D.I. 1984. Modelirovanie kul'turno-istoriceskih processov. In V. Masson (ed.), *Kompleksnye metody izucenija istorii s dvevneisih vremjon do nasih dnei,* 33-35. Moscow: Nauka.

Dolukhanov, P.M., Gey, N.A., Miklyayev, A.M. and Mazurkiewicz, A.N. 1989. Rudnya-Serteya, a stratified site in the Upper Dvina basin. *Fennoscandia archaeologica* VI, 23-26.

Dolukhanov, P.M. and Miklyayev, A.M. 1969. Paleogeografija i absolutnaja hronologija pamjatnikov neolita i bronzy v basseine Zapadnoj Dviny. In M.I.Neistadt (ed.), *Golocen,* 120-128. Moscow: Nauka.

Dolukhanov, P.M. and Miklyayev, A.M. 1977. Kul'turno-istoriceskie osnovy absolutnoi chronologii neolita i rannei bronzy v basseine Zapadnoj Dviny. *Kratkie soobscenija Instituta archeologii AN SSSR* 157, 73-81.

Dolukhanov, P.M. and Miklyayev, A.M. 1986. Prehistoric lacustrine pile dwellings in the north-western part of the USSR. *Fennoscandia archaeologica* III, 81-89.

Gurina, N.N. 1965. Novye dannye o kamennon veke severozapadnoi Belorussii. *Materialy i issledovanija po archeologii SSSR* 131, 141-203.

Khotinsky, N.A., Aleshinskaja, Z.V., Guman,M.A., Klimanov,V.A. and Cherkinsky,A.E. 1991. Novaja shema periodizatsii landshavtno-klimaticheskih izmenenij v golocene. *Izvestija Akademii Nauk SSSR - serija geograficheskaja,* No 3,30-41.

Kvasov, D.D. 1979. *The Late Quaternary history of large lakes and inland seas of Eastern Europe.* Annales Academiae Scientiarum Fennicae. Series A. III. v.127.

Loze, I.A. 1979. *Pozdnij neolit i rannjaja bronza Lubanskoi ravniny.* Riga: Zinatne.

Loze, I.A. 1988. *Poselenija kamennogo veka Lubanskoi niziny. Mezolit, rannii i srednii neolit.* Riga: Zinatne.

Machnik, J. 1970. The Corded Ware cultures and cultures from the turn of the Neolithic and Bronze Age. In T.Wyslanski (ed.), *The Neolithic in Poland,* 384-420. Warszawa: PAN.

Malmer, M.P. 1962. Jungneolithische Studien. *Acta Archaeologica Ludensia.* Lund.

Miklyayev, A.M.,Dolukhanov, P.M., and Guman, M.A. 1984. Usvyaty IV, Naumovo - ozjornye poselenija epoh neolita i bronzy v verhoviah Zapadnoi Dviny. In A.Velichko (ed.), *Arheologija i paleogeografija mezolita i neolita Russkoj ravniny,* 67-81. Moscow: Nauka.

Miklyayev, A.M., Kototkievich, B.S. and Mazurkievich, A.N. 1990. Rezul'taty arheologicheskih issledovanij na juge Pskovskoj i na severe Smolenskoy oblastej v 1962-1987 godah. In G.I. Smirnova (ed.), *Itogi arheologicheskih ekspeditsij,* 9-14. Leningrad: Ermitazh.

Miklyayev, A.M. and Semyonov,V.A. 1979. Svajnoe poselenie na Zhizhitskom ozere. *Trydy gosudarstvennogo Ermitazha* XX,5-22.

Paaver, K. 1965. *Formirovanie terriofauny i izmenchivost' mlekopitajushchih Pribaltiki v golocene.* Tartu: Akademia Nauk Estonskoi SSR.

Rimantiene, R.K.1980. *Sventoji. Pamariu kulturos gyvenvuetes.* Vilnius: Mokslas.

Schild,R. 1975. Pózni paleolit. In W. Hensel (ed.), *Prahistoria Ziem Polskich,* t.1. 159-338. Warszawa-Wroclaw: PAN.

Siiriainen, A. 1974. Studies relating to shore displacement and Stone Age chronology in Finland. *Finkst Museum* 1973, 5-22.

Vankina, L.V. 1970. *Torfjanikovaja stojanka Sarnate.* Riga: Zinatne.

Zubakov,V.A. 1986. *Global' nye klimaticeskie processy pleistocena.* Leningrad: Gidrometeoizdat.

12

AN EVOLVING REVOLUTION IN WET SITE RESEARCH ON THE NORTHWEST COAST OF NORTH AMERICA

Dale R. Croes

SYNOPSIS

Since 1950 AD, with the onset of larger-scale systematic archaeology on the southern Northwest Coast of North America, archaeologists have known that wet site deposits with perishable artefacts were occasionally encountered at the watertable depths of shellmidden excavations. The 1960s witnessed a testing of three large wet sites, Bieder-bost, Hoko River and Ozette Village. The 1970s represented a flowering of wet site exploration, with ten sites hydrauli-cally excavated and reported in an overview conference volume. This peak decade of field investigations has been followed by attempts to incorporate the unique wet site data sets into the overall picture of Northwest Coast prehistory. Numerous surprises have arisen. The perishable artefacts demonstrate very contrary patterns of cultural evolution when compared with patterns represented by stone, bone and shell artefacts, causing a complete rethinking of the meaning of previously defined phase sequences along the Northwest Coast. The understanding of prehistoric eco-nomies and of the possible continuities of ethnic traditions has been greatly revised as well.

Following England's Captain James Cook's visit to Noot-ka Sound on March 29, 1778, the Western world was first exposed to the unique and exceptionally rich hunter-fisher-gatherer cultures to be found along the Northwest Coast of North America (Fig. 12.1). Villages, or perhaps better termed towns, of thousands of people, with huge cedar plank houses, hundreds of large cedar dugout canoes, a stylized and large-scale art tradition, lived off efficient and intense fishing, hunting (including capture of even the largest mammal, the whale) and gathering of shellfish and plant foods.

Fig. 12.1 Location Map

How these coastal people had evolved into the last re-maining highly complex societies based solely on hunting, fishing and gathering fascinated the earliest North Ameri-can anthropologists, with considerable early ethnographic focus on recording their cultures. However the actual roots of this complexity could properly be approached only through archaeology, with one major problem: the majority of their often monumental structures, art and material cul-ture was made of wood and fibre. In fact Philip Drucker, one of the first anthropologists to explore the archaeological potential in this area in the late 1930s, attributed the long neglect of archaeological research on the Northwest Coast to "the belief that the coastal sites are small and few, that they are poor in artifactual material, and that much of what material they contain is so poorly preserved ... as to be irrecoverable" (1943,23).

To help counteract this view and to encourage systematic investigations Drucker further reported from his 1938 survey that "along the entire coast, sites ... are both numerous and large" and the artefactual content was good, and that not only objects of stone, bone and shell, but "even ... of wood are well preserved even in the deepest of the perpetually damp levels." He noted further that although "the wood comes out fairly sound ... on drying it tends to check and crack" (Drucker 1943, 114). But despite his lobbying attempts, Drucker left archaeology to pursue a career as a noted ethnographer on the Northwest Coast.

In the early 1950s systematic archaeological investigations began in earnest in the southern portion of the Northwest Coast. Large and deep shellmidden sites were reported, rich in fauna, and limited in quantities of stone, bone and shell artefacts. These non-perishable artefacts were adequate to begin establishing a series of archaeological phases which still frame the cultural sequences of the region (Borden 1970; Mitchell 1971).

The early shellmidden explorations often reached a watertable and commonly perishable artefacts were noted, but further investigations ceased, apparently because the basketry, cordage and wooden artefacts were quite "foreign" to the shellmidden researchers, and added little to the culture history focus of their studies. Also the problem of conservation could not, at that time, be addressed. A recent survey of site reports from lower mainland British Columbia shell middens revealed an amazing 28 wet sites encountered in these early explorations, of which only three have been given any serious archaeological attention to date (Kathyrn Bernick 1991).

During the 1950s two beautiful wood sculptures were found, providing additional interest in the possibility of preserved wooden artefacts in sites. The first and best known is the Skagit River atlatl, said to have been dredged from the river mouth area in 1952, and now radiocarbon dated to $1,700 \pm 100$ uncal BP (Fladmark *et al* 1987). The second, discovered after flooding on the Snoqualmie River in 1959, was a beautiful carved cedar bowl, now said to have disintegrated following recovery (Nordquist 1976).

In the 1960s three significant wet sites were recognized in western Washington State and preliminary attempts were made at excavation and preservation. The earliest effort, beginning in 1959, was conducted by a public archaeological group, the Washington Archaeological Society, at the Biederbost Site (45SN100) on the Snoqualmie River near Seattle, Washington and just downriver from the carved bowl (Fig. 12.2. Nordquist 1976). The amateur group used traditional trowel and shovel excavation techniques, frequently having their squares fill with water and needing to

be bailed. The perishable artefacts were cleaned in the river and then taken to a field laboratory where they were preserved by applying a 25% Plyamul Adhesive #9153 (polyvinyl acetate solution, Reichold Chemical) and 75% Firewater (50cc heavy detergent of Firewater Company of Los Altos, California mixed with 5 gallons of water), stabilizing the perishables, but leaving them brittle and hard upon drying (Nordquist 1976).

Two additional wet sites located in the late 1960s on the northwest tip of the Olympic Peninsula, Washington State, would set the stage for developing hydraulic excavation techniques: Ozette Village (45CA24) and Hoko River (45CA213). At the end of the 1967 season of shell midden excavation at Ozette, a nearby test excavation exposed the corner of a plank longhouse buried under clay at a depth of 3 m in water-saturated deposits. A carved wooden sleeping bench, mats and baskets were observed, all in an excellent state of preservation, but because of the lateness of the season this discovery could not be further pursued (Draper 1989).

At the same time, a local resident, Dave McMinn, visited the Ozette site and reported another waterlogged site buried under 3 metres of silt, sand and gravel deposits and exposed near the mouth of the Hoko River. A crew visited the site using Mr. McMinn's boat and he offered the use of a fire pump and hoses to help expose additional perishable artefacts seen at the site (Daugherty 1969, Croes 1976, 209-212). This initiated the first known use of hydraulic excavation which has become the major technique for wet site excavations along the Northwest Coast.

The 1970s experienced a wet site heyday, with at least 10 sites investigated using hydraulic excavation techniques. At Ozette, the excavators used four hydraulic pumps in tandem to begin uncovering an entire section of the waterlogged Indian village which was encased under a massive clay mudslide (method illustrated in Gleeson and Grosso 1976). Ozette and most other Northwest Coast wet sites are considered as spring-fed aquifer wet sites, with relatively rapid movement of water flowing through vegetal mat layers that have been encased within either alluvial, tidal or mudslide sediment deposits. This contrasts with wetland peat-bog sites, where water is typically slow moving or stagnant in basin-like deposits. The slope of the aquifer wet sites allows the use of hydraulic excavation techniques, since water can readily drain from the site area during excavation. (Though less commonly reported, true peat-bog sites do occur on the Northwest Coast, with good examples including the Manis Mastodon site (45CA218; Gustafson *et al* 1979) and a site in the vicinity of the Martin Site (45PC7))

In the aquifer wet sites, the waters moving into the vegetal mats have released their oxygen in upper layers (or in oxidized orange pans directly above the vegetal mats) and the environment is deep enough to remain oxygen free.

All ten investigated sites were reported in 1974 at a regional wet site symposium and a combined report pro-

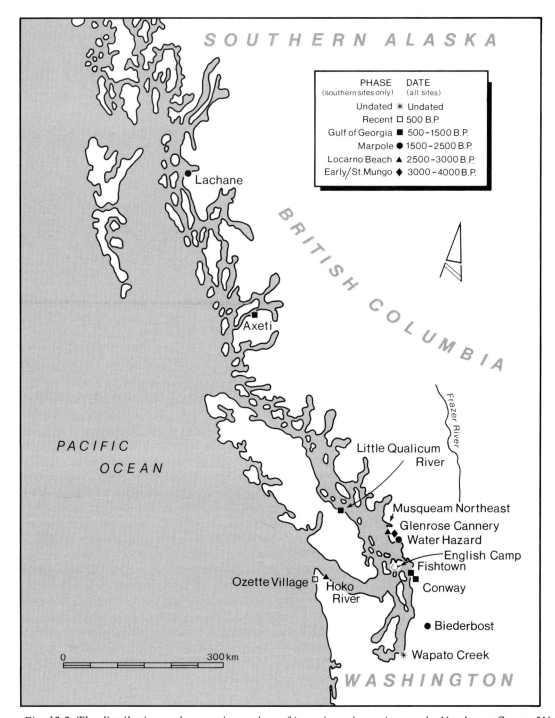

Fig. 12.2 The distribution and approximate date of investigated wet sites on the Northwest Coast of North America.

duced (Croes 1976). Much discussion centred around their significance and whether we were ready to excavate these sites. A general feeling seemed to circulate that we needed to sit back and assess their value and that we needed to perfect our conservation techniques. However, at the same time, predictions were being made concerning the future of wetland archaeology on the Northwest Coast. George Mac-Donald had reported to the Archaeological Institute of America in early 1971:

Archaeological activity on the coast is beginning to concentrate attention on sites with exceptionally good preservation, since 95% of the artistic products and all

the architecture was of highly perishable materials and can only be reconstructed by excavating such sites. I am confident that within five years we will have numerous examples of houses, carved boxes, masks, and utensils from all periods extending back 5,000 years and from all regions of the coast. At that time a definitive statement on the origin of Northwest Coast art and architecture will be possible. (MacDonald 1971:12)

Though an ambitious statement, and twenty years have now passed, we have determined that Northwest Coast wet sites typically produce 90-95% perishable artefacts, with

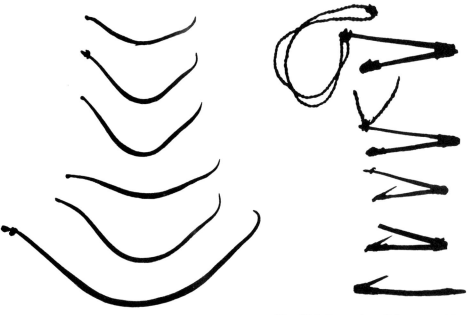

0 ——————— 10cm

Fig. 12.3 Examples of the several hundred bentwood and composite fishhooks recovered from the Hoko River wet site. Both fish-hook types are found with double twisted spruce root string leaders

only 5-10% being the previously predominant stone, bone and shell artefacts. A 90%+ rule has emerged, reflecting the emphasized use of wood and fibre as the major media of material culture on the Northwest Coast from at least 3000 years ago through to the ethnographic period. Whole houses so far have been restricted to the Ozette mudslide excavations, but large numbers of utensils and general subsistence equipment, as well as examples of clothing and dwelling components, have indeed been common. And, though not yet reaching 5000 years in age, just last summer (1990) a newly exposed wet site on the Fraser River Delta of British Columbia, Canada, in the city of Vancouver, the Glenrose Cannery Site (DgRr 6), has produced basketry and some wooden artefacts dating from 4500 uncal BP (Eldridge 1991).

The 1980s were not a period of expanded wet site field investigations, but a time of assessment of the available wet site data and how these complement the more traditional shellmidden data. As with any wet site research, the resulting surprises and contradictions, which commonly contrast to established thoughts about regional and world prehistory, have more than justified their consideration. With 90% of the material culture made from perishable materials, wet sites have been shown to be the most comprehensive medium for examining the evolution of Northwest Coast (1) subsistence technology, (2) containers, (3) shelters (housing, but also clothing), (4) transportation especially canoes, and (5) art and symbolism. I will briefly reflect on the results of research in these five areas, with particular reference to the 3000 year old wet site of Hoko River.

HOKO RIVER

This site, which lies at the mouth of the Hoko river on the northwest tip of the Olympic Peninsula, Washington State (Fig. 12.2), contains at least 45 separate and sequen-

tial vegetal mat layers deposited along a river point bar shore next to a major fishing camp, from 3000 to 2600 cal BP (Stucki 1983). The river-bottom waterlogged site deposits have been tectonically uplifted one mm per year since originally formed, now being an average 3 m higher and available for excavation during mean to low tides (Croes and Blinman 1980, Stucki 1983). Since these deposits are being rapidly eroded by a change in the river course, we have spent 9 summer field seasons (1977 through 1987) recovering an estimated 10% of the wet site deposits. The 8 main layers with 100 or more artefacts recovered demonstrated consistent mean and standard deviation percentage of the main artefact categories recovered from each layer; therefore we can predict the percentage expected of basketry, cordage, wood-working tools, fishing hooks, and other categories, from any given layer. Since this is a multi-layer wet site, we carefully compared artefacts from all layers to see if styles or types of perishable artefacts changed over the 400 year time period, but found remarkable continuity throughout.

Subsistence Technology

Northwest Coast wet site procurement artefacts, as one might expect, reflect an emphasis on fishing and secondarily hunting. Fibre nets have been found from four sites representing the past 3000 years, varying considerably in terms of construction materials, techniques and gauges (Water Hazard (DgRs 30): Bernick 1989, Stevenson 1989; Musqueam NE (DhRt 4): Borden 1976; Hoko River (45CA213): Croes 1980a; Ozette Village (45CA24): Croes 1980a). Hoko River examples are large gauge, potentially salmon gill nets, constructed of split spruce twig strands and attached to an unmodified anchor stone (Croes 1980a). Rigid lattice-work fragments, most likely used as parts of fish weirs, are also found at Hoko River and four other wet sites (Little Qualicum River (DiSc 1): Bernick 1983; Ozette

(45CA24): Croes 1980a; Conway (45SK59b): Munsell 1976b; Little Wapato Creek (45PI47): Munsell 1976a) and for examples of northern fish weir site distributions dating to as early as 3600 BP see Moss *et al* 1990.

Fishhooks were by far the most common item of fishing equipment at the early Hoko River site, with over 350 wooden fishhooks, both of bentwood (30%) and composite forms (60%), with the remaining 10% being preforms to construct bentwood hooks (Fig. 12.3). These hooks were used for offshore fishing and the faunal remains demonstrate the offshore emphasis, with 46% being flatfish (especially halibut), 32% rockfish and cod and 15% salmon (possibly also caught offshore). In combination, the abundant well preserved fishhooks and faunal remains provide very complementary data for understanding the fisheries emphasis and exact procurement equipment. This has allowed experimental behavioural studies, such as, for example, determining which types of very distinctive Hoko River hooks were used for which types of offshore fisheries. Other components of the hook-and-line equipment, including split cedar line-floats and bound anchor-stones, could also be replicated and used in these experiments (Hoff 1980).

We worked with Makah Indian people who knew how to bait the old style hooks, where the ancient fishing banks were located, and how to handle the lines once the hooks were lowered to the bottom. With little initial success in the offshore setting, the tribe and archaeologists moved to a much more controlled setting, the Seattle Aquarium, where we realized that our bone barbs needed to be set further into the V of the hook (a blatant example of not really looking closely at the prehistoric artefacts), and once adjusted we could catch anything in the aquarium.

Under these controlled circumstances we could observe the manner in which different fish took the hooks and the corresponding hooking success or lack-thereof. The archaeologically well-represented Pacific cod struck the composite hooks very aggressively, and often broke them in a manner very similar to the broken hooks at the site. The archaeologically much more common flatfish and sculpins were more cautious and rapidly sucked onto the hooks, without nearly the same striking force, and rarely broke them. From this experiment we concluded that the spring-loaded bentwood hooks were most likely for the more aggressive cod and the V-shaped composite hooks for the flatfish. Once aquarium experiments were concluded, we were able with ease to catch flatfish with the adjusted composite hooks in their natural Hoko River offshore setting

Identical bentwood fishhooks have been recorded from 3 other wet sites along the southern Northwest Coast, ranging from 1500 to 3000 uncal BP, but this exact style is not known from any later sites (Little Qualicum River (DiSc 1): Bernick 1983; Fishtown (45SK99): Onat 1976; Biederbost (45SN100): Nordquist 1976).

Another aspect of wet site subsistence technology has been identified, the fish cutting knife, consisting of split cedar stick handle with side hafted microlith flakes bound into the upper edges. The very common microliths probably could only be understood, at least in terms of function, within their wet site preserved wooden handles. Additional experimental studies, especially with the Makah ladies who were experts at cutting fish, strongly suggested that these knives were used to fillet the large quantities of flatfish being brought to the camp and prepared for sun-drying or smoking. Lithic technologist Jeff Flenniken, who organized

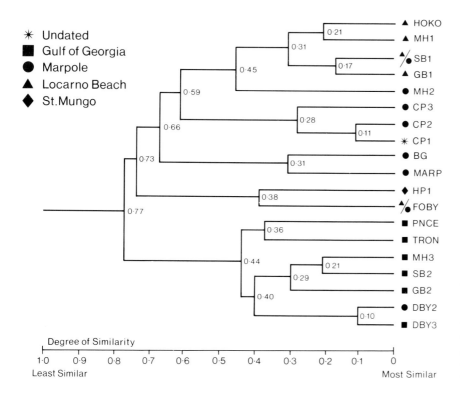

* Undated
■ Gulf of Georgia
● Marpole
▲ Locarno Beach
♦ St.Mungo

Degree of Similarity

1·0 0·9 0·8 0·7 0·6 0·5 0·4 0·3 0·2 0·1 0

Least Similar   Most Similar

Fig. 12.4 Dendrogram representing a furthest neighbour cluster analysis with 1-dice coefficient of lithic artefact types from 38 stone artefact categories common to sites in the Gulf of Georgia region and Hoko River (only sites with 11 or more types present; see Matson 1974 for site names, locations and definitions of stone categories). Note how the sites tend to cluster by established phase designations, and how Hoko River links closely with the Montague Harbour I Locarno Beach type site

103

and conducted these experiments, further believes these knives were likely made and maintained by women as the principle flintknappers (Flenniken 1981).

A less frequently encountered type of knife blade, but an important Northwest Coast phase marker, was the quartz crystal microblade. Examples were found in the dry Hoko River campsite living areas. And then, as we had always hoped, we found one, end-hafted and bound in an end-split cedar handle, giving another example of the contribution of wet sites to the understanding of the whole tool. These extremely sharp blades may have been more commonly used for fine leather cutting, or even, as some Makah Elders suggest, in minor surgery.

Projectile points include bifacially flaked and ground stone points, as well as unilaterally and bilaterally barbed carved wooden points. Typically the stone points and other lithic artefacts are used to identify the time-period and archaeological phase of site occupation. The large faceted ground slate points and the contracting-stem bifacially flaked projectile points fit well into the general 3000-2400 uncal BP Locarno Beach Phase, though Hoko River is a very western example of this typically Puget Sound/Gulf of Georgia phase (Figs. 12.4-12.5).

Seventeen barbed wooden projectile points were also recovered from the wet site area, and, though bone did

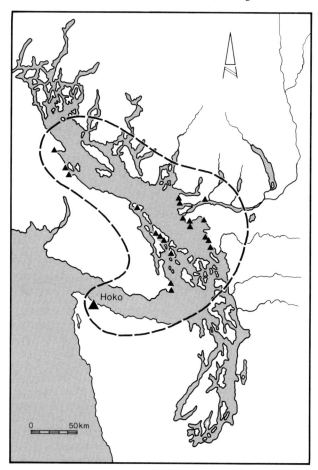

Fig. 12.5 Distribution of Locarno Beach type sites showing Hoko River's western position.

preserve in these deposits, no bone barbed projectile points were found. Therefore wooden barbed harpoon and fixed points appear to be emphasized 3000 years ago at Hoko River. These wooden points also provide much of the zoomorphically carved art at the site, to be discussed below (Fig. 12.6). Only one of these points is bilaterally barbed, with many of the remaining representing male harpoon heads, with a distinct knob on their distal ends, for socketing into the shaft or foreshaft. They commonly have a series of crescent notching as distinct line-guard edging for securing the harpoon line. Surprisingly, this form of unilaterally barbed harpoon is much more distinctive of the next archaeological phase on the Northwest Coast, the Marpole phase, although the later harpoons are made of bone and antler (type 2a and 2b, McMurdo 1972). The importance of these male harpoon heads as a Marpole phase marker has been strongly emphasised (Burley 1980).

However, as a wet site *contradiction*, the Hoko River examples indicate that this harpoon style actually was emphasized in the earlier Locarno Beach phase, *but constructed solely from wood*. In fact the evolution of these harpoons, based on presently available data, appears to go from wood in Hoko River Locarno Beach times to antler and eventually bone in the later Marpole time period (McMurdo 1972). Therefore two points (literally and figuratively) need to be emphasized: (1) all harpoons at Hoko River are wooden and so possibly were the majority at other wet sites, and (2) the use of only antler and bone examples to establish sensitive phase definitions must be discouraged until more wet site harpoons from surrounding time periods are examined.

Other parts of projectiles which occur at Hoko River and other wet sites include wooden shafts and potential atlatls. These again help in the full reconstruction of activities.

Containers: Basketry, Boxes and Bowls

Baskets are a particularly common container, characteristic of wet sites along the entire Northwest Coast for at least 4500 years. There are also some kerfed bentwood boxes and carved wooden bowls or trays. All these containers are made of fibre and wood, with ceramic containers being completely absent.

Of all artefact categories, including those of stone, bone and shell, basketry has proven to be the most stylistically sensitive and complex for comparative studies through time and across space along the entire Northwest Coast (Bernick 1988, 1989; Croes 1977, 1980b, 1988, 1989a, 1989b). All Pacific Northwest wet sites have numerous examples, and often hundreds of baskets, mats and hats. These artefacts are additive in construction, in contrast to lithics, shell and bone, which are subtractive. A wide array of construction materials, base and body construction techniques, selvages, forms, and attachments are used in combination to form basketry artefacts, providing particularly complex artefacts for comparisons.

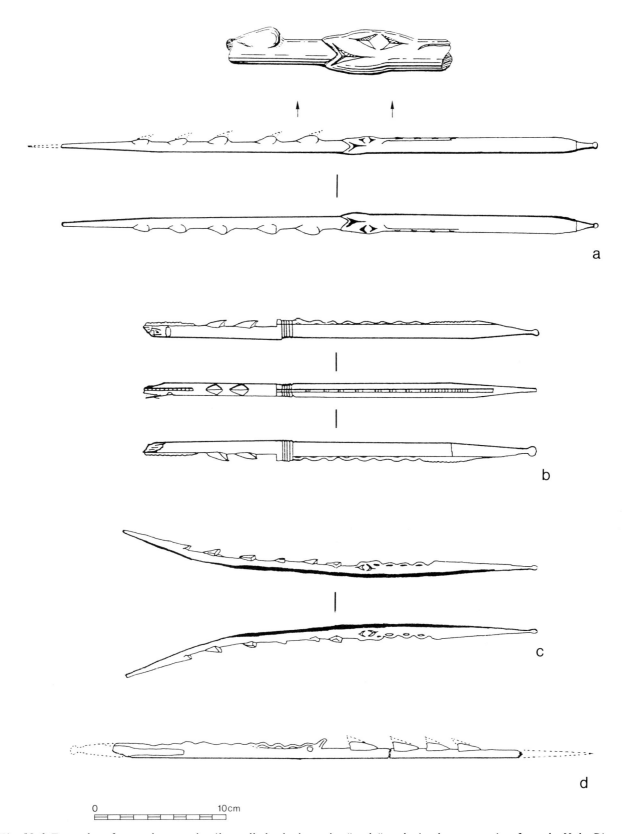

Fig. 12.6 Examples of ornately carved unilaterally barbed wooden "male" socketing harpoon points from the Hoko River wet site. a) McMinn collection #1 (water worn); b) 215/AP/1; c) Schostak collection #5 (warped from lack of preservation); d) 268/AU/2 (bird-like carving)

Probably the single most outstanding pattern derived by comparing basketry artefacts from all presently investigated Northwest Coast wet sites, is the continuity of their deep-rooted regional style in distinct coastal areas for at least 3000 years (Figs. 12.7-12.9). This contrasts sharply and crosscuts with previously established phase designations derived from changes in styles of stone, bone and shell artefacts. For example, the Hoko River lithic artefacts demonstrate a close affinity to those of the Locarno Beach Phase in the Gulf of Georgia (Fig. 12.4). However the Hoko

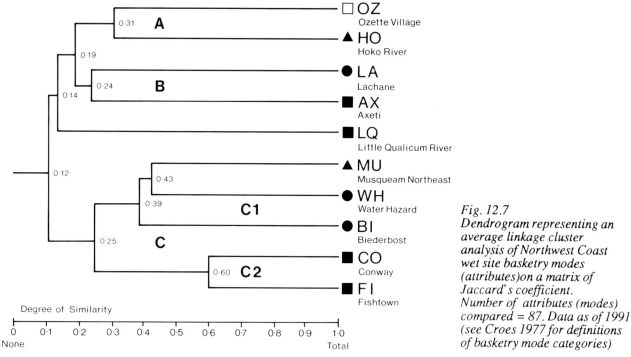

Fig. 12.7
Dendrogram representing an average linkage cluster analysis of Northwest Coast wet site basketry modes (attributes)on a matrix of Jaccard's coefficient. Number of attributes (modes) compared = 87. Data as of 1991 (see Croes 1977 for definitions of basketry mode categories)

River basketry contrasts sharply with that found at the classic 3000 year old Locarno Beach wet site of Musqueam Northeast and at the 2000 year old Marpole phase sites of Water Hazard and Biederbost in the Gulf of Georgia/Puget Sound region, and itself demonstrates complex style affinities to later Ozette wet site basketry and that distinctive of the historic period on the West Coast. The Gulf of Georgia/Puget Sound basketry illustrates its own strong stylistic continuity with sites dating from 3000 to 2000 to 1000 years and into the historic period (Croes 1989a, Fig. 1). However, the recently tested 4-4500 year old wet site of Glen Rose Cannery in the Gulf of Georgia region suggests, from a very small sample of basketry, an interesting mixing of these distinctive regional styles at this earlier period, therefore potentially styles and some aspects of ethnicity begin to diverge following this period in the southern region (Eldridge 1991).

The phase designations derived from stone, bone and shell artefacts have been demonstrated to be statistically valid (Matson 1974 and Fig. 12.4), but the regional continuity of basketry styles has required a re-assessment of *what these phase designations actually mean*. Without the wet site data, we would tend to assume the phases represent major cultural shifts and possibly replacements (e.g. Burley 1980). However the deep-set continuity exhibited by the sensitive basketry (and, to a degree, the male harpoons) tends to offset ideas of complete cultural shifts or replacements, and to reflect *in situ* ethnic continuity (Croes 1989a).

In other studies, initiated because of these wet site/non-wet site contradictions, simulation modelling of economic decision-making and its evolution in this region of the coast has provided a best-fit explanation, proposing that the defined and abrupt phase shifts represented rapid economic

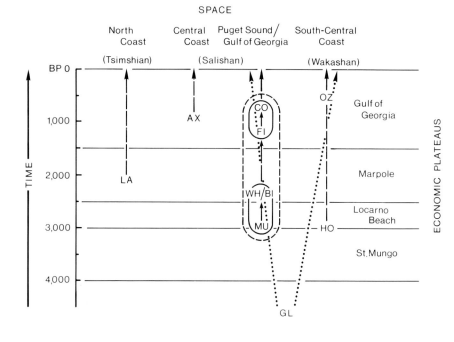

Fig. 12.8 Hypothetical stylistic or ethnic continuity patterns based on basketry and cordage artefact analyses
For full site names see Fig. 12.2

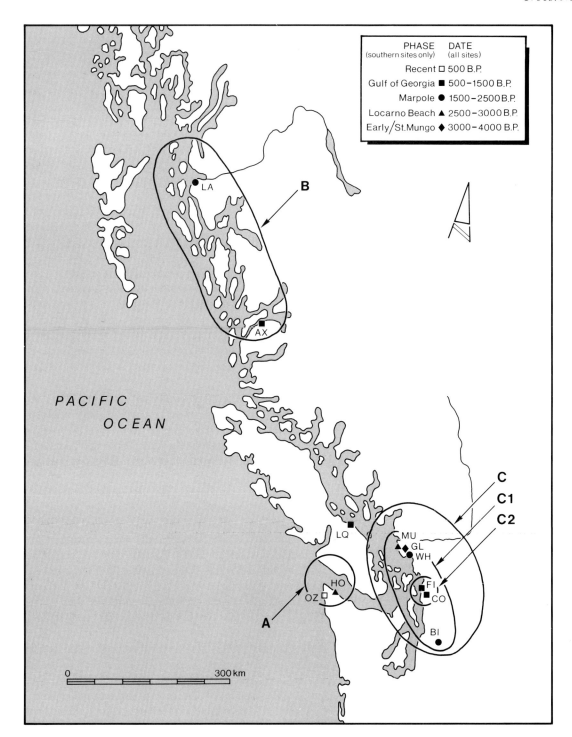

Fig. 12.9 Regional continuity of basketry and cordage styles.

adaptive shifts, which were well-reflected by the changes in subsistence-related stone, bone and shell artefacts. The previously considered cultural phases actually represent long-term stable economic plateaus or stages that were readily adapted to on a widespread basis throughout the southern Northwest Coast, regardless of the ethnic traditions, as economic solutions to the expanding and circumscribed population bases. These economic plateaus would concentrate the subsistence-related stone, bone and shell artefacts, creating a distinct phase-like marker. In this hypothetical construct the more complex and stylistically distinct basketry artefacts were not so affected by these broad and relatively quick economic shifts and most likely represent lines of ethnic continuity through time in different regions (Figs. 12.7-12.9; for the full argument, see Croes and Hackenberger 1988, Croes 1989a).

Wooden boxes and bowls are occasionally found in wet sites, though not nearly as often as basketry. Examples include, as mentioned earlier, a beautifully carved bowl washed out of the Snoqualmie River in 1959 (Nordquist 1976), and from the northern wet site of Lachane a roughed-out double bowl and distinct examples of kerfed bentwood boxes dating from 1600 uncal BP (Inglis 1976), and a corner of a dished red cedar artefact, possibly a tray, associated with the 4000 to 4500 uncal BP wet site at Glen Rose Cannery site (Eldridge 1991, 51-52). The Ozette village site produced by far the largest number of wooden containers, with 1001 wooden boxes and fragments, 120 wooden bowls and 37 wooden trays (Draper 1989). The bentwood boxes were used for storage, and also as water buckets and to hold water for cooking with heated boiling stones. The bowls and trays were likely used to serve food, or in the case of bowls to hold sea mammal oils for dipping foods.

The lack of any examples of bentwood boxes or fragments from the Hoko River site became somewhat puzzling, since the wooden wedges for splitting wood boards necessary for their construction were common and a large amount of cracked boiling stone (fire-cracked rock) was found in the campsite activity areas. This negative evidence, the lack of bentwood cooking vessels so common later at Ozette, suggested people must have been cooking in some other kind of container, which could not have been the baskets since they were not watertight. Structures that were common to the Hoko campsite areas, and quite distinctive to other sites of the Locarno Beach period, were sandstone slab lined pits. With the lack of wooden containers from all layers of the Hoko wet site, it appears these pits, probably lined with leather, formed the basins for holding water and boiling with stones. In this case the surprising *lack* of an expected wet site artefact, the bentwood box, helped to explain the use of a different type of container for cooking.

Shelter: housing, and also clothing

The most explicit examples of wet site shelters recovered are the three complete houses and three partial houses from under the mudslides at the Ozette Village site (Samuels 1983). Over 40,000 house structural elements, with many of the house planks, poles and posts broken into many pieces by the mudslide, were recovered from the encased section of a winter village dated to approximately 250 years ago by tree-ring analysis (Draper 1989; Gleeson 1983; Mauger 1978). In this encased site, the entire composition of the large shed roof houses could be characterized, from the use of C-notched upright posts carrying half-split rafter beams, to double rows of wall poles with cedar limb withies used to sling overlapping split cedar planks forming the walls, to the carefully lipped and overlapped roof boards (Mauger 1978). The inside furnishings can also be relatively easily understood, including large plank bench-bed platforms around the interior walls, central partitioned areas and family hearth areas (Samuels 1983). Of course this all needs to be reconstructed from the mudslide disturbed and redistributed setting.

Other shelters at Northwest Coast wet sites are not as directly observed, with most deposits being adjacent to living areas from where broken objects were discarded into the wet environments. The Hoko River site has been identified as a temporary spring/summer fishing station seasonally visited (Croes and Hackenberger 1988). In the actual dry campsite activity areas a dwelling area was excavated, with signs of its outline and composition (Howes 1982). Surrounding the structure was a series of large stones, assumed to anchor the walls.

As at all Northwest Coast wet sites we did find numbers of wooden wedges for splitting wood and an occasional cedar plank fragment (Croes 1980c). The wooden wedges most likely were used to split firewood for the camp. Actual cedar planks were relatively rare, and therefore not believed to be the main shelter cover material. From the shape and size of the discovered dwelling, a more likely covering would be matting, which also explains the stone weights surrounding the outline. Sewn tule mats were common at Hoko River (n = 26 examples), and found in all the major layers of the wet site. Ethnographically tule matting was a common shelter cover for temporary, pole-structure, fishing camp dwellings. The Hoko River tule mats were sewn with the most common single artefact from the site (n = 1,473 pieces), the 2-strand spruce rootlet strings, which in large part are probably deposited in the site from broken and discarded mats.

The poles used in these dwellings were most likely tied together with the second most common cordage artefacts, single strand cedar withy cords (n = 607 pieces). And the roofing material was probably stick-reinforced cedar bark shingles, also found from all major Hoko River wet site layers (n = 38 examples).

Clothing is commonly found in Northwest Coast wet sites, usually in the form of broken and discarded skirts or capes and hats. The hats particularly are interesting, since status and rank was commonly identified by the style of hat worn by the individual. Ethnographically a knob-top hat was worn by a noble or upper class and a flat-top hat worn by a commoner. At the late Ozette site this is clear (Croes 1977). From earlier sites such as Hoko River the distinction in forms is also seen, and may also be an indicator of an earlier status marking, though probably to a different degree than in the later periods (Croes 1980a). However if the hat forms did reflect some degree of status differentiation, we can assume that control of territories and their management by extended family leaders may have begun to take shape by 3000 years ago. From all indications, the emphasis and required management of procurement and storage activities, especially emphasizing sun-drying of flatfish, had been practiced by 3000 years ago at Hoko River (Croes and Hackenberger 1988).

Transportation, especially canoes

Parts of dugout canoes, and toy models of canoes in Ozette houses, have been recovered from Northwest Coast wet sites. At Hoko River we found fragments of split and carved cedar, some with lipped edges that could be gunnels from canoes, and we found tools that would be used in construction of canoes, especially wooden wedges and ground stone adze bits, and thousands of pieces of split wood and wood chip debitage indicate the active use of these tools on site, but actual large sections of damaged canoes have not been found (Paden 1980). Since the inhabitants were fishing mostly for offshore marine fish, and must have had ocean-going vessels, we can assume dugout canoes were made and used in this early period, and broken canoes probably were recycled as raw materials for other artefact manufacture.

Art and Symbolism

Art has been characterized from a number of Northwest Coast wet sites, and particularly the wealth of carved wooden art from Ozette Village (Daugherty and Friedman 1983). Other wet sites have the occasional example of art, but most of these sites are seasonal procurement camps, and large amounts of art would not necessarily be expected.

Much of the art found at Hoko River is on procurement artefacts, and especially on the wooden harpoons (Fig. 12.6). The line guards notching forms the back-bone area of zoomorphic creatures, and the area just before the barbs depicts a typically Hoko-style diamond-shaped eye and the mouth and tongue appears to be the extended series of barbs and the point. Another form of zoomorphic art at this fishing camp appears on a lure-like device probably used to attract lingcod or other fish to the surface for spearing. Other art is more geometric in nature, often with a series of notches or bands around lure-like objects, as well as on possible blanket or hair pins. This functional art might be expected from a fishing camp. Another functional example of art, but of a domestic sort, is an apparently lost (undamaged) tule mat creaser, thought to depict two birds, beak-to-beak, forming a handle. The birds are believed to be the locally common kingfisher, with the female having a band carved around her neck and the plain one being the male (Carlson 1983,205).

Other distinct and not previously mentioned art found from Northwest Coast wet sites includes a beautifully carved northern style wood handle dating from 1600 uncal BP from the Lachane site in Prince Rupert, northern coastal British Columbia (Inglis 1976). And last summer (1990) two boys contacted us with a chance-find from along the Skagit River north of Seattle, an ornately carved upright loom post made of yew wood.

CONCLUSIONS

The evolution of the wet-site revolution on the Northwest Coast has been somewhat slower than many expected, though, as I hope has been demonstrated, it now plays and will continue to play an increasingly complementary and necessary part of Northwest Coast prehistoric research and explanation. The frequent surprises and contradictions revealed through wet site excavations, besides their wealth in new information, require that their results be considered in Northwest Coast prehistory studies. We can no longer do only wet or only dry regional archaeological investigations, but we must do both, or we will not have a comprehensive perspective.

As many of the papers at the 1991 Conference have also emphasized, proper support is required to allow effective investigations, and protection of those sites endangered through erosion or drainage. Certainly their value in rounding out the picture of regional prehistories can easily justify their support by the public and funding agencies. Work also needs to continue to improve the techniques and efficiencies of preservation of perishable materials recovered. Many professionals still hesitate to enter into a wet site recovery project because they believe the most effective methods of preservation have not been developed. Probably, and fortunately for promoting this research, many wet sites need to be investigated because they are being eroded or destroyed. Those sites that must be rescued will continue to provide a needed stimulus to continually improve conservation and lead the way to vastly improved methods of preservation.

I certainly predict that after our period of sitting back and assessing the wet site resource on the Northwest Coast, we will continue to see better informed, focused, and problem oriented wet site field investigations. We have now seen part of their research potential and are only now beginning to recognize the considerable extent of this resource. We need to advance this understanding through publication of our wet site results and we need to continue efforts to evaluate and actively protect the remaining extent of the wetland cultural resource.

Acknowledgements:

The Conference Coordinators of the *Wetland Revolution in Prehistory* have made the production and presentation of this paper in Exeter, England possible. The Prehistoric Society and Bryony and John Coles are to be highly congratulated for presenting such a well organized and focused wetland conference, at a time when comparison of worldwide wet site work was most needed. In terms of this paper, the Hoko River Project research is co-sponsored by the Makah Tribal Nation, and has been made possible through support of the M.J. Murdock Charitable Trust, the National Endowment for the Humanities, and Ray and Jean Auel. Numerous project researchers, Makah community members, field personnel and students have contributed to data recovery, analysis and reporting. Though this research owes its existence to these and many previous and current researchers, the summary and conclusions remain the responsibility of the author.

BIBLIOGRAPHY

Bernick, K. 1983. *A Site Catchment Analysis of the Little Qualicum River Site, DiSc 1: A Wet Site on the East Coast of Vancouver Island, B.C.* Ottawa: National Museum of Man Mercury Series, 118.

Bernick, K. 1988. The Potential of Basketry for Reconstructing Cultural Diversity on the Northwest Coast. In R. Auger, M.F. Glass, S. MacEachern and P. McCartney (eds), *Ethnicity and Culture,* 251-257. University of Calgary, Calgary: Proceedings of the 18th Annual Chacmool Conference, Archaeological Association.

Bernick, K. 1989. *Water Hazard (DgRs 30) Artifact Recovery Project Report, Permit 1988-55.* Victoria: Archaeology and Outdoor Recreation Branch, Ministry of Municipal Affairs, Recreation and Culture, Province of British Columbia.

Bernick, K. 1991. *Wet Site Archaeology in the lower mainland region of British Columbia.* Report prepared for British Heritage Trust, Victoria, B.C., Department of Archaeology, Simon Fraser University, Burnaby, and Laboratory of Archaeology, Department of Anthropology and Sociology, University of British Columbia, Vancouver.

Borden, C. 1970. Culture history of the Fraser Delta region. In R.L. Carlson (ed.), *Archaeology in British Columbia, New Discoveries,* 95-112. B.C. Studies 6-7.

Borden, C. 1976. A Water-saturated Site on the Southern Mainland Coast of British Columbia. In D.R. Croes (ed), *The Excavation of Water-saturated Archaeological Sites (Wet Sites) on the Northwest Coast of North America,* 234-260. Ottawa: National Museum of Man Mercury Series, 50 .

Burley, D.V. 1980. *Marpole. Anthropological Reconstructions of a Prehistoric Northwest Coast Culture Type.* Burnaby: Department of Archaeology, Simon Fraser University, 8.

Carlson, R.L. 1983. Change and Continuity in Northwest Coast Art. In R.L. Carlson (ed.), *Indian Art Traditions of the Northwest Coast,* 197-205. Simon Fraser University, Burnaby, B.C.: Archaeology Press.

Croes, D.R. (ed.) 1976. *The Excavation of Water-saturated Archaeological Sites (Wet Sites) on the Northwest Coast of North America.* Ottawa: National Museum of Man Mercury Series, 50.

Croes, D.R. 1977. *Basketry from the Ozette Village Archaeological Site: A Technological, Functional and Comparative Study.* Ann Arbor: University Microfilms 77-25, 762, Ann Arbor.

Croes, D.R. 1980a. *Cordage from the Ozette Village Archaeological Site: A Technological, Functional and Comparative Study.* Washington State University, Pullman: Laboratory of Archaeology and History, 9.

Croes, D.R. 1980b. Basketry Artifacts. In D.R. Croes and E. Blinman (eds), *Hoko River: A 2,500 Year Old Fishing Camp on the Northwest Coast of North America,* 188-222. Washington State University, Pullman: Laboratory of Anthropology Reports of Investigations 58.

Croes, D.R. 1980c. Wooden wedges. In D.R. Croes and E. Blinman (eds), *Hoko River: A 2,500 Year Old Fishing Camp on the Northwest Coast of North America.* Washington State University, Pullman: Laboratory of Anthropology Reports of Investigations 58.

Croes, D.R. 1988. The Significance of the 3,000 bp Hoko River Waterlogged Fishing Camp in our Overall Understanding of Southern Northwest Coast Cultural Evolution. In B.

Purdy (ed.), *Wet Site Archaeology,* 131-152. New Jersey: Telford Press.

Croes, D.R. 1989a. Prehistoric Ethnicity on the Northwest Coast of North America, An Evaluation of Style in Basketry and Lithics. In R. Whallon (ed.), *Research in Anthropological Archaeology,* 101-130. New York: Academic Press.

Croes, D.R. 1989b. Lachane Basketry and Cordage: A Technological, Functional and Comparative Study. *Canadian Journal of Archaeology,* 13, 165-205.

Croes, D.R. and Blinman, E. (eds) 1980. *Hoko River: A 2,500 Year Old Fishing Camp on the Northwest Coast of North America.* Washington State University, Pullman: Laboratory of Anthropology Reports of Investigations 58.

Croes, D.R. and Hackenberger, S. 1988. Hoko River Archaeological Complex: Modeling Prehistoric Northwest Coast Economic Evolution. In B.L. Isaac (ed.), *Prehistoric Economies of the Pacific Northwest Coast,* 19-85. Research in Economic Anthropology, Special Supplement 3, Greenwich, Connecticut: JAI Press, Inc.

Daugherty, R.D. 1969. *Hoko River Site Research Project Proposal.* Proposal submitted to Crown Zellerbach Foundation.

Daugherty R.D. and Friedman, J. 1983. An Introduction to Ozette Art. In R.L. Carlson (ed.), *Indian Art Traditions of the Northwest Coast,* 183-195. Simon Fraser University, Burnaby, B.C.: Archaeology Press.

Draper, J.A. 1989. *Ozette Lithic Analysis.* Washington State University, Pullman, Washington 99164.

Drucker, P. 1943. Archaeological Survey on the Northern Northwest Coast. *Bureau of American Ethnology Bulletin* 133, (*Anthropological Papers* No. 20), 17-142.

Eldridge, M. 1991. *The Glenrose Cannery Wet Component: A Significance Assessment.* Permit 1990-24, Victoria: British Columbia Archaeology Branch.

Fladmark, K.R., Nelson, D.E., Brown, T.A., Vogel, J.S., and Southon, J.R. 1987. AMS Dating of Two Artifacts from the Northwest Coast. *Canadian Journal of Archaeology* 11, 1-12.

Flenniken, J.J. 1981. *Replicative Systems Analysis: A Model Applied to the Vein Quartz Artifacts from the Hoko River Site.* Washington State University, Pullman: Laboratory of Anthropology Reports of Investigation 59.

Gleeson, P. and Grosso G. 1976 Ozette Site. In D.R. Croes (ed.), *The Excavation of Water-saturated Archaeological Sites (Wet Sites) on the Northwest Coast of North America,* 13-44. Ottawa: National Museum of Man Mercury Series, 50.

Gleeson, P. (ed.) 1983. *Ozette Dendrochronological Studies.* Washington State University, Pullman: Laboratory of Anthropology.

Gustafson, C.E., Gilbow, D., and Daugherty, R.D. 1979. The Manis Mastodon Site: Early Man on the Olympic Peninsula. *Canadian Journal of Archaeology* 3, 157-164.

Hoff, R. 1980. Fishhooks. In D.R. Croes and E. Blinman (eds), *Hoko River: A 2,500 Year Old Fishing Camp on the Northwest Coast of North America,* 160-188. Washington State University, Pullman: Laboratory of Anthropology Reports of Investigations 58.

Howes, D.W. 1982. Spatial Analysis at a Northwest Coast Fishing Camp: The Hoko River Site. In D.R. Croes (ed.), *Interim Annual Report, Hoko River Archaeological Pro-*

ject, Phases XIII & XIV, Attachment N. Washington D.C.: National Endowment for the Humanities.

Inglis, R. 1976. 'Wet' Site Distribution - The Northern Case, GbTo 33 –The Lachane Site. In D.R. Croes (ed.), *The Excavation of Water-saturated Archaeological Sites (Wet Sites) on the Northwest Coast of North America*, 158-185. Ottawa: National Museum of Man Mercury Series, 50.

MacDonald, G.F. 1971. *The Origins of Northwest Coast Art and Architecture*. Paper presented to the Archaeological Institute of America, Royal Ontario Museum, Ottawa.

Matson, R.G. 1974. Clustering and Scaling of Gulf of Georgia Sites. *Syesis* 7, 101-114.

Mauger, J.E. 1978. Shed Roof Houses at the Ozette Archaeological Site: A Protohistoric Architectural System. *Washington Archaeological Research Center* 73. Washington State University, Pullman.

McMurdo, A. 1972. *A Typological Analysis of Barbed Bone and Antler Projectile Points from the Northwest Coast.* M.A. thesis, Simon Fraser University, Burnaby.

Mitchell, D. 1971. Archaeology of the Gulf of Georgia area, A Natural Region and Its Cultural Types. *Syesis* 4, Supplement 1.

Moss, M.L., Erlandson, J.M., and Stuckenrath, R. 1990. Wood Stake Weirs and Salmon Fishing on the Northwest Coast: Evidence from Southeast Alaska. *Canadian Journal of Archaeology* 14, 143-158.

Munsell, D.A. 1976a. The Wapato Creek Fish Weir Site 45PI47, Tacoma, Washington. In D.R. Croes (ed.), *The Excavation of Water-saturated Archaeological Sites (Wet Sites) on the Northwest Coast of North America*, 45-47. Ottawa: National Museum of Man Mercury Series, 50.

Munsell, D.A. 1976b. Excavation of the Conway Wet Site 45SK59b, Conway, Washington. In D.R. Croes (ed.), *The Excavation of Water-saturated Archaeological Sites (Wet Sites) on the Northwest Coast of North America*, 86-121. Ottawa: National Museum of Man Mercury Series, 50.

Nordquist, D. 1976. 45SN100 – The Biederbost Site, Kidd's Duvall Site. In D.R. Croes (ed.), *The Excavation of Water-saturated Archaeological Sites (Wet Sites) on the Northwest Coast of North America*, 186-200. Ottawa: National Museum of Man Mercury Series, 50.

Onat, A.R.B. 1976. A Fishtown Site, 45SK99. In D.R. Croes (ed.), *The Excavation of Water-saturated Archaeological Sites (Wet Sites) on the Northwest Coast of North America*, 122-145. Ottawa: National Museum of Man Mercury Series, 50.

Paden, M. 1980. Woodchip Debitage. In D.R. Croes and E. Blinman (eds), *Hoko River: A 2,500 Year Old Fishing Camp on the Northwest Coast of North America*, 273-289. Washington State University, Pullman: Laboratory of Anthropology, Reports of Investigations 58.

Samuels, S.R. 1983. *Spatial Analysis of Ozette House Floor Deposits.* Washington State University, Pullman: Laboratory of Anthropology.

Stevenson, A. 1989. Netting and Associated Cordage. In K. Bernick (ed.), *Water Hazard (DgRs 30) Artifact Recovery Project Report, Permit 1988-55*, Appendix A. Victoria: Archaeology and Outdoor Recreation Branch, Ministry of Municipal Affairs, Recreation and Culture, Province of British Columbia.

Stucki, B.R. 1983. Fluvial Processes and the Formation of the Hoko River Archaeological Site (45CA213), Olympic Peninsula, Washington. In D.R. Croes (ed.), *Interim annual report, Hoko River Archaeological Project*, Phase XIII & XIV, Attachment K. Washington D.C.: National Endowment for the Humanities.

13

FLORIDA'S ARCHAEOLOGICAL WET SITES

Barbara A. Purdy

SYNOPSIS

Waterlogged archaeological sites in Florida contain tools, art objects, dietary items, human skeletal remains, and glimpses of past environments that do not survive at typical terrestrial sites. The nonperishable components of these sites are so trivial that the sites would not have been discovered at all or their significance would be greatly diminished without organic preservation. Unfortunately archaeological wet sites are invisible since their preservation depends upon their entombment in oxygen-free deposits. As a result they are often destroyed accidentally during draining, dredging, and development projects. These sites and the objects they contain are an important part of Florida's heritage. They provide an opportunity to learn how the state's earliest residents used available resources to make their lives more comfortable and how they expressed themselves artistically. Without the wood carvings from water-saturated sites, it would be easy to think of early Floridans as culturally impoverished because Florida does not have stone suitable for creating sculptures. The prehistoric Indians of Florida were not the ancestors of the modern day peoples, but the Indians contributed to the state's heritage for more than 10,000 years before the present inhabitants arrived. In this paper I examine the probable reasons why archaeological wet sites are so plentiful and well preserved in Florida. I then describe in chronological order the locations and contents of the sites themselves.

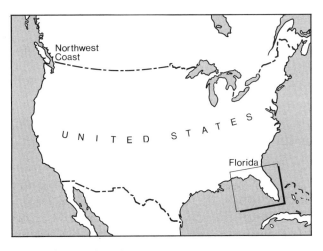

Fig. 13.1 Location Map

Florida (Fig. 13.1) is underlain by limestones of various ages. Limestones closest to the surface date from the Eocene to the Late Pleistocene depending upon their geographic location and the amount of erosion that occurred after they were deposited. In parts of south Florida, peat soils rest directly on Late Pleistocene limestone or are interbedded with marls formed during the Late Pleistocene or early Holocene. Because of the high calcium carbonate content that exists under these conditions, the organic soils are alkaline with a pH above 5.5. Preservation of archaeological remains that have been entombed in these deposits is excellent. In other areas of Florida, the organic soils are distinctly acid with a pH as low as 3.5. The immediate underlying sediments here are often quartz sands derived from Upper Miocene or Pleistocene origins. Wooden artefacts are well preserved in these acid peat soils but bone does not survive because calcium carbonate, a main constituent of bone, dissolves in the presence of acid. If shell is incorporated into the peat matrix (as in shell middens), the loss of bone is reversed. This situation occurred several thousand years ago when the aboriginal peoples of Florida began to exploit shellfish resources, especially along the St. Johns River. Above all, the survival of environmental and archaeological information in organic soils depends upon a maintenance of anaerobic conditions. A change to arid conditions allows air to enter the soil and aerobic

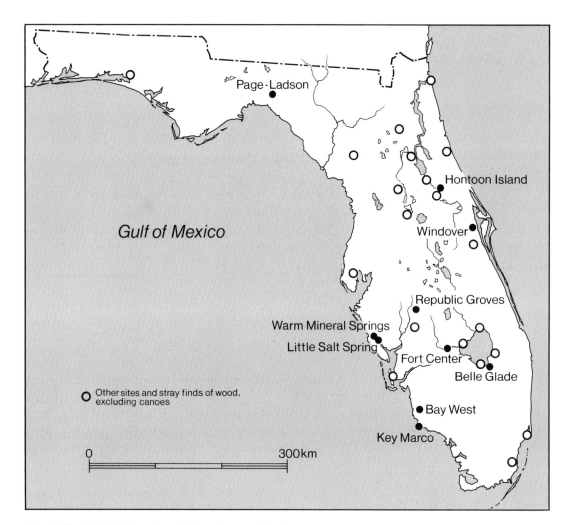

Fig. 13.2 Florida. Location of sites discussed in the text

bacteria flourish to oxidise the peat and its contents (Purdy 1991,9-20).

One would expect that the preservation of most floral and faunal material, including human skeletons and wooden artefacts, would date only to about 5000-6000 years ago when the moist conditions in Florida became widespread. This is not always the case, however, since many spectacular archaeological wet sites in Florida are older than 6000 years. The survival of these older sites may be the result of people congregating around available water supplies located in sinks or deep depressions at a time when surface water in Florida was still scarce (Purdy 1991, 19).

WET SITES IN CHRONOLOGICAL ORDER
(see Fig. 13.2 for locations)

Paleoindian: Late Pleistocene/Early Holocene *(c 10,000 uncal BP)*

Little Salt Spring and Warm Mineral Springs are located within 2 miles (3.12km) of each other in Sarasota County. Page-Ladsen is much farther north in Jefferson County (see Fig. 13.2). These three sites share a number of attributes: (1) they are all underwater which necessitates the use of SCUBA gear for investigation and recovery; (2) artefacts and/or human skeletal elements have been found in associ-

ation with now extinct Pleistocene megafauna; (3) radiocarbon analyses have yielded dates of 10,000 radiocarbon years or older; (4) faunal and floral studies have provided a clear picture of climatic conditions at the time the sites were utilized by human populations; (5) there is evidence of more recent use of the sites (see below).

Little Salt Spring is a large flooded sinkhole 60 m deep and 78 m across with a present water surface 5 m above mean sea level. A basin-like depression slopes at 25° from the land surface to 12 m in depth leaving a circular opening at the centre of the depression 25 to 30 m across (Clausen *et al* 1979,609) Through this opening one enters the main chamber of the spring. The collapsed shell of an extinct species of giant land tortoise impaled with a sharply pointed wooden stake was found on a ledge 26 m below the surface. Wood from the stake was dated at 12,030 uncal BP and the carbonate fraction of a tortoise bone was dated at 13,450 uncal BP. These dates furnish the earliest documented evidence for human habitation in Florida. Since abundant flowing surface water was scarce 12,000 radiocarbon years ago, the freshwater cenote (natural well or hole in limestone containing water) that existed at Little Salt Spring provided water for humans and animals in an oasis-like setting that contrasted with its xerophytic surroundings. It is believed that the water level in the cenote at that time was approximately at the -26 m ledge. The question remains how people got into the cavern to obtain water and to retrieve trapped animals; a bigger question is how they got out again. No human skeletal material has been reported from the -26 m ledge but numerous now-extinct animals were identified including additional tortoises, box turtles, ground sloth and mastodon along with several still extant species such as rabbit and rattlesnake.

By 10,000 uncal BP the water level had risen to about 14 m in Little Salt Spring and was only 11 to 12 m below the present surface. There is evidence that people lived around the opening to the cavern on the edge of the sloping depression. Animal and plant remains as well as bone and wooden artefacts were found there that date between 9900-9600 uncal BP. The wooden artefacts include several pointed wooden stakes made from pine, and a non-returning boomerang and carved mortar made from oak. No human skeletal remains have been found so far that date to this period of occupation. All of the animal bones are from modern species.

Little Salt Spring may have ceased to be a passive cenote and started to flow about 8500 radiocarbon years ago. The water had risen rapidly and invaded the drainage way leading into the basin from the northeast. Human utilization of the site came to an end at this time or earlier, probably because of increased availability of fresh surface water in other locations(Clausen *et al* 1979, 611-612) and perhaps because the water in the spring became too salty. The area around Little Salt Spring apparently was not reoccupied for 2000 years (see below).

In 1990, Dr John Gifford of the University of Miami was funded by the National Geographic Society to conduct a palaeoenvironmental study of the sediment deposit that lies 60 m below surface at Little Salt Spring. Gifford vibracored the sediment and obtained four cores that were 10 m or more long. A radiocarbon date received on wood removed from 1 m above the bottom of a 12 m core was 9660±160 cal BP (normalized to stable isotope ^{13}C, Beta 36591). The wood was oak. For years it was speculated that the sediment deposits at the bottom of Little Salt Spring and Warm Mineral Springs would date at least 18,000 years old to the last full glacial period and possibly more than 30,000 years. The date received by Gifford suggests that deposition of organic materials over the quartz sand core of the spring took place very rapidly. When the earliest inhabitants were at the spring around 12,000 radiocarbon years ago, the water was clear and the quartz sand bottom was probably visible to them (Gifford, pers.comm.1990).

Warm Mineral Springs, like Little Salt Spring, has yielded unprecedented information about flora, fauna, climate and human presence in Florida that may be as old as 10,000 radiocarbon years. But there are important differences. At Warm Mineral Springs hot connate water mixes with cool meteoric water to produce a year-round temperature of 30.5°C(86.9°F). These heavily mineralized warm waters are thought to be curative, the Fountain of Youth

sought by Ponce de Leon. People have been swimming in Warm Mineral Springs at least since the 1940s and the spring has been a health spa for many years (Clausen *et al* 1975). The dimensions of the spring and its underwater chamber are similar, but not identical, to Little Salt Spring.

Stratified deposits on a ledge 13 m below the present water level at Warm Mineral Springs were mapped, photographed, and sampled from 1958-1962, and a small test-excavation was conducted in 1972 (Clausen *et al* 1975, 192). Zone 3 was a leaf bed intercalated with calcitic mud layers. Numerous plants and animals were identified. The plants included pine, hickory and oak; the vertebrate animals were all extant species such as human, deer, opossum, raccoon, rabbit,squirrel, mouse and frog. The average of 11 radiocarbon dates for Zone 3 was 9700 uncal BP. Because of the excellent preservation and stratification of the Zone 3 deposits, the water level in the spring must have been at about the level of the -13 m ledge at 9700 uncal BP. This date is in close agreement with the date obtained from organic remains 12 m below surface and from the bottom deposit at Little Salt Spring. In addition many of the plant and animal species were the same. The stratified deposits at Warm Mineral Springs were subsequently damaged extensively by amateur divers. There is a lower zone of grey-green clay that contains abundant remains of extinct animals including sabre-tooth cat and ground sloth as well as extant species. This zone has not been dated but must exceed 10,000 radiocarbon years. The recovery of human remains from this zone(Zone 4) has not been verified but the examination of a female skull that probably came from the grey-green clay zone led to the suggestion that it may represent one of the earliest aboriginal human remains found in Florida.

The sediment deposit at the bottom of the spring may contain 10-12 m of palaeoenvironmental information. Unfortunately, underwater depths of 50 m or more present a formidable obstacle to efficient, safe excavation and the amount of bottom time is limited. An attempt was made to conduct a systematic excavation in the sediment deposit at Warm Mineral Springs but it progressed only to a level thought to date about 3500 radiocarbon years ago and yielded only alligator coprolites.

In addition to the damage caused by amateur divers, Warm Mineral Springs has been modified to accomodate bathers. For 30 years, sand has been dumped in the shallow water of the spring to provide a wading beach. Some of this sand has moved into the cavern where it erodes the walls and covers the sediments at the bottom. It would be beneficial to vibracore the sediment deposit as was done at Little Salt Spring in order to compare dates and depositional history. Other than such an effort, I am afraid that little remains to be studied at Warm Mineral Springs. (For a fuller discussion see Purdy 1991, 178-204.)

Page-Ladson in Jefferson County contains undisturbed sequential sediments that tell a story of interaction among flora, fauna and humans that is at least 10,000 radiocarbon years old. Prior to 5000 radiocarbon years ago, along this section of the Aucilla River, discrete sinkholes accumulated sediments of marls, clays and peats in quiet water. These sediments represent a time when the Florida aquifer was many metres below its present level. They can be distinguished easily from the more recent fluvial deposits. Ancient artefacts and Late Pleistocene fauna have been recovered in the area for several decades but always from reworked or disturbed contexts. Because of Page-Ladson's proximity to these finds, investigations were initiated at the site in anticipation of encountering a zone where Pleistocene megafauna and Paleoindian artefacts might be found together. Six test pits were excavated using both regular SCUBA gear and Kirby Morgan diving hoods with surface-supplied air, generator-supplied lights and two-way communication. Six 3-inch diameter cores were also taken to be used for stratigraphic control, radiocarbon dating and pollen and sediment analyses. The investigations of the Page-Ladson site are still underway but, at present, 86 plant species have been identified, remains of extinct and extant animals have been recovered in association with artefacts, and chronometric analyses have yielded dates on cultural material greater than 10,000 uncal BP. As at Little Salt Spring and Warm Mineral Springs, it appears that by approximately 9800 uncal BP only modern animal species survived. The investigators of Page-Ladson had the advantage of knowing ahead of time about the two southern springs and they also were aware of the large numbers of Paleoindian artefacts and Pleistocene fauna that had been recovered in the area near Page-Ladson. Using this information to construct a predictive model, they had the added benefit of being able to penetrate strata that were undisturbed by previous activities. (For a more complete description of the Page-Ladson site, see Dunbar *et al* 1988; Dunbar *et al* in press; Webb *et al* in press; Purdy 1991.)

Devil's Den in Levy County (Martin and Webb 1974; Clausen *et al* 1975) and the *Cutler Fossil* site in Dade County (Carr 1986a, 1986b) lack botanical remains but they resemble the sites described above because the sedimentary, biological and archaeological evidence they contain indicates that humans were associated with them when both sea level and/or local ground water levels were lower than present. They both contained a variety of extinct and modern animal species, remains of *Homo sapiens*, and artefacts.

Archaic: Middle Holocene
(c 8000-5000 uncal BP).

Windover in Brevard County, Little Salt Spring in Sarasota County, Bay West in Collier County and Republic Groves in Hardee County share several attributes: (1) they are "cemeteries" where the deceased were placed in shallow ponds or water-saturated organic deposits and staked down; (2) many burials, particularly those of children, were accompanied by elaborate grave goods; (3) all ages and both sexes are represented; (4) all but Bay West had human brain material preserved in some of the crania (it may have been present at Bay West also but was unobservable because of the way the site was disturbed); (5) organic materials survived in superb condition providing unprecedented insights

about cultural practices, human physical characteristics, and environment; (6) these kinds of sites occur only during the time period noted above (the average age exceeds 6000 radiocarbon years; Windover is approximately one thousand radiocarbon years earlier than Little Salt Spring, Bay West and Republic Groves).

Windover is discussed by Doran (this volume). See also Doran and Dickel (1988), Purdy (1991), and many other publications about this spectacular site.

Little Salt Spring , following about 2000 radiocarbon years of abandonment after the Paleoindian period (discussed above), was reoccupied around 6800 uncal BP. Water levels in Florida began to drop about this time and by 5500 uncal BP, were 8 m below present. The spring and surrounding area became a focus of activity for Middle Archaic period people. Their habitation area covered 10,000 to 20,000 sq. m along the higher elevations paralleling the slough or drainage way that leads into the spring from the northeast. The dead were interred in the moist soft peat of the slough and as the water level continued to drop the burial sites followed, progressing into the exposed pond basin. The most recent burial recovered at the site is 5200 uncal BP. Bodies were wrapped with grass and placed in extended fashion on biers of wax myrtle or with leafy limbs placed between the arms and the torso. Some of the human remains are in a remarkable state of preservation because of the anaerobic environment resulting from hard water and resettling of fine peat. Wood, bone, shell and stone artefacts accompanied the dead as grave goods (Clausen *et al* 1979). Some burials were recovered with brains preserved in the crania permitting DNA and mtDNA studies that have resulted in startling new, but still tentative, hypotheses about North American Indian lineages (Paabo *et al* 1988). It is estimated that 1000 individuals are buried at Little Salt Spring but, at present, only 35 have been removed. By 5200 uncal BP, the water level began to rise and fresh water again became regionally abundant ending the dependence on the spring. With the approach of sea level to its present position, heavily mineralized water began to issue from the spring; the salinity today is 3.2 per mil (Clausen *et al* 1979). There is much still to be learned from Little Salt Spring. It is hoped that extensive excavations will resume there in the near future.

Bay West provides the best example possible of the weakness of legislation pertaining to development projects that modify wetland areas. In 1980 a cypress pond was dredged to create a water source and disperse peat for use in the property owner's nursery business. The dredging operation continued uninterrupted even after artefacts and human skeletons dating 6500 radiocarbon years ago were observed. The local archaeological society was finally granted permission to salvage materials from the site as long as there was no interference with the pond clearing (Beriault *et al* 1981; Purdy 1991). The shattered bones of 37 humans and 45 animal species were identified and analyzed. Botanical species included pine, willow, wax myrtle, cabbage palm, saw palmetto, holly and staggerbrush/fetterbrush. Wooden artefacts were made primarily of pine. The small amount of cypress recovered appears to support other findings that cypress may not have been widespread in Florida 6500 radiocarbon years ago. Stone, bone and antler artefacts were also recovered from the pond. The styles of the stone spearheads as well as radiocarbon analysis were used to determine that the Bay West site was utilized around 6500 radiocarbon years ago. The destruction of the site is tantamount to desecrating King Tut's tomb. Stronger legislation and greater compensation or incentives to property owners are needed to avoid similar situations. Although stricter legislation has been enacted on paper since this site was destroyed, the actual field situation remains virtually unchanged because there is little control over a project once a permit has been granted. A landowner becomes the possessor of the entombed heritage, and it is at his mercy.

Republic Groves was a bayhead swamp that contained three springs until 1968 when canals were dug to drain the springs in order to create land dry enough to plant citrus. The spoil that was thrown up on both sides of the drainage ditches contained botanical remains and human and animal bone. Human bones with contemporary faunal remains and artefacts were seen to come exclusively from a peat layer. Some of the other animal bone belonged to extinct Pleistocene species that came from a clay deposit underlying the peat. Despite the drastic modification of the site, a great deal was salvaged and analyzed thanks to the efforts of Mitchell E.Hope, who also conducted systematic excavations in undisturbed areas at Republic Groves (Wharton *et al* 1981; Purdy 1991).

A total of 33 tapered wooden stakes made of pine and oak was recovered from the muck in direct or probable association with burials. In several instances, groups of three to seven stakes were placed in a straight line alongside interments. Many of the stakes show battering on their heads as if hammered, and many were charred. Wood stakes were found also at Little Salt Spring, Windover and the Bay West site. There may have been a larger quantity of worked wood preserved at Republic Groves but the first wood found was thought to be roots. After the original stake was found, greater care was taken in examining all of the wood before it was discarded. Several artefacts made of deer antler were recovered including four specimens that were elaborately incised ornaments or pendants. Utilitarian and ornamental artefacts made of bone included awls, knives, and beads; those manufactured from stone include beads and spearheads. It is interesting to note that 111 stone beads were found near the mandible of a child interment suggesting that they had been strung together on a necklace. The stone beads and a plummet were made of stone originating from outside Florida indicating that long distance trade was operating. The spearheads are of a variety known to belong to the Middle Archaic period in Florida,which along with radiocarbon dates places the age of the Republic Groves site at about 6000 uncal BP. A few pieces of cordage were also found and a matted impression underlying one of the burials was observed but not recovered. Several of the crushed skulls contained material that Hope suspected might be

brain tissue and this was the conclusion reached also by Dr J. Lawrence Angel of the Smithsonian Institution. Saunders (1972) studied the human skeletal material from the Republic Groves site. A minimum of 37 individuals was identified and analyzed for age at death, sex, height, pathologies, dental patterns and more.

The *Gauthier* site in Brevard County is a Middle Archaic Period cemetery that has many features resembling Windover, Little Salt Spring,Bay West and Republic Groves but it lacks the botanical component (Jones 1981).

Late Archaic/Early Ceramic (5000-2500 uncal BP)

Tick Island and Lake Monroe, both located in Volusia County along the St. Johns River, share a number of similarities: (1) their lower strata date to the period known as Mount Taylor when freshwater shellfish resources were first exploited in this area of Florida; (2) the lower components of these shell middens are late preceramic in age; (3) the earliest ceramics in North America are found in the middens 4500 cal BP; (4) the middens contain the earliest dated *Cucurbita pepo* (gourds or squash) in Florida; (5) the middens provide the first concrete evidence that human

Fig. 13.3 Tick Island. Wood carving representing a turkey buzzard: c *130 mm long*

populations were becoming less nomadic. Efficient utilization of aquatic resources probably formed the base for all later developments in Florida, including social hierarchies.

Tick Island was first reported in the 1890s. It was mined for its shell as early as the 1920s, and commercial shell mining activities nearly destroyed the site in the 1950s. The shell was used for road beds and in the drainage fields of septic tank systems. In the 1950s mining activity, the shell was transported by barge to a large pressurized washing machine that removed sand and dirt. Artefacts of bone, stone, shell, ceramic and wood were recovered as the shell emerged from the revolving washer. Animal species identified were oppossum, beaver, black bear, raccoon, otter, dog, deer, alligator, turtles, rattlesnakes and several species of bird and fish. Well preserved wooden artefacts attest to the fact that part of the mined shell was in a water-saturated environment. Fig. 13.3 shows a wooden carving that bears a strong resemblance to the Florida turkey buzzard. The skin on its head is even wrinkled. Its beak is opened in anguish because the talons of a large raptorial bird are clutching it by the throat. The exposed tongue of the distressed buzzard provides further realism. Despite the fact that the Tick Island site is badly damaged there remain undisturbed deposits on the fringes of the midden. Cores taken in 1982 and 1986 contained well-preserved fauna and flora (including gourd seeds)as well as fibre-tempered pottery sherds typical of the oldest ceramics in North America. Excavation of a portion of the water-saturated area would furnish a broader picture than is now available about the initial and developing utilization of the aquatic resources by the Indians 5000-6000 radiocarbon years ago. (For further descriptions of Tick Island see Moore 1892a, 1892b, 1893; Jahn and Bullen 1978; Purdy 1991.)

Lake Monroe probably has a history similar to that of Tick Island with regard to shell mining activities but this has not been verified as yet through existing records. The site has great potential for the recovery of a full assemblage of environmental and cultural information from the Preceramic Archaic to the early ceramic period. In February 1989, a small test excavation was conducted below the water level on the north shore of Lake Monroe. Analyses of the excavated materials revealed the presence of the oldest dated fibre-tempered pottery and the earliest known examples of *Cucurbita pepo* varieties yet found in Florida. The fauna include 20 species of snails and bivalves, 13 species of snake, salamander,alligator, 5 species of turtle, 3 species of birds, and 5 species of mammals including *Homo sapiens*. The thirty-one botanical species include cane, hickory, oak, dogwood, persimmon, ash, sweetgum, magnolia, mulberry, palm, pine, maple, willow, elderberry, cypress, elm, grape, toothache tree, bottlegourd, and the cucurbits mentioned above. Artefacts consist of fibre-tempered pottery, marine shell tools, chert flakes, several bone pin fragments and wood. Radiocarbon dates range from approximately 3000 uncal BP for the upper levels to 6000 uncal BP for Level 8 that contained no ceramics. Future excavations are planned at Lake Monroe. (For more detail see Russo *et al* in press; Purdy 1991.)

2500 uncal BP-Historic Contact (after AD 1492)

Fort Center in Glades County, Belle Glade in Palm Beach County, and Key Marco in Collier County share a number of similar attributes: (1) economy dependent primarily upon the utilization of aquatic resources; (2) little or no evidence of plant cultivation; (3) ceramics that are primarily sand-tempered plain; (4) wood carvings; (5) social hierarchy as indicated by the presence of various features that are assumed to be an indication of rank. Fort Center and Belle Glade both have an historic period component but it could not be defined adequately at either site because of disturbance by vandals and development. Hontoon Island in Volusia County falls within the same general time frame as the

Fig. 13.4 Fort Center. Wood carving of an eagle

three sites named above but it is located far north of the others and tells a slightly different story of the past.

Fort Center stretches for a mile along Fisheating Creek west of Lake Okeechobee. The site includes middens, house mounds, ceremonial mounds, earthworks, and a charnel pond. Four periods of occupation, dating from 2400 uncal BP to 250 uncal BP, were identified by William H.Sears (1982) who conducted excavations at Fort Center during the 1960s and 1970s. The second period, 1750 uncal BP to about 1150 uncal BP, is of particular interest because at that time the inhabitants constructed a special area to prepare and bury their dead. This enclosure consisted of two mounds and an artificial pond with a platform where bundled burials were placed. Sometime around AD500 the platform burned and collapsed ino the pond carrying with it approximately 300 bundled burials and about 69 wooden carvings, many of which were fragmentary. Many of these carvings supported or decorated the platform; others may have accompanied the dead as grave goods. The carvings,

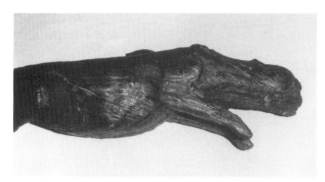

Fig. 13.5 Fort Center. Wood carving of an otter

human and skeletal remains, and animal bones were preserved because of the anaerobic conditions that prevailed in the pond. All of the carvings were made of pine, and several different styles were used to depict large birds and beasts such as eagles and otters (Fig. 13.4-13.5). Hundreds of shell and bone artefacts were also recovered from

the pond and from the two ceremonial mounds. A sample of the human remains was analyzed for age, sex, pathologies, traumas and more. Forty-three adult males, 50 adult females and 17 subadults were represented. The fauna collected from the pond was analyzed by Hale (1984); numerous species of shellfish, fish, reptiles, amphibians, birds and mammals were identified and quantified. Interestingly, floral specimens did not survive in the pond except for wood debris from the platform, the pinewood carvings and two double-ended pestles made of *lignum vitae*. Pollen analysis tended to reflect environment conditions similar to those that prevail in the area today. Sears was particularly interested in learning from pollen studies if crops were being cultivated at the site and if their presence could be used to explain the cultural complexity that existed there. Corn (i.e. maize) pollen was identified but there has been considerable debate about the pollen's identification and about the importance of corn in the diet of the people. (For

Fig. 13.6 Key Marco wooden mask.   left) 1972 photograph   right) 1990 photograph

119

greater detail about Fort Center, see Sears 1982; Hale 1984; Purdy 1991.)

Key Marco remains one of the most unusual sites in the world because of the large number of wooden masks (Fig. 13.6), figurines and decorated utilitarian items found there. In addition to the wooden objects, there were hundreds of bone and shell ornaments and tools all preserved in a "little triangular Court of Pile Dwellers" that Frank Hamilton Cushing "exploited from border to border" in the spring of 1896 (Cushing 1897). The site is located at the head of Ten Thousand Islands on the southwest Gulf Coast of Florida. A great diversity of flora and fauna were encountered. Cushing noted mangrove, buttonwood and palmetto; wood anatomist Lee A.Newsom recently identified the wood of some of the carvings as pine, cypress, mahogany, *lignum vitae*, *Bumelia* sp. and *Eugenia* sp. (Purdy 1991). The animal remains have been analyzed quite thoroughly, and they include great quantities and numerous species of marine shell, terrestial mammals, birds, turtles, alligator, whale and marine fishes. No human skeletons were found. Cushing presented his findings to the American Philosophical Society (Cushing 1897), and a thorough study of the excavations and artefacts was conducted by Gilliland (1975) who later published an account of the controversies and personalities involved (Gilliland 1989; see also Purdy 1991). Marco Island is now covered by a full-scale city of homes and resort facilities.

Belle Glade is located on the southeast shore of Lake Okeechobee. The wooden artefacts that survived at Belle Glade closely resemble some of those recovered at Key Marco and at Fort Center, as do tools and decorative items of shell and bone. The site was excavated during the Great Depression in the early 1930s using a large crew hired under the Federal Emergency Relief Program. The results of the excavation were summarized by Sterling (1935) and a complete study and a collection of the notes was published by Willey (1949). Shell, bone and wood industries were well developed. The decorative and utilitarian artefacts manufactured from each of these materials were diverse and discrete; that is, the shell artefacts did not overlap in function with those made of bone etc. Ceramics were found at the site but are not spectacular. There is no record of the number of skeletons removed at Belle Glade. The skulls of 17 males and 26 females were measured and described but these must represent only a small part of the individuals who were buried there because, as one observer states, "...stick your hand down there and there was nothing but bones. You couldn't take a pencil and stick it anywhere in the wall but what you'd find bones" (Lamme 1978). No plant remains are reported for the site and the wood of the carvings was not identified. Much of the material from Belle Glade is in the Smithsonian Institution in Washington, D.C. A house was built on the site in 1975 and the deposits are now completely desiccated as a result of the drainage necessary to stabilize the land for building. (For further details about Belle Glade see Stirling 1935; Willey 1949; Purdy 1991.)

Fig. 13.7 Owl totem recovered near Hontoon Island in 1955

Hontoon Island is located midway along the St. Johns River that runs about 300 miles through east Forida. The shell and burial mounds at Hontoon Island were visited in the 19th century by Jeffries Wyman (1875) and C.B.Moore (1893, 1894). It might not have been investigated further, especially after shell mining activities in the 1930s left only an apron of undisturbed midden on the edge of a lagoon, but a 12-foot wood carving of an owl (Fig. 13.7) was found close by in 1955 and smaller carvings of an otter and pelican were recovered during drought conditions in 1978. These discoveries prompted systematic excavations, carried out in the water-saturated lagoon area on Hontoon Island periodically from 1980 to 1988. All organic materials survived in superb condition and were recovered from stratigraphically discrete zones. Hundreds of thousands of animal bones and shell refuse representing approximately 100 species were analyzed by Dr Elizabeth S.Wing and her students at the Florida Museum of Natural History; these data have furnished a clear picture of species available and utilized by the Indians over a 1500-year period. Eleven species predominate: mussel, snail, gar, catfish, bass, mullet, slider turtle, gopher tortoise, duck, rabbit and deer (Wing and McKean 1987). Botanical species identified at Hontoon Island include 30 species of wood and 82 species of plant represented by seeds or other parts (Newsom 1987). Although *Lagenaria siceraria* (bottlegourd) and *Cucurbita pepo* (gourd/squash) seeds and rind are abundant, there is little or no evidence for cultivated plants until about 450 uncal BP when many changes occurred at the site including the introduction of pumpkin and corn. These changes are thought to represent repercussions resulting from the voyages of Columbus. Except for a few fragments, human skeletal material was not recovered at Hontoon Island. The burial mounds reported by Wyman (1875) were destroyed by shell mining activities. Artefacts were manufactured from wood, bone, ceramic, shell and stone; a few pieces of cordage were found, and European artefacts came from the topmost cultural zone. Hontoon Island, in contrast to the other sites described in this paper, except Tick Island and Lake Monroe, is a garbage midden. It offers views of the past that differ from mortuary sites and spring sites where the primary attention has been placed on answering questions about human skeletons, grave goods, and climatic changes. Hontoon Island is important for the potential it provides to study, both synchronically and diachronically, a nearly complete and unlimited assemblage of environmental and cultural "trash". It is a water-saturated, multicomponent site with a depositional sequence that is not trampled, degraded, or compressed. The terrestrial deposits on the island did not contain these well-preserved strata. (For further discussions of Hontoon Island see Purdy 1987a, 1987b, 1991.)

OTHER SITES AND ARTEFACTS

Individual Finds Numerous small carvings have been recovered in Florida. These are usually found accidentally when drought conditions prevail, or in peat mining operations or other activities that modify the wetlands. Their provenance is not known and most of them have not been

dated, but they provide an opportunity to identify wood species, observe art styles and perhaps gain insights into costumes and ornaments considered desirable by the aborigines (Purdy1991).

Canoes (Fig. 13.8) Florida has the oldest and the largest number of prehistoric watercraft in the world. Records exist for more than 200 canoes that have been found throughout the state. They date from 5000 or more years ago to the 19th century. At least six different styles are recognized that can be correlated with age and in some cases with the waterways in which they functioned. The canoes are all made of pine except for a few that date to the Historic Period after AD 1500. Studies of the canoes have provided information about the growth and utilization of aquatic resources by the Indians in post-Pleistocene Florida. The development of the technology and the behaviour associated with producing and using canoes is an analyzable part of the infrastructure of Florida's prehistoric and early historic Indians. It involves the capture of large amounts of energy and, thus, is of significant systemic importance. Most large prehistoric settlements in Florida are found along the coasts and inland waterways. The canoes functioned in many realms of Indian culture including economic, social and ritual. They were used for the transportation of people, goods, trade, warfare and exchange of ideas. Watercraft, in general, provide a way to look at continuities through time and space; in many places in the world today, for example, all major activities still occur along waterways.

The canoes, shamefully, are Florida's stepchild. They have not been given the attention they deserve. Their large size and quantity make the cost of the preservative chemicals required for conservation prohibitive and many of them have disintegrated (Newsom and Purdy 1990; Purdy 1991).

CONSERVATION

The conservation of fragile organic materials from Florida's archaeological wet sites is a major problem. There is the uncertainty of the longterm survival of previously waterlogged specimens even if conservation has been carried out and the objects curated. There is also the frustrating issue of how to reach and educate the public and developers about the immediate conservation requirements of artefacts from water-saturated sites in order to prevent results as shown in Fig. 13.6. Polyethylene glycol (PEG 540-Blend) has been used successfully for more than ten years to stabilize wood recovered from freshwater organic deposits in Florida (Purdy 1991).

CONCLUSION

In this paper I have described briefly the environmental setting and cultural inventory of archaeological wet sites that span 10,000 radiocarbon years. At many of these sites the nonperishable components are so trivial that the sites would not have been investigated at all if the organic constituents were lacking. In Florida, the Archaic Period has been particularly enhanced by the discovery of "mor-

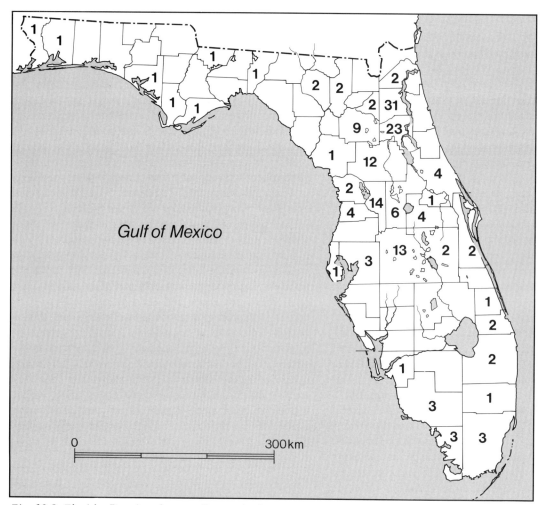

Fig. 13.8 Florida. Density of canoe discoveries by county

has been particularly enhanced by the discovery of "mortuary" sites where the dead were buried with grave goods in waterlogged deposits that ensured their survival for thousands of years. The usually perishable organic materials from wet sites provide the only broad opportunity to discover relationships between resources available and resources utilized by prehistoric groups of people. Each wet site provides more diverse information than does an upland site and each wet site is different in regard to what it reveals about its past. It is logical that information gained from wet

site excavations can be used, with caution, to make reasonable extrapolations about objects and activities that were formerly present on nearby upland sites. The contents of wet sites can be compared globally to each other and to organic materials preserved under extremely dry conditions (Purdy 1988). Most important of all, as discussed by Croes (this volume) we have not yet turned the first corner in utilizing the full potential of the added information recovered at archaeological wet sites.

BIBLIOGRAPHY

Beriault, J., Carr, R., Stipp, J., Johnson, R. and Meeder, J. 1981. The archaeological salvage of the Bay West site, Collier County, Florida. *The Florida Anthropologist* 34, 39-58.

Carr, R.S. 1986a. Preliminary report on excavations at the Cutler Fossil Site in southern Florida. *The Florida Anthropologist* 39, 231-232.

Carr, R.S. 1986b. Sinkhole yields rare view of Dade's past. *The Miami News* March 28, 13A.

Clausen, C.J., Brooks, H.K. and Wesolowsky, A.B., 1975. The early man site at Warm Mineral Springs, Florida. *Journal of Field Archaeology* 2, 191-213.

Clausen, C.J., Cohen, A.D., Emiliani, C., Holman, J.A. and Stipp, J.J. 1979. Little Salt Spring, Florida: a unique underwater site. *Science* 203, 609-614.

Cushing, F.H. 1897. Exploration of ancient Key Dwellers' remains on the Gulf Coast of Florida. *Proceedings of the American Philosophical Society* 25, 329-448.

Doran, G.H. and Dickel, D.N. 1988. Multidisciplinary investigations at the Windover site. In B.A. Purdy (ed.), *Wet Site Archaeology*, 263-289. Caldwell, New Jersey: The Telford Press.

Dunbar, J.S., Faught, M.K. and Webb, S.D. 1988. Page-Ladson: an underwater Paleoindian site in northwestern Florida. *The Florida Anthropologist* 41, 442-452.

Dunbar, J.S., Webb, S.D. and Cring, D. In press. Culturally and naturally modified bones from a Paleoindian site in the Aucilla River, north Florida. In R.Bonnischen (ed.), *Bone Modification*. Orono, Maine: Centre for the Study of Early Man.

Gilliland, M.S. 1975. *The material culture of Key Marco, Florida*. Gainesville: University Presses of Florida.

Gilliland, M.S. 1989. *Key Marco's buried treasure*. Gainesville: University Presses of Florida.

Hale, S.H. 1984. Prehistoric environmental exploitation around Lake Okeechobee. *Southeastern Archaeology* 3,187.

Jahn, O.L. and Bullen, R.P. 1978. The Tick Island Site, St John's River, Florida. *The Florida Anthropologist* 31.

Jones, C. 1981. Interview with Calvin Jones: Excavations of an Archaic cemetery in Cocoa Beach, Florida. *The Florida Anthropologist* 34, 81-89.

Lamme, V. 1978. Taped interview about the Chosen burial mound. *Palm Beach County Archaeological Society Newsletter*

Martin, R.A. and Webb, S.D. 1974. Late Pleistocene mammals from The Devils' Den fauna, Levy County. In S.D. Webb (ed.), *Pleistocene Mammals of Florida*, 114-145. Gainsville: University Presses of Florida.

Moore, C.B. 1892a. A burial mound of Florida. *American Naturalist* 26, 129-143.

Moore, C.B. 1892b. Supplementary investigations at Tick Island. *American Naturalist* 26, 568-579.

Moore, C.B. 1893. Certain shell heaps of the St Johns River, Florida, hitherto unexplored. *American Naturalist* 27, 8-13, 113-117, 605-624, 708-723.

Moore, C.B. 1894. Certain sand mounds of the St Johns River, Florida, Part II. *Journal of the Academy of Natural Sciences*, Volume X, Philadelphia.

Newsom, L.A. 1987. Analysis of botanical remains from Hontoon Island, Florida: 1980-1985 excavations. *The Florida Anthropologist* 40, 47-84.

Newsom, L.A. and Purdy B.A. 1990. Florida canoes: a maritime heritage from the past. *The Florida Anthropologist* 43, 164-180.

Paabo, S., Gifford, J.A. and Wilson, A.C. 1988. Mitochondrial DNA sequences from a 7000-year-old brain. *Nucleic Acids Research* 16, 9775-9787.

Purdy, B.A. 1987a. Hontoon Island, Florida: artefacts. *The Florida Anthropologist* 40, 27-39.

Purdy, B.A. 1987b. Investigations at Hontoon Island, an archaeological wet site in Volusa County Florida; an overview and chronology. *The Florida Anthropologist* 40, 4-12.

Purdy, B.A. 1988. Archaeological wet sites; untapped archives of prehistoric documents. In B.A.Purdy (ed.) *Wet Site Archaeology*, 325-335. Caldwell, New Jersey: The Telford Press.

Purdy, B.A. 1991. *The Art and Archaeology of Florida's Wetlands*. Boca Raton, Florida: CRC press.

Russo, M., Newsom, L.A., McGee, R.M. and Purdy, B.A. In press. Groves Orange Midden Site. *Southeastern Archaeology*.

Saunders, L.P. 1972. Osteology of the Republic Groves Site. Unpublished master's thesis. Boca Raton: Florida Atlantic University.

Sears, W.H. 1982. *Fort Center: An Archaeological Site in the Lake Okeechobee Basin*. Gainesville: University Presses of Florida.

Stirling, M.W. 1935. Smithsonian archaeological projects conducted under the Federal Emergency Relief Administration, 1933-34. *Annual Report of the Board of Regents of the Smithsonian Institution*.

Webb, S.D., Dunbar, J.S. and Watts, W.A. In press. Fauna, Flora and culture from the Pleistocene/Holocene transition at Half-Mile Rise, Florida. *National Geographic Research Reports*.

Wharton, B.R., Ballo, G.R. and Hope, M.E. 1981. The Republic Groves Site, Hardee County, Florida. *The Florida Anthropologist* 34, 59-80.

Willey, G.R. 1969. Excavations in Southeast Florida. *Yale University Publications in Anthropology* No 42. New Haven: Yale University Press.

Wing, E.S. and McKean, L. 1987. Preliminary study of the animal remains excavated from the Hontoon Island site. *The Florida Anthropologist* 40, 40-46.

Wyman, J. 1875. Fresh water shell mounds of the St John's River, Florida. *Peabody Academy of Science*. Massachusetts: Salem.

14

PROBLEMS AND POTENTIAL OF WET SITES IN NORTH AMERICA: THE EXAMPLE OF WINDOVER

Glen H. Doran

SYNOPSIS

Wet site archaeology in the United States has lagged behind that of Europe. While there are abundant wetlands in the United States two factors have limited investigations. Funding is an endemic problem in archaeology and it is a major problem for wet sites that require multidisciplinary, multiyear investigations to be truly productive. The failure of the small community of wet site archaeologists to publish in main line journals is a second major problem. As a consequence of these two shortcomings wet sites have not achieved the same level of visibility and significance they have in other areas of the world and they are not a part of mainstream United States archaeology. Wet sites in the United States, however, can be just as productive as those of Europe, particularly when events provide for both time and funding for proper investigation. Windover, an Early Archaic Florida mortuary pond (7400 uncal BP), is a case in point. Accidental discovery, non-traditional funding, and an abundance of community support have resulted in a unique picture of early burial practices and biocultural adaptation in the southeastern United States. Only by demonstrating to traditional archaeologists the importance of wet sites will their potential as unique windows on the past be fully exploited.

Wet site archaeology in the United States virtually began in Florida. Frank Hamilton Cushing in the closing years of the 19th century had heard tales of incredible artefacts in Florida's wetlands and began a series of expeditions to evaluate these materials. Preserved carved animal heads, some with the paint still adhering to the surface, wooden bowls, paddles, spoons and utensils of everyday life as well as even more fragile cordage and nets and floats were pulled

from the protecting muck soils of Key Marco (Cushing 1897). Cushing drew parallels to the European lake dweller sites that were front page news in Europe (Munro 1890; Gastaldi 1865). The preservative powers of wet sites provided graphic evidence of the sophistication and complexity of the New World's prehistoric citizens. The only kind of site which could parallel such amazing finds were the dry rock shelters scattered across the country, many of which would be excavated and plundered in the following years (Haury 1943; Guernsey and Kidder 1921).

Dry sites, entailing less difficult field conditions in general, also presented fewer problems of conservation. The desiccated materials could often go directly into museum cases. Cushing's prized artefacts, however, were and are a different story (Purdy 1974 and this volume). In time wet site materials, when improperly treated and cared for, become at best faint images of their former selves, if they survive at all. Gilliland, in the last decades, has recaptured some of the glory of Cushing's discoveries with her excellent publications (Gilliland 1975, 1989). Regrettably, Cushing, like many of his contemporaries and wet site descendants, seems to have been interested in field work but less enthusiastic about analysis, interpretation and publication. This is one of the problems that seem to plague wet site archaeology – the lack of publication, particularly in main line journals of the day. To Cushing's credit there were several articles on Key Marco (Cushing 1895, 1897; Durnford 1895), but the full value of the materials was not completely documented nor fully appreciated in the archaeological community. To a large extent the materials languished on increasingly dusty museum shelves. Others tried to duplicate Cushing's discoveries but until the last few years Florida archaeologists were largely unsuccessful and archaeological attention turned elsewhere.

The potential of Florida's wetland prehistory was, with few exceptions, largely ignored (Royal and Clark 1960; Sears 1982; Purdy 1988). The main problems facing United States archaeologists in the early part of this century, particularly problems of chronology building, ceramic trait lists and the like, could readily be accomplished without taking on the difficulties of field work and conservation that are inherent in wet site archaeology. The march of archaeological progress took place on the high ground. Boylston Street fishweir, originally discovered in 1913, is perhaps the most noticeable exception (Johnson 1942, 1949) and is still in many ways an exemplary multidisciplinary project with a diverse team of collaborators who addressed a wide variety of topics – molluscs, wood, peat, silt, pollen, changing water levels, chemistry, environmental variation, conservation and preservation, etc. The project clearly demonstrated the value of wet site investigations and the multidisciplinary approach. Even with such sterling examples, the focus of American archaeology was elsewhere – large sites, the massive middens, temple mounds of the southeast, and the pueblos of the southwest (Willey and Sabloff 1974). There was a lot of archaeology to do, and you didn't have to get your hands wet. Even in many terrestrial sites, particularly those of the Works Progress Administration epoch, with minimal conservation necessities, much of the work remains incomplete, but at least the materials have survived. In some ways, it may be a proverbial blessing in disguise that more major wet sites were not excavated during these periods. Benign neglect in museums and other storage facilities would have been far less kind to the wet sites' perishable organics.

By mid-century, there was a growing disquiet with the workings of archaeology and the failure by some accounts to "do anthropology" (Taylor 1948; Binford 1962; Binford and Binford 1968; *ad nauseam*). Expanding emphasis on multidisciplinary orientations, cultural ecology, systems theory and so forth began to shift emphasis from traditional reliance on trait lists, ceramic chronologies and descriptive analysis (Willey and Sabloff 1974). Here again, wet sites could have made a significant impact – a typical wet site almost of necessity forces the excavator to assume a multidisciplinary orientation and to deal with broader issues (Croes and Hackenberger 1988; Croes 1989). It simply can not be avoided – plant remains are readily identifiable, the tremendous volume of worked material in wood, bone, basketry and antler, etc. was ripe for the increasingly eclectic and multidisciplinary changes that were taking place in archaeology. Again, the stage was set but the actors failed to present a sustained performance and with few exceptions remained in the wings. The bulk of the money was still going to dry field work (cf. Croes, this volume).

Truly eye-opening and tremendously informative materials lurked beneath the marsh surface in America just as they did in Europe. In Western Europe particularly, the obvious potential of wet sites was central to many regional studies and multidisciplinary analyses were an integral part of wet site investigations (Coles 1984; Coles and Coles 1989). The non-recognition of wet sites in mid-century was more characteristic of the American trend.

Funding is the ever-present nemesis of archaeology but the pinch perhaps is more acute in wet site work and this may have served as a further obstacle to increased emphasis on North American wet sites. This and other forces were responsible for a very clear orientation to terrestrial sites in North America that stands in contrast to the enhanced European awareness that wet sites held the answers to questions poorly addressed much less answered in terrestrial contexts, which continues to this day (Mathiassen 1938; Hazzledine Warren *et al* 1936; Coles and Lawson 1987; Coles and Coles 1989; Dolukhanov and Miklyayev 1986; Petrequin and Petrequin 1988; Mordant and Mordant 1987 and this volume; Andersen 1985; Gramsch 1985 and this volume).

WET SITE PROBLEMS IN THE UNITED STATES

Based on a survey of articles, comments and reports in the last ten years of *American Antiquity*, only 8 of the 621 articles (1.2%) dealt with wet site issues. Since 1989 *Antiquity*, a British journal most North American archaeologists are familiar with, ran 161 articles and 18 dealt with wet site materials (11%). North American wet site archaeologists may have published more of their work in local and regional journals or in independently published volumes (Croes and Hackenberger 1988; Purdy 1979, 1987; Purdy and Hall 1981), but arguably the publication record in the most widely disseminated journal in North America, *American Antiquity*, is well below that achieved in *Antiquity*. Informal survey indicates that a disproportionate number of North American wet site investigations are either not published, or are reported in the most minimal of manners. It could be argued that, in addition to funding difficulties, the failure of wet sites to attain a more central position in North American archaeology results from the failure of the wet site archaeologists to publish their work adequately, and thereby conclusively and repetitively demonstrate that wet sites, by their very nature, are perhaps the most informative kind of site one could choose to excavate. The importance of wet sites in European prehistory and history seems more clearly established than it is in the United States and at least in part is related to a more aggressive and professional publication record than North American wet site archaeologists have achieved.

Funding of major wet site investigations, and there have been precious few, has in most cases been emphatically non-traditional. The bulk of Ozette's funding was obtained largely through political pressure at the federal level. Dale Croes has worked closely with local Indian groups for funding of his work at several Northwest Coast wet sites and some novel funding procedures have evolved (bingo archaeology – proceeds from a line on Indian-run Bingo games were donated to the Hoko Project – Croes pers.

comm.). Purdy has achieved her successes at Hontoon Island largely through small grants from her parent university, from the state, and from entities such as Earthwatch (Purdy 1987). Warm Mineral Springs (Clausen *et al* 1975; Clausen *et al* 1979) has largely been funded through political mechanisms at the state level. Windover is no exception, in this regard. The landowner's political contacts ultimately led to direct state funding of over 90% of the cost of nearly $900,000. Sear's work at Fort Center is the only major project I am aware of that was funded through traditional channels, *i.e.* National Science Foundation (Sears 1982). Could all these projects have been funded by such traditional organizations? It is unlikely given the severe limitations on NSF funding for anthropology in general and North American archaeology in particular.

For the last several years the NSF has provided between $2.2 and $2.4 million for archaeology. Based on published NSF Grants Lists between 1985 and 1989 the average project funded received around $50,000 and only 30-40% of the total funding base was directed towards North American field work, the bulk going to projects outside the United States. This is not a recent concern and funding levels at the NSF have long been an issue (Casteel 1980; Yellen *et al 1980*).

They still are. Rice has recently noted:

> *First, funding for anthropology and archaeology in real dollars has declined over the past decades since a peak in 1968 ... archaeologists and physical anthropologists are more and more dependent on interdisciplinary collaboration with colleagues in the natural and life sciences. At the same time, NSF support for these kinds of interdisciplinary research is weak ... Under current levels of funding, it is nearly impossible for the NSF to support any project for more than one year.*
> (Rice 1991,5)

What level of wet site investigations can be pursued with an average grant of $50,000? What wet site can be investigated in a single year? What wet site can be investigated without an interdisciplinary focus?

To compound the problem the majority of wet sites are found accidentally during construction, dredging or peat mining. The nature of funding cycles and proposal deadlines almost precludes effective and timely response to the serendipitous discovery of wet sites.

Based on informal tabulations, the Federal government (National Park Service, Forest Service, etc.) spent roughly $120,000,000 annually on archaeology during the late 1980s (Ehrenhard pers.comm.). Even allowing another $100,000,000 for state and Cultural Resource Management funding, this pales in comparison to the amount spent in some countries and little has been focused on wet site investigations. Japan for example, with about 5% of the area of the United States, spends roughly $500,000,000 annually on archaeology with substantial amounts directed towards wet site investigations (Matsui, this volume; Kiyotari 1986).

WINDOVER

The wet site as a case in point is Windover (8BR246) in southeast central Florida (Fig. 14.1). It typifies many of the problems, as well as the potentials of North American wet site archaeology.

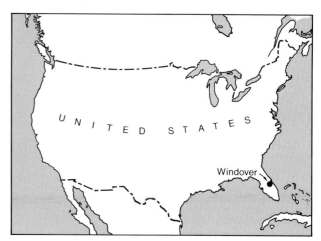

Fig. 14.1 Location Map

Windover, an Archaic mortuary pond, was discovered accidentally by developers (EKS, Inc.) constructing a road in their Windover Farms housing development near Titusville, Florida during the early summer of 1982. Ultimately EKS paid for several radiocarbon dates, rerouted the road, provided in-kind logistical and material support, and more importantly, actively lobbied for funding at the state level. Their efforts resulted in three excavation seasons running from roughly August through early January of 1984, 1985, and 1986 and one year of laboratory analysis. State funding accounted for over 90% of the nearly $900,000 excavation and research budget. Approximately 50% of the pond was investigated, and remains were recovered from a minimum of 168 individuals; it is estimated another 100-150 individuals are unexcavated (Doran and Dickel 1988a).

In 1986 and 1987 research proposals were submitted to NSF for field and laboratory analysis and both were turned down. Had it not been for the developer's interest and political contacts, Windover would never have been investigated and our knowledge of south Florida mortuary ponds in the Early Archaic period would be essentially what it was in the early 1980s. Sites like Windover were known prior to our investigations, but circumstances never allowed adequate investigation (Beriault *et al* 1981; Wharton *et al* 1981). As a result of the Florida State University investigations at Windover, the site has been listed in the National Registry of Historic Places, and Mr. Jack Eckerd, one of the property owners and project supporters, received the National Park Service's 1986 "Southeastern Archeological Conservation Award". The Florida Archaeological Council awarded Mr. Jim Swann, also one of the landowners, a "Steward of Heritage Award" for his role in supporting the Windover project. We are also trying to publish as rapidly as possible in main line journals to demonstrate the diversity of information which can come from wet sites and how they can play a unique role in understanding the past.

Excavation Plan

A basic problem was how to excavate material that was buried in peat more than 2 m below the bottom of a pond 1-3 m deep, while maintaining site integrity. A variety of excavation and dewatering strategies were considered and the one selected involved dewatering through a wellpoint installation program. During the first year a relatively small area (12 x 25 m) was encircled with sand and wellpoints placed through the sand dike. While effective, problems with seepage and the limited area for excavation were solved when the entire pond margin was encircled with wellpoints in 1985 and the entire pond was dewatered in the 1985 and 1986 excavation seasons.

Each point consists of a long pipe, or riser, connected to a perforated plastic and steel wellpoint. Points were installed by boring a hole into the peat with a high volume jet pump. A wellpoint and riser (4 – 6 m long) was then dropped into the hole and approximately 25-50 gallons of coarse sand placed around the point to act as a filter to keep fine particulate matter from clogging the well point. The points are connected to a header pipe system put under vacuum by a large rotary pump. Initial pumping volumes were around 700 gallons a minute for 2 - 3 weeks of continuous pumping. Gradually volumes tapered off to around 200 gallons per minute for the rest of the season and once into the "dry" season in Florida (less than 5 inches of rain a month) the pump could be run only at night or on alternate nights depending on circumstances. It was a very effective method of dealing with the water and has much to recommend it where necessary. A conservative estimate of the cost of wellpointing the site is approximately $120,000 (Doran and Dickel 1988a).

Chronology

The average radiocarbon date for ten samples of bone, wood and other artefactual material is approximately 7400 uncal BP (Doran and Dickel 1988b). Increased precision through radiocarbon correction studies indicates that the true age of the Windover materials should be around 8000 years BP during the Florida Early Archaic, the hunting-gathering (and fishing) aceramic tradition immediately following the Paleoindian large game hunting tradition (Milanich and Fairbanks 1980).

Conservation

During excavation all materials were kept damp by spray misting, bagged in plastic, or covered in plastic between work days. Conservation and stabilization of all organics was begun in a field lab during each excavation season. In the first year carbowax, i.e. polyethylene glycol (PEG 3350), was used. It is widely used in the preservation of waterlogged wood (Koob 1984; Brown 1974; Wing 1983).However, it is not as satisfactory for bone and antler and after the first field season Rhoplex-AC33, an acrylic emulsion, was utilized (Koob 1984; Feller 1963). Rhoplex was preferred because it lends more structural support to the fragile materials (Stone *et al* 1990).

Handwoven fabrics, unexpectedly recovered in 1986, have presented especially difficult and complex but important conservation problems and have benefited from the gracious and expert assistance of Judy Logan and David Grattan (Canadian Conservation Institute) and Joan Gardner (Carnegie Museum of Natural History, Pittsburgh). While the fabrics superficially appear to be in good shape their internal structure is severely degraded and great care is required in their conservation. Experiments using a variety of compounds have been undertaken, and it appears now that the best strategy is to freeze dry the fabrics and then stabilize them through a treatment procedure referred to as Parylene conformal coating (Gardner pers.comm; Adovasio pers.comm.). This technique involves vaporizing parylene (a solid) at high temperatures, and diffusing it under vacuum to a sample chamber at room temperature where the parylene condenses on the samples on a molecule by molecule basis creating a very thin but strong film (Humphrey 1984; Grattan 1989). The disadvantage of this technique, apart from the expensive equipment required, is that it is irreversible and no conservator likes to use techniques that can not be reversed. However, to ensure preservation of the fabrics this irreversible procedure appears to be the only reasonable course of action given the nature and condition of the material (Grattan, communication to Gardner).

Burial Practices and Paleodemography

In south Florida prior to 5000 uncal BP, burial in wet settings was apparently well established (Wharton *et al* 1981; Beriault *et al* 1981; Clausen *et al* 1975; Clausen *et al* 1979; Doran and Dickel 1988a,b; Purdy this volume). No similar burial tradition has been identified elsewhere in North America though extensive peat deposits exist particularly east of the Mississippi River. In an ongoing tabulation of the North American skeletal material which is clearly older than 5000 uncal BP (Doran and Dickel 1988b, 371, 372; Doran unpublished) and for which I would estimate 90% of all excavated materials older than 5000 uncal BP have been accounted for, several things are clear. First, there are only 51 sites coast to coast. California and Florida have the most sites, respectively 15 and 7. Generally, sites of this antiquity are represented by burials of less than 5 individuals, with the exception of Indian Knoll in Kentucky (Winters 1974) which accounts for 54% of the total sample of 2,283 individuals older than 5000 uncal BP. Illinois with 5 sites accounts for 251 individuals or 11% of the total sample, California with 15 sites accounts for a mere 6.6% of the total with 152 individuals, and Florida with 7 early sites accounts for 456 individuals, 19.9% of the total of these early examples. All but one of the Florida sites (Cutler Ridge) is a wet site or has a wet component. The full interpretation of this data is still underway but it would be tempting to suggest that, at least in part, the burial distribution reflects relatively high population densities in these regions in this early period. Such a conclusion is congruent with estimates of later population density (Ubelaker 1988, 291). With the exception of the west coast of the United States and south Florida, the dramatic population increases most apparent after 2500 uncal BP are associated with a shift to maize/bean/squash agricultural regimes (Jennings 1978). On the west coast and in south Florida population expansion also occurred, but did so without an agricultural base (Heizer and Whipple 1971; Widmer 1988; Milanich and Fairbanks 1980; and many others). These differences in subsistence regimes present interesting contrasts within which questions of population adaptation, paleodemography, paleopathology, etc. can be framed. California has a long history of productive skeletal studies (Brown 1967; Jurmain 1990; Walker 1986, 1989; Walker and Erlandson 1986); in comparison, studies of Florida skeletal material

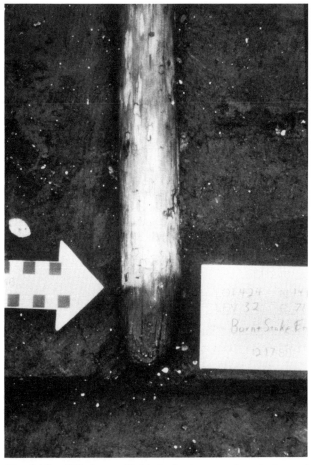

Fig. 14.2 Windover. Debarked, sharpened and charred wooden stake used to hold burial in place in pond

Fig. 14.3 Windover. Fragment of complex vegetable-fibre fabric

lag far behind, at least partly due to the scarcity of physical anthropologists in Florida (du Toit 1986; Iscan and Miller-Shaivitz 1983) though the situation is beginning to improve (Dickel *et al* 1989; Dickel and Doran 1989; Iscan 1983, 1989; Isler *et al* 1985; Maples 1987; Snow 1962).

Based on preservation of the brain tissue, bodies were placed in the Windover pond within 48 hours of death (Doran *et al* 1986). In all, 91 crania contained preserved brain tissue. Both sexes (27 females and 27 males) are represented, as well as 9 individuals of indeterminate sex. Individuals of all ages contained brain tissue. In the sloping pond margins south and west of the 1986 excavations disarticulation was common as bodies gradually slid downslope toward the deeper centre of the pond. Bodies interred on relatively flat locations on the northern margins of the pond remained stationary and were more frequently articulated. Such burials were predominantly flexed on their left side with heads oriented to the west, though there is a good bit of variation. Many bodies were apparently held in place by wooden stakes (Fig. 14.2) penetrating some of the blanket or shroud-like wrappings of the burials.

Studies of peat and water chemistry indicate that nearly neutral pH conditions provided for the preservation of the materials recovered from Windover (Stone *et al* 1990, 180,181), particularly the cancellous bone and antler materials which are less frequently recovered from wet sites than wooden artefacts.

Fabrics and Textiles

Eighty-seven examples of handwoven textile materials were recovered from 37 burials from the 1986 excavation (Fig. 14.3). Five twining or weaving types have been identified to date, including fine balanced plain weave of inner garments (possibly tunic-like garments, very finely made, one with 10 strands per centimeter). More durable, heavier materials were made with an unusual three strand twining technique. Items recovered include globular bags, mats, shrouds or blanket-like remains, cordage, twined and plaited materials. Adovasio, the director of the fabric analysis, has commented that these materials constitute:

> ... the oldest, largest and technologically most sophisticated examples of flexible fabrics found in the Americas. Older examples of rigid to semiflexible baskets, mats and sandals as well as cordage and nets are known from many places, but there is no other comparable assemblage of woven cloth like that recovered from Windover presently known to American archaeology. (Adovasio pers. comm. 1990)

Identification of the plant fibres of the fabrics is difficult. Much of the outer layer of fibre, useful in species identification, was removed during fibre processing and item manufacture. Processing of the plant material may have been facilitated by mastication and may explain some of the dental attrition patterns observed at Windover and other prehistoric sites. At present, fibres from the Sabal palm

(*Sabal palmetto*) or saw palmetto (*Seronoa repens*) appear to be the most likely source of the textile fibres (Andrews and Adovasio 1988; Andrews and Adovasio unpublished).

Bone, Antler and Dentary Artefacts

Bone awls and pins are the most commonly recovered artefact classes and were manufactured most frequently from white-tail deer and occasionally from canids and felids. One tool was made from the now-threatened manatee, and a small number of marine shells also show modification. There is also a small series of snail shells fashioned into beads.

Most of the bone artefacts are best described as pins, and some presumably could have been used in the weaving and twining activities. Some deer antler artefacts resemble atlatl weights but frequently show battering as if used as hammers which seems inconsistent with their function as atlatl weights or handles. Atlatl spurs or hooks are also present at Windover as are several other categories of bone and antler tools, such as the probable shaft straightener shown in Fig. 14.4.

CENTIMETERS

Fig. 14.4 Windover. Shaft wrench or shaft straightener for spear or atlatl, made from deer antler

Some antler tines were fashioned into socketed projectile points and one was found deeply embedded in the hip of a 35 year old male. This injury and the associated soft tissue damage led to a relatively rapid death as there is no evidence of healing.

A small series of shark teeth and dog canines were recovered, probably used as cutting tools. Some still retain the adhesive used in their hafting, while the handles themselves have not survived.

Stone Artefacts

By any measure, the stone artefact inventory, which would survive in any preservation setting, is unimpressive. It is restricted to four bifaces, one biface fragment, and fewer than 5 flakes (Doran and Dickel 1988b, 370). If the Windover burials had been placed 30 m in any direction in typical sand strata, the insignificant stone inventory would be all that was witness to a rich, diverse and informative material inventory. This emphasizes the value of wet site

investigations probably more emphatically than any other feature of Windover.

Faunal and Floral Analysis

A variety of samples of peat and floral material were collected at Windover, and most were examined with a view to environmental reconstruction and an understanding of changes in peat deposition and formation during the last 11,000 radiocarbon years (Fig. 14.5). Several of the studies, however, have direct impact in understanding the human activities and events at Windover.

Newsom's analysis of stomach contents, and comparisons to control samples, indicates the most likely time of year for the burials to have taken place is during the late summer or early fall, as fall-fruiting plants are the most common and no seeds from species fruiting in the spring have been identified (Newsom 1988 and Newsom unpublished). The plants most commonly appearing in the stomach samples include elderberry, grape, persimmon, and prickly-pear.

Wooden artefacts from Windover include the burial stakes, a double-ended pestle or muller, a spring trap with a strand or cordage attached, and a small wooden bowl. Much of the artefactual wood was compression wood which is denser, finer grained, and more resilient indicating care in selection of species and the part of tree to use in artefact manufacture.

An almost complete exocarp of a bottle gourd (*Lagenaria siceraria*) was recovered from a burial. Bottle gourds are pandemics particularly used as light, durable containers. Members of the squash family (related to the gourds) had been found north in Illinois in contexts as early as 7100 uncal BP, but the earliest archaeological presence of bottle-gourd previously recorded (also from a wet component) was dated to 4200 uncal BP (Missouri). Thus the Windover specimen pushes the appearance of bottle gourds in North America back by 3000 radiocarbon years (Doran *et al* 1990).

Petrographic analysis and subsequent reconstructions of depositional events at Windover indicate changes in water levels and pond size. During the burial epoch (8100 - 6900 uncal BP) water levels were at a low and there may have been less seasonal variation than in subsequent periods. Plant communities present at Windover and other sedimentological indicators suggest that the maximum water depth during burial activities was approximately 30 cm (Holloway unpublished; Stout and Spackman unpublished).

Osteological Analysis

The Windover collection of human bones is particularly important because it provides a much-needed biological and biocultural picture: most of the skeletal material from North America comes from the last few thousand years (Doran and Dickel 1988b), and at present the Windover

Fig. 14.5 Windover. Section through the burial deposits (c 2m high) documenting approximately 8000 years of sedimentological history

sample appears to be one of the largest and most representative of early samples (Doran and Dickel 1988b, 371, 372). A few cases are illustrative of the kinds of information that have been obtained to date.

One individual exhibited spina bifida coupled with sensory loss to the lower leg and eventual extensive osteomyelitis and loss of the foot and lower leg. Ultimately renal failure probably led to the individual's death (Dickel and Doran 1989). It seems very clear that this individual received an enhanced level of attention and relatively effective health care to have survived for what must have been several years in a severely impaired condition. This is in contravention to the classic vision of hunters and gatherers having a limited ability to maintain less productive members of their band. About 15% of the adults exhibit evidence of fractures to the upper elements, and evidence of traumatic injury is by no means rare. One individual, a 47 year old male, exhibits a classic orbital blowout fracture typically resulting from the intrusion of a sharp object into the eye (Dickel *et al* 1989). There is evidence of healing and suggestions of postural changes resulting from vision impairment.

Metric, nonmetric and paleodemographic studies are continuing and will provide a much-needed base line for comparisons with later populations in the southeastern United States.

Molecular biology – Proteins, Isotopes and DNA

Several studies of bone compounds have been undertaken and a number of bone proteins rarely identified in archaeological materials are present and include transferrin, albumin, IGG, IGN and IGA (Smith *et al* unpublished). Efforts to extract DNA from femurs have just begun (Tuross pers.comm.) Stable isotope analysis (carbon and nitrogen) indicates a freshwater aquatic dietary orientation as opposed to a strong marine orientation (Tuross *et al* unpublished). Such a pattern is also supported by faunal analysis from other nonburial sites in this region.

The recovery of preserved brain tissue in 1984 led to an assessment of structural integrity utilizing x-ray, CT scanning, and magnetic resonance imaging coupled with light and scanning electron microscopy. Tissue samples are also processed for isolation and study of remnant mitochondrial DNA and, more recently, nucleic DNA (Doran *et al* 1986; Lawlor *et al* 1991).

Isolation and identification of prehistoric human DNA truly heralds a new method of analysis of archaeological materials (Rogan and Salvo 1990; Paabo 1985, 1989; Paabo *et al* 1988; Paabo *et al* 1990). Addressing questions of population genetics may now be possible not only with living populations, but with prehistoric ones as well (Paabo *et al* 1989; Salvo *et al* 1989; Cavalli-Sforza *et al* 1988). The rate of advance and expansion of applications of this type of analysis in archaeology is particularly significant and comes at an unusual time – a time when there is a strong movement in some areas to rebury skeletal material, the very material which may provide the clearest understanding of population evolution, change, and regional genetic diversity (Ubelaker and Grant 1989; Hubert 1989; Zimmerman 1989). We are on the brink of losing materials that are only just beginning to be examined with these revolutionary techniques.

Public Education

During the three years of excavations at Windover literally hundreds of newspaper articles, television reports and radio broadcasts focused on Windover. During the three years of field work it is estimated that approximately 25,000 people (at a minimum) visited the site. In an effort to respond to the public interest in the site and to use it as an opportunity for education about archaeology, archaeological resources, and Florida sites in particular, a staff member trained in media relations was hired as a media specialist, with responsibility to coordinate and provide information to the various news entities for the last two years of investigation. This had a double benefit in that it allowed the archaeologists to perform the job for which they were trained and at the same time provided a public education component to a site that had generated immense media visibility. Creation of a similar position is strongly recommended for any project that is highly visible. This is particularly appropriate given the increasing appreciation of the importance of public education in archaeology.

CONCLUSIONS

In contrast to many countries around the world, the level of funding of all archaeology in United States is, by some measures, at the chronic level. It is particularly critical in terms of progress and funding in wet site archaeology where multidisciplinary requirements further compound the funding issue. Money specifically for surveys and inventories of wet sites seems a critical place to start, given the rapid destruction of wetland habitats. This must be followed by sufficient funding to carry out effective investigation of the sites identified. Identification and excavation, however, are not in and of themselves sufficient. Wet site archaeologists must publish in the main line journals or the value and importance of wet sites will be ignored, and they will be regarded as peripheral to the goals of anthropological archaeology.

I would like to see the day when all archaeologists look at waterlogged deposits in a site and excitedly exclaim "Fantastic, we've got wet materials!" instead of, "Stop digging, we've hit water".

Acknowledgements

Funding from the Florida Legislature provided for three field seasons in the fall of 1984, 1985 and 1986 and one laboratory season in 1987. Supplemental funding came from EKS, Inc. (owners of Windover Farms, Inc.), IBM, The National Geographic Society, the Ford Foundation, the Jesse H. Ball DuPont Charitable, Religious, and Educational Foundation, the Gannett Foundation and internal grants from Florida State University. The many volunteers of the Windover region donated thousands of hours to assist in the field work and without their help, our efforts would have been far less productive.

BIBLIOGRAPHY

Andersen, Søren H. 1985.Tybrind Vig: a preliminary report on a submerged Ertebølle settlement on the west coast of Fyn. *Journal of Danish Archaeology* 4,52-69.

Andrews, R.L. and Adovasio, J.M. 1988. *An Interim Statement on the Conservation and Analysis of Perishables from the Windover Archaeology Project, Florida.* Department of Anthropology, University of Pittsburgh, Pittsburgh, Pennsylvania.

Andrews, R. L., Adovasio, J.M. and Harding, D.G. unpublished. Textile and related perishable remains from the Windover site (8R246). In G.H. Doran (ed.), *Windover: An early wet site from Florida*, submitted to the University of Florida Press, Gainesville.

Binford, Louis R. 1962. Archaeology as anthropology. *American Antiquity* 28,217-225.

Binford, S.R. and L. Binford (eds.) 1968. *New Perspectives in Archeology.* Chicago: Aldine.

Brown, A. K. 1967. The Aboriginal Population of the Santa Barbara Channel. *Reports of the University California Archaeological Survey 69.* Berkeley: University of California.

Brown, M. K. 1974. A preservative compound for archaeological materials. *American Antiquity* 39, 469-473.

Casteel, R. W. 1980. National Science Foundation funding of domestic archaeology in the United States: where the money ain't. *American Antiquity* 45, 170-180.

Clausen, C. J., Brooks, H.K. and Wesolowsky, A. B. 1975. The early man site at Warm Mineral Springs, Florida. *Journal of Field Archaeology* 2, 191-213.

Clausen, C. J., Cohen, A.D., Emiliani, C., Holman, J.A. and Stipp, J.J. 1979. Little Salt Spring, Florida: a unique underwater site. *Science* 203, 609-614.

Coles, B. and Coles, J. 1986. *Sweet Track to Glastonbury. The Somerset Levels in Prehistory.*London: Thames and Hudson.

Coles, B. and Coles, J. 1989. *People of the Wetlands. Bogs, bodies, and Lake-Dwellers.* London: Thames and Hudson.

Coles, J. 1984. *The Archaeology of Wetlands.* Edinburgh: University Press.

Coles, J. and Lawson, A. (eds) 1987. *European Wetlands in Prehistory.* Oxford: Clarendon Press.

Croes, D. R. 1989. Prehistoric Ethnicity on the Northwest Coast of North America: an evaluation of style in basketry and lithics. *Journal of Anthropological Archaeology* 8, 101-130.

Croes, D.R. and Hackenberger, S. 1988. Hoko River archaeological complex: modeling prehistoric northwest coast economic evolution. In B. L. Isaac (ed.), *Prehistoric Economies of the Pacific Northwest Coast,* 19-85. Research In Economic Anthropology, Special Supplement 3. Greenwich, Conneticut: JAI Press, Inc.

Cushing, F. H. 1895. A preliminary examination of aboriginal remains near Pine Island, Marco, West Florida. *American Naturalist* 29, 1132-1135.

Cushing, F. H. 1897. Exploration of Ancient Key Dwellers' Remains on the Gulf Coast of Florida. *Proceedings of the American Philosopical Society* 25 (153), 329-448.

Dickel, D. N., Aker, G., Barton, B. K., and Doran, G.H. 1989. An orbital floor and ulna fracture from the Early Archaic of Florida. *Journal of Paleopathology* 2(3):165-170.

Dickel, D. N. and Doran, G.H. 1989. Severe neural tube defect syndrome from the Early Archaic of Florida (8BR246). *American Journal of Physical Anthropology* 80, 325-334.

Dolukhanov, P. and Miklyayev, A.M. 1986. Prehistoric lacustrine pile-dwellings in the north-western part of the USSR. *Fennoscandia archaeologica* 3,81-89.

Doran, G. H. and Dickel, D.N. 1988a. Multidisciplinary investigations at the Windover site. In B. A. Purdy (ed.), *Wet Site Archaeology,* 263-289. Caldwell, New Jersey: Telford Press.

Doran, G. H. and Dickel, D.N. 1988b. Radiometric chronology of the Archaic Windover archaeological site (8BR246). *Florida Anthropologist* 41, 365-380.

Doran, G. H., Dickel, D. N., Ballinger, W.E., Jr., Agee, O.F. Laipis, P.J. and Hauswirth, W. W. 1986. Anatomical, cellular and molecular analysis of 8000-yr-old human brain tissue from the Windover archaeological site. *Nature* 323, 803-806.

Doran, G. H., Dickel, D. N. and Newsom, L. A. 1990. A 7290-year-old bottle gourd from the Windover site, Florida. *American Antiquity* 55, 354-360.

Durnford, C.D. 1895. The discovery of aboriginal rope and wood implements in the mud of west Florida. *American Naturalist* 29, 1032-1039.

du Toit, B. M. 1986. *Anthropology in Florida: the history of a discipline.* Florida Journal of Anthropology, Special Publication No. 5. Gainesville: Florida State Museum.

Feller, R. L. 1963. New solvent-type varnishes. In Garry Thomson (ed.), *Recent Advances in Conservation,* 171-175. London: Academic Press.

Gardner, J. S. unpublished. Conservation of Windover fabrics and wood. In G. H. Doran (ed.), *Windover: An early wet site from Florida,* submitted to the University of Florida Press, Gainesville.

Gastaldi, B. 1865. *Lake Habitations and Pre-Historic Remains in the Turbaries and Marl-Beds of Northern and Central Italy.* Longman: London.

Gilliland, M. S. 1975. *The Material Culture of Key Marco.* Gainesville: University Presses of Florida.

Gilliland, M. S. 1989 *Key Marco's Buried Treasure: Archaeology and Adventure in the Nineteenth Century.* Gainesville: University of Florida Press.

Gramsch, B. 1985. Der mesolithisch-neolithische Moorfundplatz in Friesack, Kr. Nauen. *Ausgrabungen und Funde* 30, 57-67.

Grattan, D. W. 1989. Parylene at the Canadian Conservation Institute. *Canadian Chemical News* October, 25-26.

Guernsey, S.J. and Kidder, A.V. 1921. *Basket Maker caves of northeastern Arizona, report on the explorations, 1916, 1917.* Harvard University, Peabody Museum of American Archaeology and Ethnology Papers 8:2.

Haury, E. 1943. The stratigraphy of Ventana Cave. *American Antiquity* 8,218-223.

Hauswirth, W. W. and Dickel. C.D. unpublished. Investigations of DNA isolated from Windover brain tissue: methods and implications. In G. H. Doran (ed.), *Windover: An early wet site from Florida,* submitted to the University of Florida Press, Gainesville.

Hazzeldine Warren, S., Piggott, S., Clark, J.G.D., Burkitt, M. C. and Godwin, H. and M.E. 1936. Archaeology of the submerged land-surface of the Essex Coast. *Proceedings of the Prehistoric Society* 2, 178-210.

Heizer, R.F. and Whipple, M.A. (eds) 1971. *The California Indians: a Source Book,* (second edition). Berkeley: University of California Press.

Holloway, R. G. unpublished. Pollen analysis of Holocene sediments from the Windover pond peats (8BR246). In G. H. Doran (ed.), *Windover: An early wet site from Florida,* submitted to the University of Florida Press, Gainesville.

Hubert, J. 1989. A proper place for the dead: a critical review of the 'reburial' issue. In R. Layton (ed.), *Conflict in Archaeology of Living Traditions,* 131-166. One World Archaeology, Vol. 8. London: Unwin Hyman.

Humphrey, B. J. 1986. Vapor phase consolidation of books with the Parylene polymers. *Journal of the American Institute of Conservation* 25, 15-29.

Iscan, M.Y. 1983. Skeletal biology of the Margate-Blount population. *Florida Anthropologist* 36, 154-166.

Iscan, M.Y. 1989. Odontometric profile of a prehistoric southeastern Florida population. *American Journal of Physical Anthropology* 78, 3-8.

Iscan, M.Y. and Miller-Shaivitz, P. 1983. A review of physical anthropology in the *Florida Anthropologist. Florida Anthropologist* 36, 114-123.

Isler, R., Schoen, J. and Iscan, M.Y. 1985. Dental pathology of a prehistoric human population. *Florida Scientist* 48, 139-145.

Jennings, J. D. (ed.) 1978. *Ancient Native Americans.* San Francisco: W.H. Freeman and Company.

Johnson, F. (ed.) 1942. *The Boylston Street Fishweir.* Papers of the Peabody Foundation for Archaeology, Vol.2. Boston, Mass.

Johnson, F. (ed.) 1949. *The Boylston Street Fishweir II.* Papers of the Peabody Foundation for Archaeology, Vol.4. Boston, Mass.

Jurmain, R. 1990. Paleoepidemiology of a Central California Prehistoric population from CA-Ala-329: dental disease. *American Journal of Physical Anthropology* 81, 333-342.

Kiyotari, T. 1986. Problems concerning the preservation of archaeological sites in Japan. In R.J. Pearson (ed.) and G.L. Barnes and K.L. Hutterer (co-editors), *Windows on the Japanese Past: studies in archaeology and prehistory,* 481-490. Ann Arbor: Center for Japanese Studies, University of Michigan.

Koob, S. P. 1984. The consolidation of archaeological bone. In N.S. Brommelle, E.M. Pye, P. Smith and G. Thomson (eds), *Preprints of the Contributions to the International Institute for Conservation of Historic and Artistic Works, Paris Congress (Adhesives and Consolidants),* 96-102. London: The International Institute of Historic and Artistic Works.

Lawlor, D. A., Dickel, C.D., Hauswirth, W. W. and Parham, P. 1990. Ancient HLA genes from 7500-year-old archaeological remains. *Nature* 349, 785-788.

Maples, W. R. 1987. *Analysis of skeletal remains recovered at the Gauthier site, Brevard County, Florida.* Miscellaneous Project Report Series No. 31, Florida State Museum, Dept. of Anthropology.

Marquardt, W. H. 1986. The development of cultural complexity in southwest Florida: elements of a critique. *Southeastern Archaeology* 5l, 63-70.

Mathiassen, T. 1938. Some recently found Reindeer antler implements in Denmark. *Acta Archaeologica* 9.

Milanich, J. T. and Fairbanks, C.W. 1980. *Florida Archaeology*. New York: Academic Press, Inc.

Mordant, C. and Mordant, D. 1987. Noyen-sur-Seine, site mesolithique en milieu humide fluviatile. *112th Congres National des Societes Savantes, Lyon, Pre-et Protohistoire*, p. 33-52.

Munro, R. 1890. *The Lake - Dwellings of Europe*. Cassel: London.

Newsom, L. A. unpublished. The Paleoethnobotany of Windover. In G. H. Doran (ed.), *Windover: An early wet site from Florida*, submitted to the University of Florida Press, Gainesville.

Paabo, S. 1985. Molecular cloning of ancient Egyptian mummy DNA. *Nature* 312, 644-645.

Paabo, S. 1989. Ancient DNA: extraction, characterization, molecular cloning, and enzymaticamplification. *Proceedings of the National Academy of Sciences, U.S.A.* 86. 6196-6200.

Paabo, S., Dew, K, Frazier, B.S. and Ward, R.H. 1990. Mitochondrial revolution and the peopling of the Americas. *American Journal of Physical Anthropology* 81, 277.

Paabo, S., Gifford, J.A. and Wilson, A.C. 1989. Ancient DNA and the polymerase chain reaction. The emerging field of molecular archaeology. *Journal of Biological Chemistry* 264, 9797-9712.

Petrequin, A-M. and Petrequin, P. 1988. *Le Neolithique des Lacs. Prehistoire des lacs de Chalain et de Clairvaux (4000 - 2000av. J.-C.)*. Paris: Editions Errance.

Purdy, B. A. 1974. The Key Marco, Florida collection: experiment and reflection. *American Antiquity* 39, 105-109.

Purdy, B. A. 1979. An evaluation of wet site resources of Florida. *Florida Anthropologist* 32, 104-113.

Purdy, B. A. 1987. Investigations at Hontoon Island, An Archaeological Wetsite in Volusia County, Florida: An Overview and Chronology. *Florida Anthropologist* 40, 4-12.

Purdy, B. A. (ed.) 1988. *Wet Site Archaeology*. Caldwell, New Jersey: Telford Press.

Purdy, B. A. and Hall, S. 1981. Investigations and stabilization of wooden artifacts from Florida wetsites. *Southeastern Archaeological Conference Bulletin* 24, 16-17.

Rice, P. M. 1991. In "Organizational review at NSF", A partial text of the SAA's oral testimony before the NSF Organizational Task Force. *Society for American Archaeology Bulletin* 9, 4-5.

Rogan, P.K. 1990. Study of nucleic acids isolated from ancient remains. *Yearbook of Physical Anthropology* 33, 195-214.

Rogan, P.K., and Salvo, J.J. 1990. Molecular genetics and pre-Colombian South American Mummies. *Molecular Evolution, UCLA Symposium on Molecular Cellular Biology* 122, 223-234.

Royal, W. and Clark, E. 1960. Natural preservation of human brain, Warm Mineral Springs, Florida. *American Antiquity* 26, 285-287.

Salvo, J.J., Allison, M.J., and Rogan P.K. 1989. Molecular genetics of pre-Columbian South American mummies. *American Journal of Physical Anthropology* 78, 295.

Sears, W. H. 1982. *Fort Center: an archaeological site in the Lake Okeechobee Basin*. Ripley P. Bullen Monographs in Anthropology and History, Number 4. Gainesville: University Presses of Florida.

Smith, D. G., Lorey, F.W., and Rolfs, B.K. unpublished. Serum Albumin Phenotypes for the Prehistoric Population of Windover and their Anthropological Significance. In G. H. Doran (ed.), *Windover: An early wet site from Florida*, submitted to the University of Florida Press, Gainesville.

Snow, C.E. 1962. *Indian burials from St. Petersburg, Florida*. Contributions of the Florida State Museum, Social Sciences. 8. Gainesville: University of Florida.

Stone, T., Dickel, D. N. and Doran, G. H. 1990. The preservation and conservation of waterlogged bone from the Windover Site Florida: a comparison of methods. *Journal of Field Archaeology* 17, 177-186.

Stout, S. A. and Spackman, W. unpublished. Paleoecology of the Windover site interpreted by peat petrology and chemistry. In G. H. Doran (ed.), *Windover: An early wet site from Florida*, submitted to the University of Florida Press, Gainesville.

Taylor, W. W. 1948. *A Study of Archaeology*. Memoirs of the American Anthropological Association, No. 69.

Tuross, N., Fogel, M., Newsom, L. A. and Doran, G.H. unpublished. Subsistence in the Florida Archaic: the stable isotope and ethnobotanial evidence from the Windover site. Submitted to the *American Journal of Physical Anthropology*.

Ubelaker, D. H. 1988. North American Indian population size, A.D. 1500 to 1985. *American Journal of Physical Anthropology* 77, 289-294.

Ubelaker, D. H. and Grant, L.G. 1989. Human skeletal remains: preservation or reburial? *Yearbook of Physical Anthropology* 32, 249-288.

Walker, P. L. 1986. Porotic hyperostosis in a marine dependent California Indian population. *American Journal of Physical Anthropology* 69, 345-354.

Walker, P. L. 1989. Cranial injuries as evidence of violence in prehistoric California. *American Journal of Physical Anthropology* 80, 313-324.

Walker, P. L. and Erlandson, J.M. 1986. Dental evidence for prehistoric dietary change on the Northern Channel Islands. *American Antiquity* 51, 375-383.

Wharton, B.R., Ballo, G.R. and Hope, M. E. 1981. The Republic Groves site, Hardee County, Florida. *Florida Anthropologist* 34, 59-80.

Widmer, R. J. 1988. *The evolution of the Calusa, a non-agricultural chiefdom on the Southwest Florida coast*. Tuscaloosa: University of Alabama Press.

Wing, E. S. 1983. *A guide for archaeologists in the recovery of zooarchaeological remains*. Florida Journal of Anthropology, Special Publication No.3, Gainesville: Florida State Museum.

Winters, H.R. 1974. An introduction to the new edition. In W.S. Webb *Indian Knoll*. Knoxville: University of Tennessee Press.

Willey, G. G. and Sabloff, J.A. 1974. *A History of American Archaeology*. London: Thames and Hudson.

Yellen, J. E., Greene, M.W., and Louttit, R.T. 1980. A response to "National Science Foundation funding of domestic archaeology in the United States: where the money ain't". *American Antiquity* 45, 180-181.

Zimmerman, L. J. 1989. Made radical by my own: an archaeologist learns to accept reburial. In R. Layton (ed.), *Conflict in Archaeology of Living Traditions*, 60-67. World Archaeology, Vol. 8. London: Unwin Hyman.

15

THE *PFAHLBAULAND* EXHIBITION, ZÜRICH 1990

Ulrich Ruoff

SYNOPSIS

Pfahlbauland, *organised by the Gesellschaft für Schweizer Unterwasserarchäologie in 1990, was a combination of an exhibition and numerous activity points.* Pfahlbauland *offered the visitors a vivid picture of the daily life of the people in the Neolithic and the Bronze Age. It was the most comprehensive presentation of this subject that has ever taken place in Switzerland.* Pfahlbauland *covered 20,000 sq. m and was situated on the edge of lake Zürich and just offshore on a little island.*

The best known prehistoric remains of Switzerland are certainly the so-called Lake Villages. The first settlements of this type were discovered in the 1850s in Obermeilen, in the neighbourhood of Zürich. The great numbers of piles standing in the lake were interpreted to have supported platforms, on which the villages were built. This interpretation seemed so self-evident, that it was not very much discussed until almost a century later. Today we know that most of the villages were originally built on dry land or on ground flooded only seasonally. The remains of these villages were covered by water only later on, partly because the shores on which they were built sunk and partly because the water levels of the lakes have risen. The innumerable piles discovered are, in fact, remains of different villages built on the same sites at various times and of alterations, or repairs of the individual houses, which seem to have been undertaken quite frequently. These wetland sites are especially important for study of the life of Neolithic and Bronze Age man, because of the great variety of well preserved finds, which they invariably yield. For instance, textiles and objects of wood and bone and of other organic materials, which usually perish on dry land, often remain in a very good condition under water for thousands of years. Equally important from the archaeologist's point of view is the fact that one prehistoric village after another was often built on

more or less the same site, the remains of which are usually separated from each other by layers of sand and lake marl. Thus the great number of cultural layers and the clear stratigraphy of these sites make their study a very worthwhile undertaking.

Thanks to new developments within dendrochronology it has been possible to accumulate much fundamentally new evidence about the length and the relative chronology of the various prehistoric cultures and individual settlements in the recent years (Chronologie 1986; Becker *et al* 1985). At the same time a new picture of the character of the early settlements has emerged. We can now truly say that we know more about several aspects of the Swiss Neolithic and Bronze Age villages built on the lake shores or in the bogs than for example the Early Mediaeval settlements in this country. So far, however, the general public has known little about the latest discoveries of the archaeological research work. Even the school books have not been appropriately revised, though people are in general interested in archaeology (Osterwalder Maier 1990). Excavations and important finds always attract publicity. Nevertheless, many antiquated ideas about prehistoric man still stubbornly persist. Even educated people often seem to think that outside the Mediterranean area people lived more or less like savages up to the Roman period. Prehistoric man is popularly presented as a dishevelled cretin brandishing a club.

PLANNING PFAHLBAULAND

In 1988 the Society for Swiss Underwater Archaeology began to plan a large archaeological exhibition in order to try to remedy such misconceptions[1]. The aim of the exhibition was to show the most important discoveries of recent research on the Swiss Neolithic and Bronze Age settlements from the lakesides and in the bogs (Suter 1987; Gross *et al* 1987; Eberschweiler *et al* 1987; Gross *et al* 1990). From the very beginning the Committee of the Society decided that the exhibition must not consist only of showing finds. So it began to plan a kind of trial ground exhibition, where the visitors could try for themselves how prehistoric tools were used and what kind of results ancient working methods produced. In that way they could get a clearer impression of the skills of prehistoric man than just by looking at the ancient implements in show cases. The Committee also wished to have a kind of open air museum built in the manner of an Early Bronze Age lake village in the exhibition area. Remains of unusually well preserved villages from that period and other prehistoric epochs had been discovered during a rescue excavation at Zürich-Mozartstrasse in 1981. So a reconstruction of one such village could be ventured upon (Fig. 15.1. Gross *et al* 1987).

When we tried to define the goals of such an exhibition project, we realized that they could not be attained only by setting up an experimentation area complemented by the reconstructed village. As the only prehistorian on the Committee I also felt responsible for the correctness of the scientific information, and I was afraid that, for example, the experimental workshops could all too easily degenerate into a rather perfunctory show. Moreover most aspects of the main theme - life of the prehistoric farming societies - could not very well be illustrated with experimental workshop activities only. They had to be supplemented with more ordinary exhibitions and other means of conveying information to the visitors.

Very soon the project outgrew the modest dimensions which the Committee of our small Society had originally foreseen. The main problem was the financing of the project. We realized that in order to make it commercially viable we had to organize it on a large scale. For if we had only a small exhibition and spent only a moderate amount of money for advertising it, too few people would visit it. This would mean that the admission fees, the contributions of the sponsors, as well as those of the City and the Canton of Zürich (about 1/4 of the Budget) would not cover the expenses of the setting up of the necessary buildings and the wages of the people, who we would have to employ to run it. However, a large exhibition which would attract plenty of visitors would also be much more expensive to build. In the end Mr. U. Wenger, appointed to take care of the planning and management of the exhibition, calculated that the most profitable relation between the costs of putting it up and the expected income from the admission fees would mean that the exhibition ought to attract about 400,000 visitors within the six months, for which we could have the right to use the grounds. The Committee was slightly staggered at this piece of news, because we knew that no exhibition in Switzerland had ever pulled in such a vast number of people, but we decided, nevertheless, to push ahead. We had, of course, hoped from the very beginning that even such people who did not usually visit museums or cultural shows would come to this exhibition. Now it became a vital necessity. Incidentally, the above calculation proved more or less correct. Because of a disastrous fire three weeks after the opening of the exhibition we

probably lost about 100,000 visitors, but by the end of the October, when *Pfahlbauland* closed its doors, 380,000 people had visited it.

It would, of course, have been possible to make the exhibition a financially quite viable show by letting space for souvenir shops and many other kinds of commercial activities. There was, indeed, no lack of suggestions concerning such possibilities, and it was at times really difficult for the archaeologists to fend off most of these offers, which, in their opinion, would have spoilt the atmosphere of the exhibition and distracted the visitors from its actual purpose. To reconcile conflicting ideas about popular appeal, financial viability, and the scientific message of *Pfahlbauland* seemed indeed at times even more difficult than the finding of ways and means of conveying the archaeological and historical information to the general public in an easily understandable form.

The City of Zürich allowed the exhibition to be built in a lakeside park, which lies a little outside the city centre, in the neighbourhood of the well known Lake Dwelling settlements of Zürich-Wollishofen. The area at our disposal was a little over 20,000 sq. m including a small artificial island just off the shore. The island was an ideal place for the reconstruction of the Early Bronze Age village (Fig. 15.2).

The area of the *Pfahlbauland* was planned as follows: the reconstruction of the Early Bronze Age village was to be built on the island and there were to be three large, identical wooden exhibition centres in the park (Fig. 15.1). In the middle of each complex there was to be a large pyramidical room. It was to be used for audiovisual shows, which introduced the specific themes of each particular exhibition centre to the visitors. The middle room was surrounded by a wide, covered passage through which the visitors could enter the three exhibition halls of each centre. On the fourth side of each 'pyramid' there was a covered workshop area. It was enclosed by a palisade-like wooden fence. In each workshop there was a long table for demonstrations as well as stools, small tables and necessary gadgets for the visitors. There were also information panels and show cases with explanatory material.

We preferred to have small workshops at each exhibition centre rather than a larger experimentational area. In that way it was easier for the visitors to see the connection between the prehistoric tools in the show cases, the information on display in the exhibition halls, and the specific workshop areas where they could use lookalike tools and try ancient working methods for themselves (Fig. 15.3). The experimentations in the workshops had not been planned to offer the visitors perfunctory leisure activities, but to help them gain insight into the skills of prehistoric man. The placing of the workshops with their bustle and demonstrations in the immediate vicinity of the exhibition halls was also seen as a means of catching the attention of those visitors who had primarily come to see only the exhibitions in the halls. So we hoped that even the most

Fig 15.1 Aerial view of the exhibition area. In the left hand corner the restaurant and the entrance area, between the trees the three exhibition centres with the 'pyramids' in the middle, on the island the burnt remains of the first reconstruction of the Early Bronze Age village from about 1600 BC

Fig 15.2 A view of the reconstruction of the Early Bronze Age village. Evidence for the groundplans and the heights of all the houses was discovered at Zürich-Mozartstrasse in 1981

Fig 15.3 Children trying to work an upright weaving loom under the guidance of a trained weaver at the textile workshop

Fig 15.4 Melting down bronze in a crucible in a pit with pieces of glowing charcoal. The demonstrator works with two bellows to pump air into the charcoal until a temperature is reached at which the metal melts down

casual visitors would carry away some impressions which would contribute to a better understanding of the life of ancient man and help displace the above-mentioned primitive ideas about the lake dwellers.

Groups of nearly life-size figures placed in prehistoric everyday situations between the two entrances of each exhibition hall were meant to dispel old ideas of the lake dwellers as carefree hunters and of village life as romantic as a party by the lake shore on a nice summer day. The groups shown included a woman milking a cow, a smith hammering bronze and a man sowing corn. There was also a big model presenting the area around the Lake of Zürich in the Neolithic, when it was still largely covered by primeval forests.

Knowledge about the economic circumstances of Neolithic and Bronze Age man is equally or even more important for the understanding of these periods as typological and chronological information about the different 'cultures'. Economic aspects were also emphasized in the small guide book written for the visitors. Information on the typological differences between ceramics or tools of the different prehistoric cultures or cultural groups were mentioned only in passing. Instead, references to the agricultural methods and to the domestic animals kept during the various periods were added to the presentation of the chronology of the Lake Dwelling sites around Lake Zürich.

Experimental Workshops

Information about the Neolithic and Bronze Age lake dwellers' astounding dexterity at handicrafts was presented to the visitors through original finds as well as copies made especially for this exhibition. These showed the various stages of making such objects. Practical demonstrations in the workshops complemented the exhibitions in the buildings. It could be shown for instance on the basis of numerous wooden objects that Neolithic man was extremely knowledgeable about the suitability of various parts of different kinds of trees for special purposes. He seems unfailingly have been able to choose the right piece of the right kind of wood for each of the manifold objects he was obliged to make of this material. Also the archaeologists involved in the project gained many new insights into Neolithic woodworking practices when they were making the copies of the prehistoric objects needed for *Pfahlbauland*. We had, for instance, no idea how difficult it would be to try to find really suitable pieces of trunks and branches for the various axe shafts, similar to those used by Neolithic man. The pieces of wood that our expert, a trained carpenter, managed to discover after much effort, scarcely came up to the exacting average Neolithic standards.

It was fascinating to watch a bronze cast being made on the work-site (Fig. 15.4). A group of students from the University of Zürich under the direction of a specialist and prehistorian, Walter Fasnacht, demonstrated it several times each week. This was not just an exhibition demonstration but a real piece of experimental archaeology. The most surprising part was perhaps the simple apparatus necessary for such a casting, a pit with charcoal (we also found that just wood could be used, but then it was more difficult not to miss the right moment for taking out the molten metal), two air channels leading into the pit, two leather bellows and a crucible. The crucibles used were reconstructions of originals from the Neolithic Pfyn and Horgen cultures. In all of this Walter Fasnacht and his team profited from the long experience of the French archaeologist Philipe Andrieux. This is not the place to recount the details. However, it should be mentioned that despite a lot of practice, only half of the casting attempts were successful in reaching a product which met prehistoric standards (Fig. 15.5). As a colleague of mine rightly observed with refer-

Fig 15.5 One of the knives of Urnfield type, cast by the students of Prehistory in the workshop, together with the form used for its casting

ence to the workshops in *Pfahlbauland*, nowadays we try to develop special technical equipment for every kind of work, but if one looks at less developed or ancient peoples, however, one finds very simple apparatus, but a lot of 'know how' and skill.

This is also true of much of the everyday work in the household, such as the pounding and grinding of grain. Only when two African women had told us that we should remove neither the corn nor the chaff from the mortar until the very end were we able to produce useful results, and by using the correct movement when grinding on a simple saddle quern, they did the job in half the time that it had taken our people to do the same amount. It is, indeed, advisable to be cautious when calculating man-hours for various kinds of work in prehistoric and historic times. One's own attempts may not be comparable.

Other serious experiments were also taking place in *Pfahlbauland* in the pottery workshop under the direction of excavation technician, Johannes Weiss. Superb copies of Neolithic and Bronze Age vessels, fired in simple pits, were produced (Fig. 15.6). Through these experiments we became better judges of genuine prehistoric pottery. Above all, there was experimentation using different tempers. Some of the vessels were used for cooking, and it was noted whether the burnt-on remains of food and the overflow of

Fig 15.6 A potter decorating a bowl thrown in the manner of the vessels of the Urnfield Culture

cooking liquids had the same effect as it had on prehistoric originals.

Experimentations with the working of wood and bone also took place in the exhibition. Children, above all, were fascinated by seeing how stone or bone chisels, awls and other such tools were made by polishing. They were given rectangularly sawn pieces of soft soapstone instead of the harder stones typically used for the prehistoric originals so that they were able to produce finished objects during their visit. Many visitors liked to try their hand at making small copper vessels. They could be produced by working sheets of copper with hammers which were exact copies of the authentic Bronze Age socketed hammers. Several fires were kept burning all through the day around the workshop so that the metal which had become hard and brittle through hammering could be heated again and again.

Displays and Talks

In order to illustrate various activities of the lake dwellers we tried to find ethnological parallels in European history rather than in primitive societies of today. We did this for three reasons:

1. even if parallels were drawn only between certain interesting similarities between the techniques used by the lake dwellers of the Swiss Bronze Age and a primitive people of today the visitors would tend to think that these people would also otherwise have lived in a more or less identical manner.

2. the comparisons made between examples taken from Swiss prehistory and from later periods of European history would give the spectators a feeling of a closer emotional connection with the subject matter than parallels drawn between the lake dwellers and some far-off tribes would have done.

3. parallels drawn between the circumstances of the lake dwellers and those in the not-so-very distant past in one's own country would show clearly how slowly for example some agricultural practices changed over long periods of time before the mechanization of farming caused its relatively recent enormous changes.

The School Programs Department of Swiss Television had made three twenty minutes long films about the Lake Dwellings as well as about Neolithic and Bronze Age working methods[2]. Short lectures and audiovisual shows took place in each of the 'pyramid' rooms every quarter of an hour. The purpose of the short lectures was to inform the visitors about one or another special theme connected with the Lake Dwelling studies. We wished the lectures to be as ingenious and diverse as possible so that they would help to stimulate the visitors to reflect on the related problems themselves. The lecturers, most of whom were students, were free to decide for themselves if they wanted to tell the visitors about enigmatic prehistoric objects and also to let them handle them, or if they wanted to inform them about the differences between the death rates of the prehistoric times and those of today, or to talk to them about primitive agriculture on the basis of ethnological comparisons. They might also describe the rigours of living in a prehistoric lake village in winter time. Many of the old well-known pictures of the Lake Dwellings depict their inhabitants like guests at a romantic lake shore party on a beautiful summer day. The various possibilities concerning the lectures were, of course, discussed with each student, and all of them took part in a special three day training course organized by the Society. We noticed later on that this training had, however, been too rudimentary. Some of the lecturers turned out to be too pedantic, while others felt obviously unsure about themselves or about their subject matter, or both. Yet, it must also be stated that quite a number of the students understood really well how to inspire the visitors to think about the circumstances in which prehistoric man lived and the difficulties he encountered in his daily life. Anyway, the main idea behind these lectures proved correct: short and relatively detailed talks on specific aspects of the Lake Dwellings obviously helped the visitors to understand the challenges and problems of modern archaeological research better than a very general synopsis would have done.

In general the visitors seem to have appreciated the fact that not only most of the lecturers, but also most of the other people involved in the running of the exhibition, were students of archaeology, excavation technicians, archaeologists or restorers, i.e. people who had first hand knowledge of one kind or other about the Lake Dwellings. Experts, not showmen, were sought after. Quick-witted repartee by the personnel does not necessarily encourage visitors to ask questions or help them to overcome their diffidence about displaying their ignorance of prehistory. It was also important that the people who conducted the workshop activities were experts in their own respective fields and could answer questions in a serious way on the basis of their own experience, and did not conceal the problems involved with prehistoric working methods.

In addition to the exhibition buildings there was a number of additional activities like drives in ox-drawn Bronze Age type carts, Lake Dwelling lookalike dugouts for canoeing on the lake, a laboratory for dendrochronology, a Neolithic bake-oven and, last but not least, the above mentioned Early Bronze Age village on the small island.

RESULTS OF RECENT RESEARCH

All the prehistorians involved in the preparations of the *Pfahlbauland* considered it very important to try to convey a new view of Neolithic and Bronze Age subsistence economy to the visitors. So the Swiss National Museum in Zürich, the Direction of which had decided to mount a simultaneous archaeological exhibition in the Museum, chose as its theme 'Lake dwellers – the First Farmers of Europe'. The two volumes of articles written on this and related subjects by archaeologists from various European countries give a comprehensive view of the present state of their studies (*Die ersten Bauern* 1990). Since the 1960s archaeobotanists have been co-operating closely with the 'Büro für Archäologie' of the City of Zürich on all its underwater and lake shore excavations. At the beginning

they concentrated primarily on the environmental studies, later the study of agriculture and the gathering of wild edibles during the Neolithic and Bronze Age gained precedence. The most important results of these twenty-five years of archaeobotanic research in Zürich were published in 1989 (Jacomet *et al* 1989). Also archaeozoology has played a very important part in the study and evaluation of finds from the large scale rescue excavations in Zürich (Schibler and Suter 1990). At the excavation of the Zürich-Mozartstrasse alone we discovered around 100,000 bone fragments, which were subsequently analyzed (Gross *et al* 1987).

The latest results of these studies were at our disposal to show to the public in the three halls of the first exhibition centre. They were respectively called 'To Sow and to Reap', 'Over the Water and through the Primeval Forest', and 'Domestic and Wild Animals'. The agricultural methods used and some aspects of the economics of gathering wild plants were presented in the first hall. Corn was most probably the main source of nourishment for Neolithic man. The place outside the hall where corn was threshed was a great attraction, especially for children. The botanist responsible for the section on plants and botanic exhibits had stored the year before sheaves to last through the whole six months of the exhibition. After threshing the corn was pounded in a mortar and then ground in the Neolithic manner between a concave stone and a grindstone. The next steps were to make the dough and then to bake small flat cakes on a hot stone in an open fire or in a bake-oven like the ones in the Neolithic Bavarian bog settlements.

The second of the above mentioned displays was a survey of the Neolithic and Bronze Age landscape. The third exhibition showed what the most important domestic animals were, namely cattle, swine, sheep and goats, and their importance as sources of meat and milk as well as the significance of cattle as draught animals for prehistoric man. The same exhibition provided a survey of the wild animals that Neolithic man liked to hunt at times when there were not enough domestic animals to be slaughtered. Fish was, of course, an important source of nourishment. However, we gave rather little space to the presentation of hunting and fishing in *Pfahlbauland*, because most people think anyway that these activities were the main occupations of ancient man. It may, therefore, have come as quite a surprise to many visitors that one of the first things they encountered inside the gates of *Pfahlbauland* was a small garden, where flax was growing along with other plants. In due time the flax was harvested, the fibres prepared for spinning and eventually also spun in the textile workshop of *Pfahlbauland*.

The cows, bulls, goats, sheep and swine kept on the small island beside the reconstructed Bronze Age village certainly left a lasting impression on visitors about the kind of domestic animals kept by the lake dwellers. The Society *Pro Specie Rara* helped to choose animals for the exhibition which were more or less similar to the prehistoric breeds. We also constructed a cart on the basis of the fragments of disc wheels and an axle which were found in a Corded Ware layer during the excavation of the Zürich-Pressehaus site in 1976 (Ruoff 1976). We wanted the cart to be drawn at regular intervals through the exhibition area by oxen, but where was the farmer to be found who knew how to handle a yoke and draught oxen? And what further problems would we encounter even when we had found someone who was prepared to drive an ox? It never occurred to us that we might have used a cow. How surprised I was when I read in a book which was still in constant use in our agricultural schools fifty years ago 'The cow is a cheap source of animal power and has become the draught animal of the small and medium-sized farm in the alpine lands. 70% of small and medium-sized farms in southern Germany work with draught cows'. This same handbook mentioned that Austria's cows drew the harvest wagons, that in Northern Italy and Southern France draught cattle were used for ploughing and that in Switzerland around 100,000 cows, bulls and bullocks provided the draught power.

In the absence of oxen, we had to stick with a bull. Luckily, it was a good-natured animal, and the difficulties we had envisaged did not occur. There was another problem though: the animal refused to pull! We had to be content with two or three circuits a day (Fig. 15.7). Happily, fathers frequently took on the role of the bull and pulled their children around in the stone-age cart. The cart proved itself exceptionally stable and usable on rough ground. Incidentally, the first prototype was even used on a mountain farm for shifting muck. During the six months of the exhibition one of the wagons must have covered 100 km on rough asphalt without major repair. Our bull was a constant reminder to us that in order to keep domestic animals usefully, you need experience.

Lake Villages

It was in the 1950s that many archaeologists came to the conclusion that the old idea of these villages standing on large platforms built on piles in the lakes, must be wrong. Excavations of various bog sites had shown that very often the floors of the houses were not raised above ground level at all. Evidence for this is provided by the many hearths that lay directly on the ground. These results did not, however, find acceptance outside archaeological circles. It was obviously hard even for some archaeologists to give up the cherished view of the 'romantic' lake villages of old. This attitude influenced the course of further research in a positive, but also in a negative way. It was certainly good for prehistorians to study the evidence against the old interpretation of the piles as supporting posts for large platforms in great detail again and again. During these repeated investigations they discovered evidence for a number of different manners of constructing houses which nobody had been aware of earlier. They also became aware of the fact that

Fig 15.7 A bull of a rare old breed drawing a cart reconstructed on the basis of the remains of a vehicle found in a Corded Ware layer at Zürich-Pressehaus in 1976

houses which had simply been considered 'Lake Dwellings' may originally have been built in very different kinds of situations. There were obviously villages which had been built on ordinary dry lakeshores, others which consisted of houses built on 'stilts' and stood very near to the water – the sites of such villages were periodically inundated. Last but not least, there also seemed to be villages which had really been built in the water, and also any number of combinations between the various locations and the manners of construction.

In the opinion of our team the question of whether the villages were built on dry land or in water has, however, dominated Swiss Lake Dwelling studies far too much. In the exhibition this problem was, therefore, not presented in great detail. The structure of the villages and their 'genesis' was expounded much more circumstantially. It has recently been possible to investigate and clarify such matters at quite a number of different sites thanks to new advances in dendrochronological studies. Among the most surprising new findings are the examples of a couple of villages with very regular ground plans. Certain traces at other sites also indicate that such ground plans may have been quite normal during the Neoltihic and Bronze Age. The houses stood in rows and usually very close to each other. A further interesting fact which has recently emerged is that the villages were usually built over a period of several years. We built a model of a such a village for the exhibition. The first of the houses of this particular village, which dated from the Corded Ware period, had been built in 2605 BC, and the complete village with its regular rows of houses stood ready only after seven years (Gross and Ruoff 1990).

In the reconstructed Early Bronze Age village on the small island it was easy for visitors to get a good idea of the regularity of a prehistoric village and of the confined space in which ancient man lived. It consisted of eleven buildings. Previously during excavation we had discovered not only the foundation beams of the houses, but also one ridge post and some of the corner and centre posts, which had supported the roofs, lying on the ground. On the basis of their length we had been able to calculate the heights of the walls and the slope of the roofs. During the reconstruction of the village we realized that each row of houses must probably have shared a common roof. There was simply not enough space between the walls of the individual houses for separate roofs to have been constructed. Such a row of houses would therefore in reality have looked like a long house.

Most people who visited the village seem to have wondered in what kind of way the small community was once organized. It was very evident that nobody living in such a confined village was able to act freely according to his or her individual wishes. I think that the significance of *Pfahlbauland* lay, indeed, in its providing not only modern views on prehistory but also factual information presented in such a way that the visitor more or less had to start asking himself questions about the life of early man. I cite here only one such question posed by a friend of mine. He asked me whether the curved Late Bronze Age objects which the archaeologists call 'keys' really fulfilled this function. I told him that one such object at least worked like a key on the model door in the exhibition. The mechanical details were, however, of little interest to him. He was remembering the villages in the Pacific Islands where he had lived for long periods of time. He said he had never seen a locked door in native villages. Who would want to steal anything, when anyone within the small community could discover the stolen article straightaway in the thief's house? What would the lake dwellers want to lock up? The community storehouse? The temple? Soon a whole group of town administrators of Zürich who chanced to be in the exhibition was disscussing the matter. The incident illustrates how little we still know about everyday life in prehistoric times even in cases where we believe to have clinched a seemingly definite interpretation for an object. Re-thinking may be necessary.

Non-material aspects

Today many archaeologists prefer to avoid clear statements about the non-material side of prehistoric cultures. In a prehistoric context the word 'culture' is anyway most of the time used only to denote complexes of features and objects which are considered typical in a definite area at a certain time. Subjects like religious beliefs, social traditions and other traces of non-material culture are dealt with cursorily by describing burial places and objects, which may possibly have had a 'cultic purpose'. In *Pfahlbauland* such concise descriptions would not have been appreciated. The visitors would want to know much more about prehistoric man's outlook on life and death. As we began to mount the displays dealing with the themes 'Friend and Foe', 'Supremacy of Nature', 'Life and Death' and to plan the events where conceptions like culture, society, cult and magic would have to be presented we realized that the prehistorians themselves have discussed these matters far too little. These subjects, have, of course, been dealt with in a large number of theoretical studies with numerous models. There is, however, a dearth of critical appraisals of concrete archaeological findings in this field. So it was quite a challenge to try to portray such issues in a way which, we hoped, would be intelligible to a broad public. What kind of occurrences brought about the emergence and the dissolution of the various 'Cultures' (the word is here used in its archaeological meaning)? In what way did we consider the society to have been organized? What could the objects found in the graves have meant?

Furthermore, we wanted to correct the still wide-spread view that the lake dwellers would have been an ethnical group of their own. Time and again most prehistorians have probably been disconcerted at realizing how easily the uninitiated give free rein to fantasy and what a large number of half-truths are flying about. Swiss archaeologists are, for instance, often asked whether the lake dwellers were Celts. Why? Probably because people generally connect the Celts with an enigmatic culture, and it gives a certain lustre to the history of Switzerland to imagine that the Celts once lived here. It is certainly no accident that we encounter the mysterious figure of a Druid in most of the stories and novels about the lake dwellers. So it was necessary to point out to the visitors that quite probably the inhabitants of the lake and bog villages never represented a closely knit society. Within the large geographic area of the presumed 'Lake Dwellings Culture' there were people living in one area whose cultural traditions differed widely from those of the inhabitants of another area. It was also important to show to visitors that our ideas about the past would be distorted if they were based only on certain aspects borrowed from totally separate cultures which prevailed in different places during diverse periods and were in other aspects dissimilar to each other. Later on, during an archaeological conference organized in *Pfahlbauland*, I was again struck by the tendency of the scientists to describe findings without discussing their historical testimony at all. For instance one prehistorian had detected conspicuous traces of use on battle-axes, but he did not discuss the dark implications.

Speaking about the battle-axes I may mention the reasoning that led to our having the display 'Friends and Foes'. Our portrayal of the past is always influenced by the ideals of our own time at least to some extent. We believe to find in the past either encouraging or deterrent parallel developments. Our view of the past is further influenced by the propensity to record such occurences which are either exemplary or somehow out of the ordinary, rather than everday life. A display of prehistoric weapons and pictures of the defence structures excavated would, therefore, easily give the impression that the Neolithic and Bronze Age inhabitants of our country were belligerent. If, however, we underplayed the bellicose element altogether there was the converse risk that the visitiors would probably regard those prehistoric farmers as all-too-peaceful and egalitarian. It was therefore decided to present the information in contrasted pictures. For example the photograph of the skeleton of a Neolithic man who had been shot in the back was displayed together with a wedding picture of a happy couple with their guests. In order to survive it is namely necessary not only to be able to conquer one's foes but equally important to have good relations with one's fellow men. Another contrasted pair of pictures showed modern people who wore outfits that conform to the average and others who had tried through wearing unusual clothes and accessories to differ from their neighbours. The pictures were connected with information on traces of similar tendencies discernible in prehistoric finds.

The display called 'Life and Death' was dominated by charts showing the duration of life of prehistoric men and the Swiss of today. The first chart was based on the statistics derived from the study of Mid-European Neolithic and Bronze Age burial sites. Life-sized photographs of modern people of different ages, starting with a toddler and ending with an eighty year old man, covered the walls. In front of the photographs we placed models of Neolithic people of various ages: a small child, a ten years old boy, a twenty years old woman and a man aged about thirty. On the other side of the room, in front of the photographs showing people

from forty to eighty years there was only a reconstructed stone cist with the skeleton of a young pregnant woman. The grave was excavated at Rapperswil on Lake Zürich. A visitor remarked after studying the display that obviously quite a few children and young people were orphans. It was exactly the kind of reflection we had hoped to be able to awake with the display.

The display 'Power of Nature' was to remind the visitors of the fact that though little concrete evidence survives of cultic rites, we may fairly confidently presume that prehistoric man believed in existence of supernatural powers and in life after death in one form or other. Did the pendants of deer teeth and imitations carved from bone belong to a form of hunting magic? And what is the significance of the fact that our hunters today still honour their wives with deer tooth pendants? Should we call Late Bronze Age pendants 'amulets' and compare them, as Professor Müller-Karpe has done, with Egyptian healing charms? Was it permissible to see signs of a fertility cult in the gynaecomorphic vessels of the Cortaillod? We could only draw our analogies from religious history or from ethnology and folk-lore, that is, from areas in which all of us had little experience. In spite of all this, we ventured to express some views to direct the visitors. We felt it important also to give clues to the many areas of which little, or only incomprehensible traces remain. What was the importance, for instance, of the lovely neolithic ceremonial axes which were found in the river Limmat which flows into Lake Zürich? A river sacrifice? What for? When we were looking for comparative ethnological pictorial material, we came across the picture of a man with a similar axe blade in a bunch of leaves. Who could have guessed that, as was explained to us by the ethnologists, he was just in the act of performing some rain magic?

Involuntary experiments

Two three-dimensional pictures – combined with sound effects – showed the flooding of one village and the conflagration of another. Traces of both kinds of catastrophe have been discovered at numerous Lake Dwelling sites. The aim of the pictures was to illustrate how prehistoric man was more or less at the mercy of natural forces which he could not control. However, it was more difficult for us to imagine how prehistoric people confronted these forces. Skeletons of three Neolithic lake dwellers, who obviously lost their lives when their village burnt down, as well as Late Bronze Age objects partly consumed with fire, were on display. Remains of the settlement with the skeletons were excavated at Zürich-Mozartstrasse 1981. It seemed almost an irony of fate, that we should witness two fires in *Pfahlbauland* ourselves. A couple of weeks after opening the managing team of the exhibition was sitting in the restaurant *Hirschkeule* built on the premises, when a thunderstorm broke out over Zürich. Storm clouds raced across the lake and the rain pelted down. A television crew who had just been recording, was now obviously seeking shelter in the reconstructed Early Bronze Age village. We wondered whether the TV crew might actually take advantage of the situation because we kept seeing dark figures hurrying over the bridge, and, indeed, they were creating the effects of a fire. Above the nearest row of houses a bright glow appeared, like the licking flames of a new fire, then a flame seemed to run across the gable. Whilst we were wondering how the film people had managed this in the midst of a downpour, another flame blazed up. 'It's really burning!' someone shouted. We ran out into the darkness and onto the island. The people who had stayed on in the workshops fetched fire extinguishers. We fought the flames from the outside and the inside, but whenever we thought we had it under control, the next gust of wind rekindled the glowing embers in the roof. Finally the fire brigade appeared and set up their hoses. The damage was not very extensive. From the outside all one could see was blackened thatch with a burnt out hole at the gable, but the incident had given us a good idea of what a fire really meant in a village where the houses stood very near to each other. In the Early Bronze Age the village would certainly have burnt hopelessly to the ground.

A week later our village really burnt down. This time it was deliberate arson and even the fire brigade was unable to save much. Before reconstructing the houses again we carried out a small excavation. Only two sticks and the loom weights remained of the loom. There was not a trace of the baskets, nets and other things which we had stored in the large roof space of one house. The hazel rods and posts in the walls fared better, being protected by the daub. It may be no coincidence that daub cladding has also been noted on the ends of beams in lake-side and bog dwellings, i.e. the lake dwellers may have tried to protect the beams of the houses against fire by daubing them. Some unusual aspects were noted: a pot had fallen from its stand quite undamaged, and the corn in a storage vessel was carbonized only against the edge of the pot, while remaining unharmed in the interior. Just how dangerous a fire could be to the inhabitants of such a closely constructed village was shown, for instance, by the enormously heavy collapsed gable wall of one house. Our disaster also gave rise to certain ques-

tions. Had the prehistoric settlers kept all their vital grain stores, including a quantity of seed for the next sowing, in villages with such a high fire-risk? Were the little houses which we thought of as granaries really intended to store grain? Where did the people go after such a conflagration? Who took them in? Why did they build their houses so close to each other anyway? Many questions still remain to be answered.

Notes

1. The exhibition *Pfahlbauland* took place in Zürich from April 10th to October 15th 1990. The President of the Society is Dr Kurt Burkhart, Zürich. The first draft for an open air archaeological show combined with exhibition halls, workshops and audiovisual programs was drawn up by the author of this article. He was also responsible for the themes selected for the specific exhibitions and the first sketches of the groundplans for the buildings and their placement on the site. The graphic artists' office 'Atelier Fabrik am Wasser' in Zürich, the exhibition specialist and designer Markus Riegert in Winterthur and various other exhibition experts were commissioned to design and build the exhibition with the workshops. Dr Edi Gross, 'Büro für Archäologie' of the City of Zürich, was an adviser in archaeological matters. He also wrote most of the texts for the information panels in the exhibition as well as the guide book. Mr Beat Eberschweiler, Stud. Phil I., was responsible for the filmshows, lectures and special activities. Mr Urs Wenger took care of the general administration and financial management of the project.

2. *a)* Thomas, Franziska und die Archäologen, Stumme Zeuge vergangener Jahrtausende. *b)* Franziska vor 5000 Jahren *c)* Prähistorisches Handwerk: studiert und ausprobiert (Experimentelle Archäologie). Schweizer Fernsehen DRS in Co-Produktion mit der Gesellschaft für Schweizer Unterwasser-Archäologie, 1990. Wissenschaftliche Leitung: Beat Eberschweiler, Guido Lassau. Regie: Roger Burckhardt.

BIBLIOGRAPHY

Becker B. *et al* 1985. Dendrochronologie in der Ur- und Frühgeschichte. Die absolute Datierung von Pfahlbausiedlungen nördlich der Alpen im Jahrringkalender Mitteleuropas. *Antiqua 11*, Basel.

Chronologie 1986. Archäologische Daten der Schweiz. Datation archéologique en Suisse. *Antiqua 15*, Basel.

Eberschweiler, B., Riethmann, P. and Ruoff, U. 1987. Greifensee-Böschen, Kanton Zürich. Ein spätbronzezeitliches Dorf. *Jahrbuch der Schweizerischen Gesellschaft für Ur- und Frühgeschichte* 70, 77-100.

Die ersten Bauern 1990. Pfahlbaufunde Europas. Forschungsberichte zur Ausstellung im Schweizerischen Landesmuseum und zum Erlebnispark / Ausstellung Pfahlbauland in Zürich, 2 volumes. Exhibition catalogue of the Swiss National Museum, Zürich.

Gross, E., Brombacher, Ch., Dick, M., Digglemann, K., Hardmeyer, B., Jagher, R., Ritzmann, Ch., Ruckstuhl, B., Ruoff, U., Schibler, J., Vaughan, P.C. and Wyprächtiger, B. 1987. Zürich "Mozartstrasse". Neolithische und bronzezeitliche Ufersiedlungen. *Berichte der Zürcher Denkmalpflege, Monographien* 4.

Gross, E. and Ruoff, U. 1990. Das Leben in neolithischen und bronzezeitlichen Dörfern am Zürich- und Greifensee. *Archäologie der schweiz* 13, 101-112.

Gross, E., Jacomet, S. and Schibler, J. 1990. Stand und Ziele der wirtschaftsarchäologischen Forschung an neolithischen Ufer- und Inselsiedlungen im unteren Zürichseeraum 'Kt. Zürich, Schweiz). In J. Schibler, J. Sedlmeier and H. Spycher (eds), *Festschrift für Hans R. Stampfli*, 77-100. Basel: Helbing and Lichtenhahn Verlag AG.

Jacomet, J., Brombacher, C. and Dick, M. 1989. Archäobotanik am Zürichsee. Ackerbau, sammelwirtschaft und

Umwelt von neolithischen und bronzezeitlichen Seeufer-siedlungen im Raum Zürich. *Berichte der Zürcher Denkmalpflege, Monographien* 7.

Osterwalder Maier, C.1990. Schüler-Robinsonade im Pfahlbau Urgeschichte im Schulunterricht.In J. Schibler, J. Sedlmeier and H. Spycher (eds), *Festschrift für Hans R. Stampfli*, 173-180. Basel: Helbing and Lichtenhahn Verlag AG.

Ruoff, U. 1978. Die schnurkeramischen Räder von Zürich-"Pressehaus". *Archäologisches Korrespondenzblatt* 8, 275-283.

Ruoff, U. 1987. Archaeological Investigations beside Lake Zürich and Lake Greifen. In J. M. Coles and A. J. Lawson (eds), *European Wetlands in Prehistory*, 55-73. Oxford: Clarendon Press.

Schibler, J. and Suter, P. 1990. Archäozoologische Ergebnisse datierter neolithischer Ufersiedlungen des schweizerischen Mittellandes. In J. Schibler, J. Sedlmeier and H. Spycher (eds), *Festschrift für Hans R. Stampfli*, 205-240. Basel: Helbing and Lichtenhahn Verlag AG.

Suter, P. J. 1987. Zürich "Kleiner Hafner". Tauchgrabungen 1981-1984. *Berichte der Züricher Denkmalpflege, Monographien* 3.

16

THE WETLAND REVOLUTION: A NATURAL EVENT

John Coles and Bryony Coles

The need for archaeological action in wetlands is today recognised in a growing number of places. The richness of sites preserved in waterlogged conditions has been demonstrated repeatedly, and the dire threats posed by drainage have been acknowledged, underlined by a more general recognition of the environmental losses consequent on desiccation. In Britain and Ireland the last decade has seen wetland survey and excavation teams and projects initiated at an encouraging rate, and the papers in this volume describe recent wetland work in a number of other locations around the world. It is not enough, much is being destroyed unrecorded, but at least some relevant action is being taken.

At the same time, the techniques of wetland archaeology have seen rapid development, both at the field stages of survey and excavation and at the laboratory stages of post-excavation and conservation. Many aspects of field techniques in particular are discussed in the papers above, with references to the discoveries consequent on advances in scuba-diving, or coffer-dams and well-points, and for an example of the rewards of structured field survey readers should turn to the results of the Fenland Project (e.g. Hall 1987). The developing range of post-excavation techniques is seen in projects such as the Windover investigations (Doran, this volume and references therein), or in the diverse specialists called upon, some years ago now, to assist in the investigation of the prehistory of the Somerset Levels as reported in *Somerset Levels Papers*.

Charavines

One site which illustrates well the potential avenues of investigation open to the wetland archaeologist, but which may not be familiar to prehistorians, is Charavines-Colletière, dated *c* AD 1000 and essentially proto-historic. It is a small, defended lakeshore settlement of 2-3 rectangular buildings, close to the neolithic hamlet of Charavines-Les

Baigneurs, and currently under investigation by Colardelle and Verdel (1988). When lake levels are high, excavation takes place underwater but if the levels fall open-air excavation becomes practicable. The quantity of physical information yielded is highlighted by the fact that two divers, excavating possibly more slowly underwater than would their open-air counterparts, require 10-15 people on-shore to keep pace with the preliminary sorting and processing of the excavated material. In due course, this is passed on to the relevant specialists; their work, which as yet is far from complete, has already produced results which show how a site of this nature can amplify the existing record, both through what *is* preserved and because the conditions of preservation are good enough to argue that missing evidence has not simply decayed, but was never part of the site assemblage.

The techniques applied to date the site, used independently and as a check on each other, include typology, numismatics, radiocarbon dating and dendrochronology. The last-named also provides an estimate of site duration, at about 20 years, and indicates a genuine contemporaneity with the two other known early medieval settlements on the shores of the lake ('genuine contemporaneity' is discussed further below). Pollen analysis indicates the dryland vegetation and diatoms indicate the condition and level of the lake; interpretation of these aspects is reinforced by O_{18} analysis of wood cellulose to determine rates of photosynthesis and hence rainfall. As the wood is also dated by dendrochronology, and the O_{18} analyses can be carried out on samples consisting of just a few growth-rings, it becomes possible to suggest decade-by-decade conditions of rainfall and, in this instance, to relate the construction of the lakeshore settlement to a relatively dry phase.

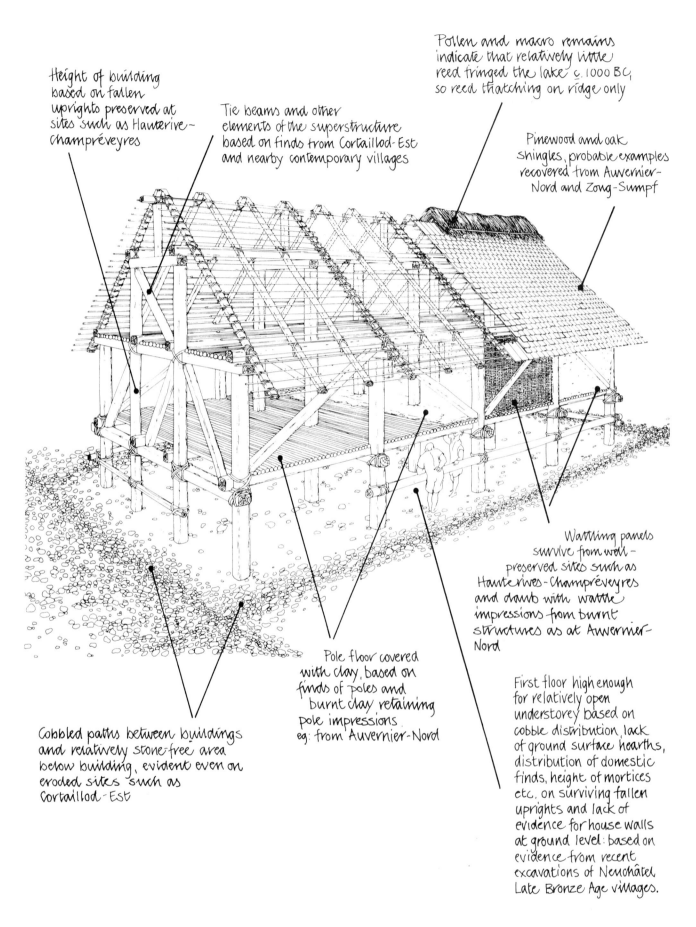

Height of building based on fallen uprights preserved at sites such as Hauterive-Champréveyres

Tie beams and other elements of the superstructure based on finds from Cortaillod-Est and nearby contemporary villages

Pollen and macro remains indicate that relatively little reed fringed the lake c. 1000 BC, so reed thatching on ridge only

Pinewood and oak shingles, probable examples recovered from Auvernier-Nord and Zong-Sumpf

Wattling panels survive from well-preserved sites such as Hauterives-Champréveyres and daub with wattle impressions from burnt structures as at Auvernier-Nord

First floor high enough for relatively open understorey based on cobble distribution, lack of ground surface hearths, distribution of domestic finds, height of mortices etc. on surviving fallen uprights and lack of evidence for house walls at ground level; based on evidence from recent excavations of Neuchâtel Late Bronze Age villages.

Pole floor covered with clay, based on finds of poles and burnt clay retaining pole impressions eg: from Auvernier-Nord

Cobbled paths between buildings and relatively stone-free area below building, evident even on eroded sites such as Cortaillod-Est

Fig 16.1 Reconstruction drawing by Béat Arnold of a house from Cortaillod-Est c 1000 BC, based on evidence from Cortaillod and from contemporary sites in the vicinity; annotated by BJC (Arnold 1990, fig.69)

The artefacts from Charavines-Colletière include very few agricultural tools, but pollen, macroscopic plant remains and bones reveal a varied economy based predominantly on cultivated plants and domestic animals, with some gathering of wild fruits and nuts and a very little (*c* 1%) hunting. Horses were not eaten and so do not enter the faunal record, but their significance to the inhabitants is registered in the artefact assemblage which includes numerous pieces of horse-harness, shoes, spurs etc.; this suggests that the horse was important for riding, maybe in war. It is interesting that the range of artefacts does not reflect farming, and the range of animal bones does not reflect horse-riding, but both activities were of major significance to the people who lived at the site.

There is direct evidence for leather-working, iron-working, wood-working and textile production, and the artefact range is extended with imported pots, musical instruments, gaming pieces, ornaments, swords and crossbow bolts as well as the horse-gear mentioned above, all of which provides material for study by many specialists. It also poses problems of conservation, especially for composite artefacts made of both organic and inorganic materials.

Charavines-Colletière provides so much to work on, which will flesh out the regional archaeological and documentary record for the period, that it is disconcerting to learn that the excavators have so far uncovered no evidence for either literacy or Christianity, both of which one would have taken for granted for wealthy Burgundians of AD 1000. Were these wetlanders illiterate heathens? Or is the archaeological record, excellent though it is, simply deficient in these respects? Whatever the answer, it is the conjunction of archaeological and historical evidence which shows up the problem and in doing so reminds us that wetland sites, however startling, nevertheless still present an incomplete reflection of the past.

It is also important not to exaggerate the claims of wetland archaeology. Very dry sites and frozen sites preserve similarly diverse ranges of high-quality evidence (e.g. Mons Claudianus: Peacock and Maxfield 1990). Dryland sites may contain well-preserved evidence under certain conditions, for example the débris from the production of inorganic artefacts deposited in disused pits at Gussage-All-Saints on the dry chalk downlands of southern England (Wainwright 1979), and there are dryland sites with a great diversity of evidence, such as the neolithic tells of south-eastern Europe. The results of wetland and dryland archaeology might therefore be considered to be essential similar, yet wetland archaeology tends to maintain a degree of separateness in many respects, which is not necessarily well-advised (Coles 1991).

Integration

What is essential now is to consider the integration of wetland results into the wider archaeological framework, and to ask whether this has been done, whether it can be done and whether it should be done. If a Wetland Revolution exists at all, it is in the answers to these questions.

It can be argued that there has been very little real integration of the results from wetland work. Many wetland archaeologists have been pre-occupied on the one hand with the threats to their sites and on the other with the enormous demands of the resulting post-excavation work, and they have had little time to spare for matters beyond the wetlands. As for the majority of 'other' archaeologists, few have studied the results of wetland survey and excavation in depth, perhaps because they do not immediately perceive any link between what is familiar to them, i.e. dryland evidence, and alien categories of information from a hostile environment. A brushwood trackway or a wooden mallet may have curiosity value, but what bearing do they have on the interpretation of postholes in a different environment? And how does a settlement in a peat-bog illuminate one's understanding of the society that farmed the surrounding drylands?

There have been exceptions, especially when it comes to studying artefacts rather than settlements, as for example with Bradley's recent analysis of artefact deposition (Bradley 1990). And some regions are still sufficiently aware of and endowed with water, however controlled, to take for granted the normality of wetland evidence. In north western Europe, this can be said particularly of the Netherlands and also of Denmark, as reference to their archaeological journals will illustrate.

Sometimes, the evidence from a wetland site appears to be well-integrated into the study of a particular period or region, but the appearance may be deceptive. Star Carr is the classic example here, a site whose domination of Early Mesolithic studies in Britain is reflected in the numerous re-interpretations attempted subsequent to Clark's mid-century excavations and publication (Clark 1952, and for reference to the many reinterpretations see Legge and Rowley-Conwy 1988). In the early 20th century, the Iron Age Lake Villages of Somerset, Glastonbury and Meare, had dominated studies of the British Iron Age in a similar fashion, but by the 1970s they had ceased to be regularly used as examples of Iron Age settlements, despite providing better-preserved evidence than most subsequent discoveries. Their fall from fashion was partly just that, when what was once fresh became hackneyed as an example, and also little attempt had been made to relate either Glastonbury or Meare, in their particular and peculiar wetland contexts, to what was going on in the drylands around them. When David Clarke came to reinterpret Glastonbury (Clarke 1972) he was reviving a forgotten site, that had been so little integrated into the interpretation of the British Iron Age that it could be dropped without apparent damage to the overall picture. The same could happen to Star Carr except that from the time of excavation onwards some attempt has been made to consider its links with the surrounding drylands and, more prosaically, there is still little evidence to put in its place.

Other wetland sites, far from dominating, have never fully risen from the waters of oblivion. Key Marco, from Florida, has remained almost as obscure after as before its excavation although Cushing published one long descriptive paper in 1897 and anyone reading Gilliland's recent publications (1975 and 1989) will appreciate the significance of the site (see also Purdy, this volume). Doran's contribution to this volume discusses some of the possible causes for the general neglect of wetland information in mainstream North American archaeology, and between them he and Purdy document the marginalisation of wetland sites and the evidence retrieved from them. Many wetland sites in other regions have suffered similar fates: excavated, published and then ignored for no good reason.

Nevertheless, there is one major assemblage of wetland evidence relatively well-known to prehistorians, and that is the material from the circum-Alpine lake settlements of Neolithic and Bronze Age date. Its quality is exceptional. Here, for example, one can determine from dendrochronological analyses the stages of construction of a small neolithic hamlet, and estimate within a few years the lengths of occupation, abandonment and renewed occupation - all this is known for Charavines-Les Baigneurs (Bocquet *et al* 1987). Around Lake Neuchâtel, for some periods, prehistorians are confident that they have identified all the settlements of certain phases, and through dendrochronology they can demonstrate definite contemporaneity (e.g. see Magny and Schifferdecker 1980 for the late Neolithic). For one relatively eroded and impoverished later Bronze Age site, Cortaillod-Est, Arnold has developed the house reconstruction drawing shown in Fig. 16.1, and in this instance virtually every element of the structure is based on contemporary local archaeological evidence, even to the roofing shingles (Arnold 1990). Few dryland sites of any period can provide such reliable documentation for a reconstruction, and yet the circum-Alpine evidence for structures and settlements is used by archaeologists mainly in the study of local, lakeside prehistory, and scholars have been wary, perhaps rightly so, of applying it more widely.

Chronology

There is one aspect of wetland archaeology, in particular, which seems likely to change our understanding of prehistoric evidence from all contexts. The increasing availability of precise dendrochronological dates, directly related to archaeological contexts and cultural items, makes it possible to be certain of the exact contemporaneity of sites or artefacts, however far-flung. At the moment, in many instances establishing such contemporaneity seems to have little more than curiosity value. It was exciting, when the dendrodate for the Sweet Track came through, to hunt through the literature to see what else was built with wood felled in 3807/6 BC and to find that the Somerset Levels trackway was constructed while people were building on the shores of Lake Neuchâtel at Hauterive-Champréveyres and at Twann on Lake Bienne (Hillam *et al* 1990). There is no cultural link between the sites, but to know that they

existed at the same time puts the Sweet Track evidence into a slightly new and perhaps more European perspective.

Similar opportunities exist with the dendrodates now available for the trackways from central Ireland (Raftery, this volume), especially from the 1st millennium BC, and in this case it may well prove relevant to a better understanding of the technology and the function of the Irish trackways to be able to compare them with tracks that crossed the bogs of Lower Saxony (Hayen 1987), knowing for each region the dates of construction within a decade, if not closer. For example, the great Corlea I roadway (148 BC) was apparently built about 20 years before a similarly massive and equally enigmatic trackway across the Wittemoor (XLII Ip, *c* 129 BC). The trackways from the Netherlands, by contrast, are at present dated by radiocarbon (Casparie 1987, 62-64), and there can be no certainty of their chronological relationship to the Irish or the Saxon trackways.

Raftery discusses above and elsewhere (Raftery 1990, 40) the identification of a second stretch of trackway, across Derraghan bog, which continues the route of Corlea 1 and which has a dendrodate of 156 ± 9 BC (for an explanation of ± 9 see Baillie 1988), placing it close in time and maybe exactly contemporary with Corlea I at 148 BC. Thus it is reasonable to interpret the two lengths of trackway as part of a single building project. With radiocarbon dates, there can be no such certainty (see Coles, Caseldine and Morgan 1980, 26-28, for an example of the problems).

If the above are signs of a new quality of chronology for prehistory, it could be argued that it will apply only to a few favoured sites. Preservation of wood suitable for dating by dendrochronology is much rarer than preservation of organic material suitable for radiocarbon samples. But the number of dendrodates from European sites north of the Alps is steadily increasing, and as local chronologies build up even isolated wooden structures have a chance of being dated, as with the recently-discovered well at Kückhoven, a settlement of early farmers in northwest Germany. The oak-timbers lining the well were felled in 5303 BC (Bahn 1991). Secondly, a number of the wetland sites with dendrodates provide closed contexts of known short duration. This can be seen for the Sweet Track, dendrodated to 3807/6 BC and calculated to have been in use for at least a decade on the basis of identified repairs, but abandoned within two decades of building given the limited decay of the structure prior to its burial by natural agencies, and the absence of repairs after the first decade (Coles and Coles 1986). A number of the circum-Alpine settlements, especially the earlier ones, are also shown by dendrochronology to be of short duration, for example Charavines-Les Baigneurs, mentioned above (Bocquet *et al* 1987). Both the Sweet Track and the Charavines houses are directly associated with a range of artefacts, including pottery and stone axes and arrowheads. Typological studies allow the dendrodate for the wetland finds to be applied to dryland examples of the same types, at least in a general sense (e.g. Hillam *et al* 1990, 218). This may seem to be taking the evidence to extremes but the practicality of such dating for sequences of artefact types is already apparent from the well-dated circum-Alpine Bronze Age (see, for example, discussion in Arnold 1990). There is no reason why it should not apply equally to earlier sites and finds. This wetland revolution in dating promises a widespread effect in Europe, and there is potential for similar developments in the study of prehistory wherever the dendrochronological dating of archaeological sites is practicable.

Different prehistories

There is another aspect of wetland archaeology which has revolutionary implications for the study of prehistory, although at first these may seem less self-evident than with dendrochronology. The possibilities can be approached via a brief glance at one aspect of the economic evidence available from wetland sites. Many of the earliest neolithic settlements around the Alpine lakes have yielded abundant evidence for the exploitation of wild resources alongside the use of domestic plants and animals (e.g. Bodensee: Becker *et al* 1985). Dolukhanov (this volume) discusses a similar situation in northeastern Europe, as Louwe Kooijmans (1985) has done for the Netherlands. It is often assumed that their wetland location renders the economy of these sites irrelevant for understanding the adoption of farming on a European scale, particularly as the wetland picture contrasts with the dryland one of heavy reliance on domesticated plants and animals. But the wetland microregion is not necessarily any less representative than others within a broader region (see Evans, this volume, for further discussion of allied points), and study of the transition to farming in the very diverse wetlands of the Rhine/Meuse delta, the shores of the Bodensee and the Usvyaty basin is surely as illuminating as study of sites confined to loess soils. Both are needed for a balanced investigation of early farming.

The potential of wetland archaeology for revealing a different prehistory is touched on in several of the contributions to this volume. Doran points out that the only trace that Windover's men, women and children would have left in a dryland environment consists of two or three undiagnostic stone artefacts. Gramsch disentangles the cultural affinities of successive groups who settled at Friesack via analysis of the methods of hafting bone points used in different occupation layers. Again, this is evidence that would not survive under normal dryland conditions. Croes demonstrates that the cultural history apparent from the organic artefacts of the Northwest Coast is different to the traditional lithics-based reconstruction of culture change. Seeking a reason for the difference, he argues that changes in lithics stem from a shift to a new economic plateau, with widespread technological change allied to changes in the exploitation of the environment. Organic artefacts, on the other hand, are more amenable than lithics to stylistic variation and hence they are more commonly used for the expression of cultural affiliation. The development and distribution of basketry and wooden artefacts therefore perhaps better reflect the human populations who made

them than do stone tools. If Croes is correct, then it is one of the misfortunes of prehistory that so often only lithics survive, and where there is wetland evidence available, that evidence is crucial in the *general* study of prehistory.

Wet lives

However much we argue for the wider significance of wetland results, to us of the 20th century the idea that people in the past should deliberately choose to live in wetlands appears daft. Who among us would now prefer to pad over the damp grasses or through the reeds, or slog across the mudflats, or wade in shallow water on our daily rounds - going to work, going to shop or gather supplies, going home. And who would like to live and sleep over damp ground, even if raised above it by a wooden or clay floor? We, conditioned by our dread of 'rising damp', and by our centrally-heated upbringing, find it difficult to understand those who squatted like ducks in the lakes, or perched upon mounds of mud along the tidal shores, or camped on river levees, or built huts in a swamp. Yet is this any more inexplicable to us than those who wilfully dragged huge boulders and massive timbers to build forts on the tops of hills? And each day slid down to work the fields below and carry out their other activities, and staggered back up with heavy loads of food and wood, and water? To us, avowed wetlanders, the hillfort people made the more work for themselves and the lowlanders had the easier lives.

The papers in this volume have demonstrated the virtues of a wetland life, in the variety and quantity of materials available to those who deliberately chose to live their lives in or near the wet and damp - the lakes, seashore, river valleys and marshlands of the past. The question is surely not now why they did it, but why we as archaeologists have taken so long to accept it as a normal response to environmental opportunities. It happened - all over the world and at all times throughout prehistory - so why have we failed to exploit the widely acknowledged values of wetland archaeology? Organic survival, environmental detail, chronological precision, structural/cultural evidence far in advance of that from almost any other site wherever found - this volume is full of examples of those who have capitalised on the wetland opportunities.

Anyone seriously considering the vast array of evidence from wetland excavations may well conclude that most of the benefits of waterlogging lie *within* the sites rather than in wider aspects. In providing evidence for the internal arrangements and composition of sites (e.g. houses, streets) and their occupants (e.g. stomachs, brains), wetlands perform at their highest level, and perhaps this is one of the reasons why relatively little effort has been made to develop profound theoretical stances for wetland archaeology. The absence of any real body of theory specifically designed for wetland evidence is a serious handicap, and will become increasingly so.

Let us now glance at some of the opportunities both found and lost, accepted or ignored. Let us begin with another reference to the homeland itself – the Alpine lakes of Europe. There can be no argument about the facts of preservation, of material culture in abundance or the presence of unusual things, and there has been much attention paid to site location – out of the water or in the water; Ruoff has drawn attention to this overkill. But with a few notable exceptions, there has been relatively little attention paid to the economic basis, land extent and use, settlement structure, movement within settlements, travel and communication to the mountains and valleys, and to social relations - evidence for all of which survives, some well some badly, within and near the waterlogged sites. Alpine wetland archaeology needs some wider viewpoints.

We might look next at the Great Lakes of Poland, focussed on Biskupin and its contemporaneous fortified settlements (see Niewiarowski *et al*, this volume). There is a great opportunity here, now beginning to be grasped, to develop models of interaction, to explore the economic and social relationships of the satellite settlements to the major strongholds, to consider the exploitation of both water and land in this fertile region. The lakes area with its wealth of environmental and cultural evidence could sustain and supply any number of predictive and speculatory models, to help explain how and why the landscape was divided, and incidentally to help maintain and augment the interest of the public in this national monument.

Less specific comment can be made about the earlier episodes of human settlement in Europe and beyond. Although the caves, shelters and open-air settlements of the Upper Palaeolithic period have preserved quantities of lithic and bone materials, what revolutionary information might be revealed by the discovery of a waterlogged site where organic evidence survived? What wooden tools, handles, bindings, containers and plant foods might be displayed? How would the archaeological organisation of the existing evidence into typological, technological and cultural groups stand if we had an indication that, as suggested above, organic materials formed the defining features, being more malleable and expressive of human preferences, intentions and accomplishments? Some attempts to discover such sites would seem overdue.

Comment has already been made about the rather few archaeologists working the wetlands of North America, and the difficulties faced by them in the integration of their data into those of mainstream (odd word in this context) North American archaeologists. On the Northwest Coast where human occupation is attested over the past 10,000 years, and where the preservation of organic evidence has been truly remarkable, the archaeological response at all levels (from survey to publication) has been weak apart from the very few exceptions described by Croes. Yet the strong historic traditions of the people who occupied and shared the land, and who once lived in balance with nature, offer an unique opportunity to interpret the traces of ancient exploitation, to infill the still fragmentary archaeological evidence by judicious analogy and to demonstrate cultural, environmental and economic continuities where appropriate. And here the interaction of alien culture (us) with indigenous culture, both in the recent past (shameful) and at present (? better), must be encouraged and controlled, not for our puny purposes but for the future well-being of the region and its people.

Across the continent, in Florida, we are on less hopeful ground. No native people representative of the prehistoric indigenes have survived the onslaught of the European colonists. Yet Florida, apart from a few elevated places, is nought but a vast wetland of lakes, rivers, marshes and swamps. Human settlement, extending back at least 10,000 years ago, was extensive, and wetland survivals demonstrate the richness of the ancient cultures. But, as we have seen, the integration of this evidence, so laboriously gained over the past 100 years, within the prehistory of eastern North America is barely begun. Key Marco was indeed a 'freak' in this context, but scarcely more than, say, Star Carr in the British Mesolithic, Biskupin in the Iron Age of central Europe, and so on. We cannot sit back and wait for those of dryland mentalities to convert themselves – the message has to be taken out to the unbelievers. Only by hammering home, time and again, the wetland message will our evidence come to be accepted as the gospel, or a gospel, to be ignored at anyone's interpretive peril.

The message

What is the message that wet sites carry? It is that there once existed a sustainable balance between humans and the natural world, altered over time and varying with opportunities and circumstances. The choice of wetland environments, as offering abundance and variety, was therefore logical and unsurprising. For economic reasons, both in the supply of materials for a structured life and in the day-to-day acquisition of the needs for subsistence, lakesides, river valleys and coastlands were favoured for their individual reasons. Interaction with other environments, less wet but with their own special features, was obvious and practical, and few wetlanders remained fixed and immobile in their own patch. In the same way, those who chose for very good reasons to occupy lands mostly raised and dry, were not static, tied to the land. A feature of humans in the past, as in the less-mechanised parts of the present, is their sense of the dynamic, of the need and curiosity to move about, to augment and satisfy their real and imagined needs, and to respect nature; in this last, we of the mechanised world fail the test. The grass may have always looked greener in the next field - especially if that field was a water meadow.

In conclusion, we would argue that it is no good looking only in immense detail at a wetland site, so full of data – you will drown, submerged by evidence. It is even less use seeking full explanations of human behaviour in a dryland site – you will starve to death. The crucially important grains of evidence surviving on the latter site, when nourished by the waters of the former, will flourish, and the shoots will be both sturdy and abundant. Those you don't like, you can prune away. In less botanic terms, we need both dryland and wetland sites in concert to get a real idea of how and why humans lived and died as they did, over time and within the multitude of environments themselves evolving. This is not revolutionary – it is common sense, and therefore it may require a revolution for some to accept.

BIBLIOGRAPHY

Arnold, B. 1990. *Cortaillod-Est et les villages du lac de Neuchâtel au Bronze final.* Archéologie neuchâteloise 6. Saint-Blaise: Editions du Ruau.

Bahn, P.G. 1991. The great wooden well of Kückhoven. *Nature* 354, 269.

Baillie M.GL. 1988. The dating of the timbers from Navan Fort and the Dorsey, Co. Armagh. *Emania* 4, 37-40.

Becker, B., Billamboz, A., Dieckmann, B., Kokabi, M., Kromer, B., Liese-Kleiber, H., Rösch, M., Schlichtherle, H. and Strahm, C. 1985. *Berichte zu Ufer-und Moorsiedlungen Südwestdeutschlands* 2. Stuttgart: Kommissionsverlag. Konrad Theiss Verlag.

Bocquet, A., Brochier, J.L., Emery-Barbier, A., Lundstrom-Baudais, K., Orcel, C. and Vin, F. 1987. A submerged Neolithic Village: Charavines 'Les Baigneurs' in Lake Paladru, France. In J.M.Coles and A.J. Lawson (eds), *European Wetlands in Prehistory*, 33-54. Oxford: Clarendon Press.

Bradley, R. 1990. *The Passage of Arms.* Cambridge University Press.

Casparie, W. 1987. Bog trackways in the Netherlands. *Palaeohistoria* 29, 35-65.

Clark, J.G.D. 1954. *Excavations at Star Carr.* Cambridge University Press.

Clarke, D.L. 1972. A provisional model of an Iron Age society and its settlement system. In D.L. Clarke (ed.) *Models in Archaeology*, 801-869. London: Methuen.

Coles, B. and Coles, J. 1986. *Sweet Track to Glastonbury.* London: Thames and Hudson.

Coles, J.M., Caseldine, A.E. and Morgan, R.A. 1982. The Eclipse Track 1980. *Somerset Levels Papers* 8, 26-39.

Coles, J.M. 1991. *From the waters of oblivion.* C.J.C. Reuvens-Lezing 2. Groningen: Stichting voor de Nederlandse Archeologie.

Colardelle, M. and Verdel, E. 1988. Un village de l'an mil retrouvé sous l'eau: Les fouilles de Charavines. *Dossiers histoire et archéologie* 129, 4-84.

Cushing, F.H. 1896 .Exploration of Ancient Key Dwellers' Remains on the Gulf Coast of Florida. *Proceedings of the American Philosophical Society* 35, 329-448.

Gilliland, M.S. 1975. *The material culture of Key Marco.* Gainesville: The University Presses of Florida.

Gilliland, M.S. 1989. *Key Marco's Buried Treasure.* Gainesville: University Presses of Florida.

Hall, D. 1987. *The Fenland Project, Number 2: Fenland Landscapes and Settlement between Peterborough and March.* East Anglian Archaeology Report No.35, 1987. Cambridge: Fenland Project Committee.

Hayen. H. 1987. Peatbog Archaeology in Lower Saxony. In J.M. Coles and A.J. Lawson (eds), *European Wetlands in Prehistory*, 117-136. Oxford: Clarendon Press.

Hillam, J., Groves, C.M., Brown, D.M., Baillie, M.G.L., Coles, J.M. and Coles, B.J. 1990. Dendrochronology of the English Neolithic. *Antiquity* 64, 210-220.

Legge, A.J. and Rowley-Conwy, P.A. 1988. *Star Carr Revisited.* London: Birkbeck College.

Louwe Kooijmans, L.P. 1985. *Sporen in het land.* Amsterdam: Meulenhoff Informatief.

Magny, M. and Schifferdecker, F. 1980. Essai sur l'occupation du sol au Néolithique: le groupe de Lüscherz. *Bulletin de la Société Préhistorique Française* 77 (1), 18-25.

Peacock, D.P.S. and Maxfield, V.A. 1990. *Archaeological Reports from Mons Claudianus.* (Unpublished interim: Universities of Exeter and Southampton)

Raftery, B. 1990 .*Trackways through Time.* Dublin: Headline Publishing.

Wainwright, G.J. 1979. *Gussage All Saints. An Iron Age settlement in Dorset.* Department of the Environment Archaeological Reports No.10. London: Her Majesty's Stationery Office.